Vivencio O. Ballano

Gender Ideology and the Contemporary Catholic Church

A Sociological-Synodal Exploration and Inculturation

Springer

Vivencio O. Ballano
Polytechnic University of the Philippines
(PUP)
Manila, Philippines

ISBN 978-981-97-8123-2 ISBN 978-981-97-8124-9 (eBook)
https://doi.org/10.1007/978-981-97-8124-9

This Springer imprint is published by the registered company Springer Nature Singapore Pte Ltd.
The registered company address is: 152 Beach Road, #21-01/04 Gateway East, Singapore 189721, Singapore

His Holiness Pope Francis, Members of the Dicastery of the Doctrine of the Faith, and the LGBTQI Community

About This Book

This book sociologically investigates the contemporary Catholic Church's stance on gender diversity and "gender ideology" and explores ways to adapt the social science perspectives on sex, gender, and gender fluidity in the Church's moral teachings, applying Pope Francis's inductive synodal theology. Using the sociological theories on gender, moral panics, and morality and drawing on secondary literature, media reports, and church documents, it specifically unpacks the "gender ideology's" alleged grave threats to humanity, family, children, and human dignity as moral panics as well as examines the Catholic morality of gender-enhancement treatment and sex change. Ultimately, this volume aims to inculturate or adapt the contemporary sociological gender theory and research in the Catholic Church's moral doctrines as a synodal response to the "signs of the times." It therefore appeals to church authorities, moral theologians, LGBTQI leaders, as well as scholars and students of sociology, religion, and gender studies.

Contents

About the Author

Vivencio O. Ballano is the Program Chairperson of the Master of Arts in Sociology, Graduate School Program, Polytechnic University of the Philippines (PUP), Manila. He received advanced degrees in theology and sociology from the Ateneo de Manila University. To date, he has published 6 Scopus-indexed monographs with imprints Springer Nature and Routledge. His forthcoming volumes for 2024 include "Pope Francis's Synod on Synodality and Modern Sociology" (Routledge) and "LGBTQIA Inclusivity, Homosexuality, and Same-Sex Marriage in the Catholic Church" (Springer Nature). Ballano has also published several Scopus and Web of Science-indexed journal articles on the sociology of law, religion, clerical sexual abuse, bioethics, and Catholic social teaching.

Part I
Overview of the Book and Unpacking Gender Ideology in the Catholic Church

Chapter 1
Introduction: Overview of the Book

Abstract This chapter introduces the main arguments, methodology, and theoretical foundation of the book, together with an overview of the social background, research gap, and contribution to the literature. The book is a critical investigation of what has been called "gender ideology" (GI) in the Catholic Church as a moral panic, and of its alleged serious threats to humanity, family, children's welfare, and human dignity. Both Pope Francis's synodality and inductive synodal theology, and sociological perspectives on gender, gender theory, gender diversity, and LGBTQI inclusivity are explored. The chapter outlines the major areas of conflict between the proponents of GI, led by Catholic bishops and moral theologians, and advocates of gender diversity, led by pro-gender sociologists, feminists, activists, and LGBTQI leaders, seeking to find common ground for synodal dialogue and inculturation.

Keywords Synodality · Synodal listening · Sociology · Gender ideology · Gender theory · Synodal church

Introduction

In March 2024, during a two-day gender conference in the Vatican entitled "Man-Woman Image of God: For an Anthropology of Vocations," Pope Francis reiterated Pope Benedict XVI's concept of gender and gender theory as "gender ideology" (hereafter called GI). To him, GI advocates gender diversity that allows people to alter their God-given gender. It erases the gender differences between a man and a woman and thus constitutes the greatest threat to humanity's survival (Zengarini 2024).

This remark was made just after the Roman Catholic Church (RCC) had finished its first roundtable discussions in Rome for Pope Francis's ecclesiastical reform project, the Synod on Synodality (SoS), a long consultation process involving different representatives of the Catholic Church on adapting the Church's mission in contemporary society. The SoS aims to establish a synodal church in accordance with the reforms of the Second Vatican Council (Vatican II)—a church that is welcoming to marginalized

V. O. Ballano, *Gender Ideology and the Contemporary Catholic Church*,
https://doi.org/10.1007/978-981-97-8124-9_1

sectors of society, which may include gender-diverse individuals or members of the lesbian, gay, bisexual, transgender, queer, and intersexual (LGBTQI)[1] community.

Pope Francis's synodality offers "everyone—especially those who for various reasons find themselves on the margins—the opportunity to express themselves and to be heard in order to contribute to the edification of the People of God" (Synod of Bishops 2021, 3). In a synodal church, Francis envisions that a "whole community, in the free and rich diversity of its members, is called together to pray, listen, analyze, dialogue, discern, and offer advice on taking pastoral decisions, which correspond as closely as possible to God's will" (ITC 2018). This vision of an inclusive church implies listening and welcoming nonbinary people or individuals with diverse gender identities such as the LGBTQI community.

However, the persistent labeling of gender and diversity as part of GI makes one wonders whether Pope Francis and the RCC are serious in pursuing synodality and greater integration of the gay community into the Christian community to achieve a synodal church. Synodal listening to marginalized groups or people at the periphery of the Church and society, such as the LGBTQI community, is one of the hallmarks of Francis's pontificate. Marginalized groups in the Church includes gender sociologists, social scientists, feminists, and LGBTQI leaders, whose empirical views on sex and gender often contravene the RCC's philosophical concepts of sexuality and gender, which are founded predominantly on the Thomistic natural law theory (TNLT).

Synod, Synodality, and Inculturation

In order to realize his vision of an inclusive and listening church that welcomes all to the Christian community, Pope Francis introduced the theological term "synodality" to stress the Church's openness to cultural diversity as well as divergent views of marginalized groups in society, which may include members of the LGBTQI community, sociologists, feminists, and gender activists. The term "synodality" originates from the word "synod"—meaning "assembly" or "meeting," from the Greek word σύνοδος—and refers to the common responsibility of all the members of the People of God for the life of the Church (Pope Francis 2015).

Synods or meetings of bishops with the Pope have always been part of the tradition of the RCC and from the earliest times have been used by the Catholic hierarchy to update the Church in response to the changing times. Pope Paul VI's document, *Apostolica Sollicitudo* (1965), institutionalized them as a papal instrument for church reforms. Pope Francis has broadened the concept of a synod, introducing some innovations to expand its consultation process to include ostracized and unwelcomed members of the Church and society. Through synodality, he intends to adapt Christian teachings to contemporary society in the spirit of the Second Vatican Council's

[1] Although aware of the evolution and nuances of this term, the book only uses the acronym "LGBTQI" throughout for consistency.

(Vatican II) *aggriornamento* [church renewal], which is part of the RCC's evangelization process, known as inculturation. Pope Francis wants "the church brought up to date in order to meet the new challenges of the modern world" (Hahnenberg 2007, 5).

Fr. Pedro Arrupe, S.J. (1978) formally introduced the concept of inculturation into the RCC in a letter entitled "The Work of Inculturation of the Faith and Promotion of Christian Life" to encourage Jesuits to advance it in their apostolate. To Fr Arrupe, inculturation is the incarnation or adaptation of Christian life and of the Christian message in a particular local cultural context. To Pope John Paul II, inculturation is of utmost significance in evangelization. To him, "an inaccurate adaptation of the Christian faith in human cultures can lead to a bad theology and defective pastoral policies and practices" (Ballano 2021, 1).

Inculturation is embedded in synodality, which refers to the common responsibility of all the members of the People of God for the life of the Church (Pope Francis 2015). Synodality implies adapting the Church's teachings to the concrete lives of Catholics in the contemporary world: first by listening to and learning from the lived experiences of people, especially those at the margins of the Church and society, such as people with diverse genders and sexualities, and then by creatively applying the moral doctrines based on this synodal listening.

Inculturation involves entering into the thought and cultural patterns of the hearers of the Gospel. It is not merely judging cultural personal appearance and externals acts of people with diverse genders but also involves identifying their personal struggles and motives for their actions. In one of his media interviews, Pope Francis expresses this synodal concern for the LGBTQI community, maintaining that "If a person is gay and seeks God and has good will, who am I to judge?" (BBC News 2013, para. 4).

To concretize his synodal concern and inculturate church teachings for gender-diverse people in contemporary times, Pope Francis's declaration *Fiducia Supplicans* [Supplicating Trust] (FS) approved the giving of pastoral blessings by priests to homosexual couples and allowed them to act as godparents in baptism (DDF 2023). He even went as far as encouraging gay couples to seek legal protection and enter civil unions to protect their rights. Listening to people at the peripheries has been a hallmark of his pontificate and a central concern of his synodality. Sadly, despite his synodal support for the gay community, and LGBTQI inclusivity in the Church and society, Francis still opposes campaigns for gender diversity and transgenderism by sociologists, feminists, and activists.

Pope Francis and GI

Pope Francis has given GI and anti-gender movements a new visibility by describing them in the early part of his papacy as an "ideological colonization" (Francis 2015). To him, the contemporary concept of gender and GI are part of a Western neocolonial project in which gender activists and their governments impose decadent secular values on non-Western societies (Patternote and Kuhar 2017). GI promotes gender diversity, transgender sexuality, and non-traditional forms of family structure perceived to be contrary to traditional Catholic moral beliefs and values.

Indeed, Pope Francis has provided new "tactics and strategies for this war, with his rhetoric of anticolonialism and warm receptivity to individuals" (Case 2019, 659). Like his predecessor Pope Benedict XVI, he subscribes to Pope John Paul II's "theology of the body" and labels as GI any attempt by critical scholars, feminists, activists, and sociologists to subvert the Church's gender complementarity teaching.

In an interview with the Argentine daily newspaper *La Nación* [The Nation] on March 10, 2023, Francis reiterated the exaggeration of gender as GI or what sociologists call "moral panics" (Cohen 1972) as the "most dangerous" (Mares 2024) and "ugliest ideology of our time," because it cancels all distinctions between a man and a woman (Zengarini 2024). To him, "God created man and woman; God created the world in a certain way… and we are doing the exact opposite…This is the age of sin against God the Creator" (Francis 2016a, b, para. 42).

To characterize gender and gender theories as the ugliest and most dangerous ideology of the times runs counter to the scientific gender approaches of modern sociology and the social sciences. Gender sociologists, behavioral scientists, and feminists basically view gender theories in scientific research as tentative explanations—subject to data confirmation—of the various gender relations in society, as well as the social injustices against women and gender-diverse people in today's world. They generally understand gender theories as tools for research and to achieve societal reforms and social justice—a cause that is within the purview of the RCC's social doctrines and Francis's synodal priorities of protecting the human dignity of the downtrodden in society (Pope Francis 2016a; DDF 2024).

However, the broad and complex concept of GI has created a barrier both to meaningful inculturation or adaptation of the social science and feminist perspectives on sexuality and gender in the RCC and to synodal dialogue between Catholic bishops and gender advocates. How can Pope Francis's openness to divergent views in his synodality and his friendly stance towards gender-diverse people such as the LGBTQI community be reconciled with GI's rigid philosophical view of gender based on the RCC's doctrine on gender complementarity? How can an inculturated and synodal view of sex and gender that incorporates contemporary sociological gender research be reconciled with GI?

The struggle between those who attack GI and those who support it is complex. The history of GI reveals "a complicated interchange between the constellation of liberatory movements castigated by the Vatican as 'gender ideology' and the constellation of reactionary movements the Vatican and other religious conservatives developed to counter them" (Case 2019, 659). The RCC tends to interchange GI and gender theory (GT) as if they are of the same nature. Scholars agree that GI is a complex and difficult signifier to define that is primarily used by the RCC as a political tool against a common enemy in its war against gender and feminism, rather than a sociological term that conceptually interprets empirical gender relations in society. To Graff (2016), conservative Catholics use GI as a signifier and unifying concept to interpret the evils of liberalism in human sexuality (Graff 2016).

One might therefore wonder whether the RCC is talking about facts in GI, or merely exaggerating to create a political label that will mobilize conservatives and traditionalists to resist the empirical and scientific approaches to gender of sociologists, feminists, and gender activists, and to defend its purely deductive and philosophical view on sex and gender. The Vatican opposes any attempt to change the Church's traditional view that sex and gender are immutable, ontologically linked, and ordained by God based on TNLT—a view that ignores not only LGBTQI gender experience in society but also the current scientific research on biological sex, gender, and gender identity.

GI is not an accurate description of gender in society but an exaggeration that defends the RCC's doctrine on gender complementarity, which denies any form of transgenderism and gender diversity in society. Thus Agnieszka Graff (2016) suspects that there is something "delightfully demonic about GI" that exaggerates its alleged dangers to humanity, human dignity, family relations, and children's welfare. GI also exaggerates the threats of gender to the fundamental differences between men and women that may end civilization. In this case, GI then acts as a magnet for the various fears, anxieties, and obsessions of cultural conservatism that constitute what sociologists call "moral panics" (Cohen 1972). Historically, it is said to be part of the conservative turn that followed the Second Vatican Council (Vatican II).

Research Gap and Contribution

Sociological research that applies Pope Francis's synodality and synodal theology to gender studies appears to be missing in current Catholic theological literature. GI, a recent development in the RCC, became a global signifier when Pope Benedict XVI began to circulate the term within Catholicism and in global fora to resist scientific approaches to gender. Existing literature is either against or sympathetic to GI's agenda. Anna Gwiazda (2020) illustrates this divide in her comparative gender and politics study of those who advocate GI in the Central and Eastern European context and those who challenge it using populist rhetoric.

Other scholars view GI as stifling women's rights in society and advancing equality for women through legislation. In an edited volume, *Gender Equality,* Leal Finho et al. (2021) address UN Sustainable Development Goal (SDG) 5 which addresses gender disparity and aims to safeguard women's rights to equal opportunities in society. Toldy and Garraio (2020) also argue that GI is inimical to women's rights, "betrays" the most important role of women (maternity), and hinders women's participation in public discussions and political decisions that directly affect them.

There is also a large and growing body of critical sociological literature investigating the current anti-gender expressions of individual countries around the globe (e.g., Garbagnoli and Prearo 2017; Graff and Korolczuk 2018), as well as collections or edited volumes that examine GI campaigns in entire regions (e.g., Kováts and Põim 2015; Bracke and Paternotte 2016; Paternotte et al. 2016; Paternotte and Kuhar 2017).

Despite this growing literature, it is apparent that no sociological study that investigates the empirical aspects of GI in relation to Pope Francis's synodality and inductive synodal theology, separating the facts from fiction or exaggeration concerning gender theories and gender relations. There is also a paucity of sociological literature that inculturates or adapts the social science perspectives on sex and gender into the RCC's moral magisterium. Pope Francis's synodal inductive approach encourages interdisciplinary study and the incorporation of scientific methods in understanding the moral situations and lived experiences of people, including those of nonbinary persons or LGBTQI people, before theological reflection.

To date, no sociological literature has analyzed the areas of conflict and common ground between the Vatican's views on gender as reflected in GI and those of sociologists and feminists. GI is not as simple a concept as it seems. It is a highly complex term covering a range of issues that require a sociological and inductive analysis. GI, as understood in the RCC, is not about theorizing gender inequalities in the world for scientific research purposes. It is rather a social and political signifier that originated within Catholicism and has spread swiftly to Europe, the United States, and other parts of the world.

Since it is not a product of a thorough interdisciplinary scientific investigation and sophisticated theorizing, but a social construction, GI is a political signifier against those who oppose the RCC's philosophical and theological understanding of sex and gender as immutable, inseparable, and ordained by God. To Krzysztof Charamsa, the emergence of GI is a sign of intellectual failure on the part of Catholic theologians and scholars to engage in dialogue with gender experts and reformers to update the RCC's traditional moral teachings on gender. "Instead of re-assessing concepts such as 'natural law' in the light of gender studies and confronting new social reality, the Church cut off the very possibility of discussion" (cited in Graff 2016, 269).

Garbagnoli (2016) also explains that GI only aimed to construct a single enemy, assembling both religious and non-religious actors, when in fact its groups and movements are varied. Legitimizing itself as a discourse defending "what is human," GI is highly flexible and difficult to pin down. Gender scholars have criticized it as bereft of theoretical content. Mayer and Sauer (2017) view GI as an empty signifier, a mere symbolic glue against a common enemy, and a flexible concept which can be shaped in various ways in the service of political protest. Since it is not clearly defined by the RCC, GI has become a flexible umbrella term that creates an impression of conspiracy theories and is connected to "everything and anything from marriage equality and sexual education to reproductive and adoption rights and abortion" (Kuhar and Zobec 2017, 33).

Catholic theologians and clerics, mostly educated in the normative disciplines of philosophy and natural law theory and lacking expertise in scientific gender studies, could not assist Pope Francis and the RCC's moral magisterium to understand gender from sociological and feminist perspectives, engaging in dialogue with gender social scientists and feminists. Francis's synodal process and inductive synodal theology, however, can be a potent conceptual tool with which to establish an interdisciplinary dialogue between Catholic moral theologians and sociologists to inculturate scientific approaches to sexuality and gender in the RCC.

This book attempts to critically examine GI from an inductive, synodal, and sociological perspective, separating fact from fiction or exaggeration, or what sociologists call moral panics. It also intends to distinguish the philosophical and metaphysical conception of sex and gender from the sociological and scientific understanding in order to provide ways to inculturate the social science perspective into the RCC's traditional teachings on sex, gender, and gender complementarity and to realize Pope Francis's vision of a synodal church.

Objectives and Main Arguments

The monograph sociologically investigates the nature of GI in the contemporary Catholic Church as a moral panic and explores a common ground whereby empirical perspectives concerning gender, gender diversity, and LGBTQI inclusivity can be adapted to fit within the Church's moral teachings as a new "call of the times." Pope Francis's synodality and inductive synodal theology are employed as the primary conceptual framework, and the book draws on secondary literature, media reports, and church documents. It specifically aims to critically unpack "GI's ideology's" alleged grave threats to humanity, family, children, and human dignity, as well as to explore the sociological morality of gender-enhancement treatment (GET) and sex change. It attempts to find a common ground between the RCC's fundamental position on gender and sexuality in society and that of sociologists, feminists, or people behind GI to realize a synodal church in the realm of gender.

It theorizes that the RCC's GI is a form of moral panic and a misconception of the sociological difference between ideology and gender theory as used in sociological and feminist research studies. It argues that the dominance of the normative philosophical approach to gender and sexuality that is founded on TNLT remains the primary obstacle towards a synodal and inculturated understanding of gender and sexuality in the RCC.

Pope Francis's prescriptive assessment of gender as GI is a negative unintended consequence reflecting the prevailing normative clerical thinking in the RCC caused by the philosophical and theological priestly education that tends to disregard empirical and scientific research on gender and sexuality in society by sociologists and feminists. Despite this disciplinary limitation, Pope Francis is pushing boundaries in his synodality and inductive synodal theology, challenging deductive philosophical reasoning to resolve moral and theological issues in the RCC, and encouraging an interdisciplinary approach that is open to the scientific approaches of the social sciences.

In his *motu propio* document entitled *Ad Theologiam Promovendam* [To Promote Theology] (*ATP*), Francis (2023) manifests openness to the approach of the inductive theological method that begins with people's lived experiences—thus welcoming the sociological and social sciences' inductive research—as the starting point of theologizing. In dealing with moral issues, Francis's inductive approach implies first knowing the empirical reality or moral situation before theological reflection or application of moral principles to resolve them. This method is in line with his latest Church reform project called the SoS, which encourages dialogue and consultations with Catholics, the marginalized, and even representatives of humanity who are rarely heard in the Church.

Ultimately, this book contends that inculturating or adapting sociological and social science perspectives into the Church's moral teachings on sex and gender is necessary for greater acceptability of gender diversity and LGBTQI inclusivity in the RCC. It recommends a synodal dialogue between the Catholic hierarchy, moral theologians, and gender sociologists and feminists to achieve a common and holistic understanding of the nature of gender and sexuality in the contemporary world, so that GI can be discarded as an inaccurate signifier in the RCC.

Methodology

This book relies largely on archival or documentary data from published secondary literature and studies (see Long-Sutehall 2010; Largan and Morris 2019). It mainly uses textual data from RCC documents, peer-reviewed journal articles, books, and media reports. These sources were collated and analyzed to construct the main argument and attain the research objectives of the book. Secondary data analysis (SDA) is employed, which is a recent approach in qualitative research comparable to the well-established tradition of re-using quantitative data (Long-Sutehall et al. 2010).

SDA re-uses data produced for prior purposes to gain new social scientific and/or methodological knowledge (Irwin and Winterton 2011). In SDA, researchers use data collected by others in previous studies to answer new research questions (Wickham 2019). This volume used SDA and a systematic literature review to formulate its overall objectives and arguments.

The process of finding relevant textual data for the study began with a preliminary survey of online materials and familiarization with the research field. Pertinent databases and search terms were then sought, and a search method determined to identify online scholarly materials for study (Booth, Papaioannou, and Sutton 2012). Peer-reviewed journal articles, books, Church documents, and media reports that deal with gender, GI, gender complementarity, synodality, inductive synodal theology, and sociological and feminist theories and methods were evaluated, analyzed, and synthesized to pursue the book's objectives.

Overview of Major Parts and Chapters

This book has three Parts and nine chapters. Part I provides an overview of the book and unpacks gender and GI in the RCC using the sociological-synodal approach. This chapter introduces the background to the study, research gap and contribution, objectives, main arguments, and the methodology and theoretical framework of the study.

Chapter 2 unpacks the concept of GI as a political signifier and source of moral panic in the RCC, applying the critical and inductive analysis of sociology and Pope Francis's inductive synodal theology. It identifies the basic conceptual conflict between the RCC's doctrinal understanding of sex and gender and that of sociologists and feminists, exploring common ground to reconcile them. It specifically distinguishes the RCC's traditional philosophical approach to gender, gender complementarity, and gender theory from the sociological and feminist method using a sociology lens and Francis's inductive theology.

Chapter 3 analyzes the misconceptions and exaggerations of GI concerning gender, separating the factual from the fictional. It particularly characterizes GI as a moral panic and identifies some of its distorted perspectives on the scientific nature theory and ideology, as well as the correct role of theory and gender theory in sociological and feminist research. It argues that sociological and feminist gender theories are diverse and tentative, thus they cannot be inaccurately categorized under one banner of GI and characterized as directly attacking the RCC's moral doctrines.

Part II explores the major theoretical areas of conflict between the RCC's position on GI and that of those who advocate feminism and gender diversity using synodal-sociological perspectives. It specifically unpacks GI's alleged grave threats to humanity, family, and children's welfare. It begins with Chap. 4, critically investigates the alleged GI's threat to human anthropology. It argues that seeing gender as a threat to humanity is an ethnocentric social construction based on the philosophical tradition of the Church's moral teachings. It contends that GI's threat to humanity's survival is not physical but epistemological, one that challenges the RCC's metaphysical and philosophical view on sex, gender, and gender complementarity based on natural law. This chapter attempts to find a common ground between the sociological and Francis's synodal approach.

Chapter 5 attempts to sociologically unpack GI's alleged threat to the family as a foundational social unit of society, applying Pope Francis's inductive synodal theology. It contends, first, that there is no credible empirical evidence of the alleged threat, and second, that various forms of human family aside from the Catholic heterosexual family model existed long before the advent of GI. This chapter recommends the adoption of cultural relativism as well as the synodal and sociological approaches to resolve the moral panic over the perceived negative impact of GI on the family.

Chapter 6 debunks the moral panic of the alleged dangers of GI to children's welfare based on the RCC's heterosexual model of the family and on gender complementarity teaching, referencing research studies that show how new emerging forms of family structures in the LGBTQI community do not necessarily jeopardize children's welfare. It argues that seeing the welfare of children as being threatened by same-sex families and parenthood is an overreaction rather than a realistic assessment of gender's impact on children, applying sociological research and Pope Francis's inductive synodal theology.

Part III examines the RCC's understanding of human dignity vis-à-vis the current gender issues in society, according to DDF's latest document *Dignitas*

Infinita [Infinite Dignity], as well as exploring ways in which the RCC can inculturate the sociological and feminist perspectives on gender, gender diversity, and LGBTQI inclusivity in its moral teachings. Specifically, it re-evaluates the morality of transgenderism, gender-enhancing treatment (GET), and sex change, applying the sociological method and Pope Francis's inductive theology.

Chapter 7 assesses the exaggeration of gender's threat to human dignity and evaluates the morality of transgenderism, GET, and sex change. It argues that the traditional philosophical moral approach grounded in natural law theory is inadequate for moral analysis of these contemporary sexuality and moral issues. It recommends the sociological approach of inquiring into motives before moral judgment, as well as the application of the principle of double effect to fully understand the morality of transgenderism, sex change, and gender diversity, and to dissolve GI's moral panic in the RCC.

Chapter 8 sociologically analyzes how the RCC's teaching on human dignity can be applied in today's sociological research on sexuality and gender in accordance with Pope Francis's inductive synodal theology and the recent Vatican declaration entitled *Dignitas Infinita* [Infinite Dignity]. It argues that application of the teaching on human dignity in concrete moral situations requires inductive and sociological assessment, discernment of the complex moral situations involved, and an inquiry into the motives of actors before determining which options affirm or reject human dignity. It also sociologically re-examines the empirical basis of the traditional interpretation of gender complementarity in the Book of Genesis—the root cause of why transgenderism, GET, and sex change are ultimately seen as transgressions of human dignity.

Finally, Chapter 9 attempts to sociologically argue that the recognition and acceptance of gender diversity and LGBTQI inclusivity is a synodal call of our times for today's RCC, which requires inculturation in light of Pope Francis's synodality and sociological gender studies. It specifically contends that gender diversity has existed since ancient times but has only been emphasized in recent decades owing to growing media campaigns, biotechnological advances, and pro-gender and LGBTQI activism. It recommends that the RCC re-evaluates its philosophical stance on sex and gender and adapts some of the sociological and social science perspectives to recognize gender diversity and LGBTQI inclusivity as synodal response to call of the age.

Theoretical Orientation

Origin and Theological Foundations of GI

Pope Benedict XVI is said to have played a key role in the adoption, circulation, and legitimation of the term GI in the RCC (Vaggione 2020). His reading of the anti-feminist pamphlet "Gender: The Deconstruction of Women" by the American journalist-activist Dale O' Leary allegedly influenced his negative attitude toward feminism and gender theories (Graff 2016). Case (2019) theorizes that an alternative scenario could have occurred in the RCC had Cardinal Joseph Ratzinger, before becoming Pope Benedict XVI, not read O'Leary's pamphlet.

Thus, the term GI originated within Catholicism (Vaggione 2020). GT and GI are terms "invented" by the RCC through Pope Benedict XVI to understand and counter the influence of the feminist and LGBTQI movements that were growing in popularity in the United States, Europe, and Latin America. GI became a concept, a signifier of the perceived evils of liberalism in the realm of human sexuality by conservative Catholics." Although Benedict XVI introduced GI in the RCC, it was John Paul II's ideas about 'culture of death,' 'bad feminism,' and "a close companion of 'natural rights and 'complementarity'" that were said to be the underlying assumption behind this concept (Graff 2016, 282).

Pope John Paul II saw male and female as naturally complementary in his "theology of the body," which became the theological foundation of GI. To John Paul II, "When considered together [as man and woman], they produce a unified reality, forming a whole that neither of them could form alone: "Masculinity and femininity express the twofold aspect of man's somatic constitution… [which] consists in reciprocal enrichment" (Ford 2018, 81).

The doctrine on gender complementarity that views biological sex and the socio-cultural role of sex (gender) as mutually inseparable realities became deeply embedded in the RCC's moral magisterium, and herein lies the fundamental moral principle of GI (Francis 2016a, b). Even the progressive Pope Francis, who welcomes members of the LGBTQI group into the Church (DDF 2023), upholds this theology. In his post-apostolic synodal exhortation on the pastoral care of families entitled *Amoris Laetitia* [The Joy of Love], Francis (2015) declared that sex and gender are distinguishable but immutably linked with one another as ordained by God.

GI can pose a major obstacle preventing the inculturation or adaptation of sociological and social science perspectives on sex and gender. Strictly maintaining the RCC's philosophical and metaphysical view of sex and gender and gender complementarity, it resists synodal listening and dialogue with gender-diverse people as well as gender sociologists, social scientists, feminists, and LGBTQI activists.

Philosophy, Sociology, and Contemporary Morality

GI is a complex moral issue that cannot easily be resolved within the RCC to advance the Church's mission in today's society by mere deductive philosophical reasoning. In an increasingly complex and globalized world, developing an interdisciplinary approach called sociological theology that creatively integrates and maintains disciplinal limits between theology and sociology is necessary for evangelization (Gill 2012). Crucially, this approach will enhance the theological and empirical thinking of the Catholic hierarchy of clerics as spiritual leaders of the RCC as they seek to deal with contemporary moral issues such as gender, gender diversity, and LGBTQI inclusivity.

In the medieval period, with St. Thomas Aquinas's adaptation of Aristotelian philosophy in the Christian faith, philosophy became so embedded in Catholic theology that eventually the RCC accepted the idea that reason is the cognitive path of faith and that philosophy, as a science of reasoning, is its essential tool. Just before the Second Vatican Council (Vatican II), "most Catholic thinkers…assumed that Catholic theology was a firm structure built on the foundations of scholastic philosophy and accepted this idea as the de facto situation" (Vanderhaar 2012, 71). The RCC ultimately views faith and reason as two cognitive paths of revelation and human nature (Pontifical Council on Justice and Peace 2005, para. 75). Philosophy became the handmaid of theology. Philosophical theology became the main discipline in clerical education, overlooking the importance of behavioral sciences such as sociology in dealing with and evangelizing in the evolving modern world.

To apply the RCC's moral principles to the increasingly complex globalizing world of today requires both a sociological approach and Pope Francis's inductive, synodal, and interdisciplinary theology. As a normative discipline, philosophy fundamentally relies on a priori knowledge and metaphysical criteria to judge human behavior. It basically asks conceptual rather than empirical questions and thus as an academic field is limited in its ability to deal with behavioral aspects of contemporary morality.

Philosophy cannot scientifically account for social behavior and the growing complexity of the cultural systems of people who receive Church teachings in modern and postmodern times (Frodeman 2013; Ballano 2020). And yet, the Catholic hierarchy of bishops who act as moral guardians in the RCC is still largely educated in the normative disciplines of philosophy and theology, lacking the descriptive, scientific sociological and social science knowledge that greatly sharpens empirical thinking on contemporary moral issues such as gender relations. The result of this normative education is that Catholic bishops and moral theologians largely view the world and human behavior in a prescriptive and philosophical manner that tends to overlook the empirical reality, failing to appreciate how the descriptive and scientific lens of sociology and behavioral sciences can greatly assist them in understanding the empirical and cultural dimensions of moral behavior.

Enhancing the empirical thinking of Catholic clerics, professed religious, missionaries, and theologians through intensive training in sociology in seminaries and houses of formation is crucial if they are to accurately comprehend the empirical character of the complex moral issues of contemporary society such as gender, gender diversity, and LGBTQI inclusivity and guide the ecclesiastical reforms of the SoS. In today's fast-paced societal transformation, institutions such as the RCC that are often seen as the vanguard of religious traditions, are usually left behind when it comes to scientific and sociological knowledge.

Role of Sociologists in Studying Religion

Sociology does not aim to colonize the RCC's religious beliefs and doctrinal systems but to provide an accurate scientific assessment of the moral aspects of gender issues to assist the RCC's moral magisterium and moral theologians to apply the Church's moral principles in today's complex and globalizing world. The persistent moral issues of gender, GI, gender diversity, and LGBTQI inclusivity represent a new synodal call of our times for the RCC's inculturation to achieve Pope Francis's synodal Church.

The devout Catholic sociologist of religion Thomas Luckman cautions sociologists never to argue with theologians, pointing out a basic distinction between religion and science. To him, it is not the function of the sociologist to defend, attack, justify, or delegitimate people's religions or the belief systems of any society (Luckman 2022). Luckman's warning is apposite. Sociologists have no business attacking, justifying, or delegitimizing people's religion or belief systems. They can, however, assist religion, as part of human culture, to clarify the empirical dimensions of some of its belief systems to promote greater religious understanding for people in society. After all, religious thought and practice are human activities (Pugh 2009).

Sociologists can also help religion's theologians to ground some of their theologizing, especially if it involves moral or behavioral issues. Sociology is a descriptive rather than a prescriptive discipline. Using the scientific method, it studies society and people's behavior, primarily using what the German sociologist Max Weber calls value-free judgment, although it respects the value-laden knowledge of theology in society.

Although religion, including Catholicism, is understood as having transcendent origins, being based on divine revelation in the Scriptures, it is also nonetheless a human activity. Thus, Dietrich Bonhoeffer and other religious scholars think that religious thought and practice, albeit done in response to a perception of a divine transcendence, are nonetheless human actions (Bonhoeffer 1953; Pugh 2009). In his doctoral thesis, *Sanctorum Communio*, Bonhoeffer (2009) specifically thinks that Christianity has a sociologically and empirically definable essence despite its supernatural origins. To Haight (2008), the Church is first and foremost a human institution grounded in human society and culture, although its ultimate mission is supernatural.

In the RCC, sociologists are among the people who are not always listened to by Church authorities, theologians, and ecclesiastical scholars. They are among the voiceless in the RCC, as characterized by the SoS. With an apparent lack of sociologists who can directly relate their sociological research on current Catholic moral and ecclesiastical issues, the sociological voice remains weak in the RCC. And yet Vatican II was open to the exact sciences and various disciplines that study the human being for evangelization (Pontifical Council for Justice and Peace 2005, para. 76).

Pope Francis' current vision on synodality aims to understand historical context, epochal changes, complexity of social context, and "signs of the times" in order to interpret them in the light of the Gospel:

> The synodal journey unfolds within a historical context marked by epochal changes in society and by a crucial transition in the life of the Church, which cannot be ignored: it is within the folds of the complexity of this context, in its tensions and contradictions, that we are called to "scrutinize the signs of the times and interpret them in the light of the Gospel" (GS, no. 4). (Synod of Bishops 2021, 7)

The engagement of sociology with religious phenomena does not seek to colonize theology or people's religious belief systems, nor to delegitimize religion. In most cases, sociological work on religion entails clarifying and providing the empirical foundations of some theological and religious claims on human behavior and society. The scientific methodology of sociology is necessary to accurately describe the empirical reality or moral situation in order for theologians to appropriately judge and apply in society the social doctrines of the Church, known as Catholic social teaching.

Pope Francis's Inductive Theology and Sociology

In his latest apostolic letter, *APT*, Pope Francis revised the statutes of the Pontifical Academy of Theology in Catholic theology (PATH) "to make them more suitable for the mission that our time imposes on theology." It encourages a "'paradigm shift' in Catholic theology that takes widespread engagement with contemporary science, culture, and people's lived experience as an essential starting point" (Liedl 2023, para. 2). "This means that theology must be "capable of reading and interpreting the Gospel in the conditions in which men and women live daily, in different geographical, social and cultural environments" (The Pillar 2023, *para.* 20).

This paradigm shift implies the engagement of sociology in Catholic theology. In *APT,* Pope Francis has recognized the need for Catholic theology to dialogue with other branches of knowledge such as sociology and the social sciences to understand people's lived experiences. Thus, Catholic theologians who assist Francis in his SoS should welcome the contribution of sociology to the enhancement of inductive synodal theology.

Francis's inductive theological approach coincides with the inductive sociological method that begins with accurate understanding of human experience before theorizing. However, sociologist are not moralists, generally describing behavior and social phenomena but refusing to pass moral judgment over them as "right" or "wrong," and "good" or "evil." Sociological knowledge is descriptive rather than prescriptive.

Unlike Catholic moral theologians who judge human behavior with a fixed set of metaphysical beliefs such as the natural law theory, sociologists usually adopt an attitude of moral neutrality in judging people's actions and social situations. To them, moral claims and truth claims are not self-evident or absolute but are relative to the cultural conventions in which those who utter them are embedded (Jarvie 2007).

While Catholic theologians tend to absolutize their theological paradigm to analyze behavior, sociologists tend to be relative and adopt a sociological theory which they find appropriately to describes or explains a social or moral phenomenon, acknowledging that there is a plurality of normative norms to judge the empirical dimension of social behavior. Relativism is often understood as "cultural relativism," which means that the values, knowledge, and behavior of people must be judged according to their cultural context (Cole 2019) and not based on a fixed metaphysical or philosophical theory.

In contrast, Catholic theologians and moralists generally adopt an absolutist position in evaluating social phenomena. Absolutism generally makes normative ethical decisions based on perceived "objective rules," maintaining that some things are always "morally right" or "morally wrong," regardless of the cultural context. Moral theologians believe that there are universal moral truths relevant across all contexts and all people, based on divine law and human reason.

Catholic Theology, Sociology, and Morality

Catholic moral theologians and philosophers are not obliged by their disciplines to support their theorizing with scientific data following their normative disciplines. But sociologists as social scientists are required to support their theorizing to test its applicability to empirical reality through the scientific research method. Data are necessary to confirm or disconfirm theoretical assessment in sociology. This scientific approach is different from the prescriptive philosophical and theological theorizing that generally only occurs at the conceptual level without data support.

When dealing with the morality of homosexuality, for example, Catholic moral theologians would usually approach it using the traditional TNLT and deductive philosophical reasoning. Thus, they would morally conceptualize homosexuality as "unnatural" and intrinsically disordered in the metaphysical sense, using reason and logic rather than first inquiring into its factual nature. In the RCC's moral teaching, which is promoted by Catholic moral theologians, homosexuality is "naturally disordered," not because it violates certain laws of nature in the empirical sense, but because it contravenes the metaphysical and theological conception of "nature" as understood in scholastic philosophy and TNLT.

The theological-philosophical approach to morality does not normally gather empirical data through the scientific method to support moral judgment. It adopts the deductive method that uses philosophical reasoning rather than the inductive approach that seeks empirical evidence before judging the morality of a human action. Instead of investigating and scientifically evaluating the moral situation of the ethical issue before passing moral judgment, Catholic moralists generally resolve moral issues through deductive reasoning, regardless of the lived experiences of people and social science research studies.

This deductive theological and moral approach is contrary to Pope Francis's (2023) new inductive synodal theology as expounded in *ATP*. *ATP* calls for a paradigm shift in Catholic theology. Instead of applying the deductive method of the past, Francis wants an inductive theological method that prioritizes the accurate understanding of peoples' lived experiences before theological reflection. This has serious implications for resolving complex moral issues such as homosexuality, same-sex marriage, and LGBTQI inclusivity.

For the sociologist and priest Fr Andrew Greeley (2012), theology combines professional reflection according to the methodology of its discipline with extremely amateur observations about the world (Greeley 2012). "The dependence of Catholic moral theology on philosophy… has inadvertently sidestepped the contribution of sociology and social sciences in providing an empirical account of the social order, which is necessary for attaining a sound moral judgment and analysis. Philosophy, as a discipline, lacks scientific methodologies to test the appropriateness and applicability of its theories in the empirical world" (Ballano 2019, 4–5). Sociological research can therefore be utilized by Catholic moral theologians as an empirical foundation for moral judgment and application of the RCC's moral principle and prescription.

RCC's Moral Panic in GI and Francis's Synodal Theology

Post-Vatican II papal documents have acknowledged the significant contribution of the social sciences to Catholic moral theology and Church discipline. In the post-synodal exhortation entitled *Pastores Dabo Vobis* [I Shall Give you Shepherds], for instance, Pope John Paul II (1992) recognized the contribution of sociological research in the human formation of Catholic priests. Pope Francis's (2023) *ATP* further recommends a paradigm change in Catholic theology that needs to use other branches of knowledge such as the social sciences to understand the cultural revolutions occurring in society and to update Church teachings for the establishment of a synodal church.

Understanding human behavior and resolving moral and ecclesiastical issues by starting with human experience and empirical data before theological reflection are concerns that are common to Pope Francis's inductive synodal theology and the inductive approach of modern sociology. Given the growing complexity of today's globalizing world, the cultural revolution, and the emergence of complex moral issues concerning sexuality, gender, and LGBTQI inclusivity, an inculturated Catholic moral theology that combines Francis's inductive synodal theology and the sociology of morality to address the complex gender issues of GI is becoming imperative.

As Brickell (2009, 466) argues:

> The study of sexuality has grown rapidly in recent decades, and the literature is vast. Some scholars have explored the history and meaning of sexual identities and some the dissemination of sexual advice, while others focus on the patterns and politics of sexual activity in historical and contemporary context.

Because of the strong influence of the theology of the body espoused by Pope John Paul II and reaffirmed by Pope Benedict XVI and Pope Francis, the RCC has inappropriately and indiscriminately categorized all views and explanations that oppose this theology and the official Church teachings on gender and sexual teachings by the magisterium as GI (Ford 2018). This labeling does acknowledge, however, the basic difference in perspective and method between traditional Catholic morality and the sociology of morality.

The struggle between those who attack GI and those who support it is complex. The history of GI reveals "a complicated interchange between the constellation of liberatory movements castigated by the Vatican as 'gender ideology' and the constellation of reactionary movements the Vatican and other religious conservatives developed to counter them" (Case 2019, 659). The Vatican tends to use GI and GT interchangeably as if they are the same terms.

Yet, scholars agree that the RCC's exaggerated description of GI's threats to the family, church, and society are being used as a political tool to create a common enemy and moral panic in its war against gender and feminism. The concept of moral panic was elaborated by the sociologist Stanley Cohen in his book "Folk Devils and Moral Panics." To him, a moral panic is:

> a condition, episode, person or group of persons emerges to become defined as a threat to societal values and interests; its nature is presented in a stylized and stereotypical fashion by the mass media; the moral barricades are manned by editors, bishops, politicians and other right-thinking people; socially accredited experts pronounce their diagnoses and solutions; ways of coping are evolved or (more often) resorted to; the condition then disappears, submerges or deteriorates and becomes more visible. (Cohen 1972: 1)

A moral panic is an exaggeration of a perceived threat to societal values by authorities or mass media to generate urgent mass support for political action rather than an accurate description of a societal problem. Crossman (2019: para. 1) sociologically defines a moral panic as "a widespread fear, most often an irrational one, that someone or something is a threat to the values, safety, and interests of a community or society at large."

If GI is RCC's inaccurate term for the complex gender problems of the current age, used to instill fear of its alleged dangers and to generate urgent action, then it fits into the sociological criteria of being a moral panic that requires sociological and inductive synodal analysis to sift fact from fiction. As Agnieszka Graff (2016) contends, GI "tends to magnify its negative impact on people such as its threat to children, the danger of 'collapsing' differences between men and women, the prophesied end of civilization that serves like a magnet of the various fears, anxieties, and obsessions of cultural conservatism." Thus, without a sociological clarification, GI can be confusing to ordinary Catholics who need synodal pastoral guidance in today's world.

In his *ATP,* Pope Francis (2023) manifests openness to the inductive theological method that begins with empirical reality rather than theories. This method commences with people's lived experiences—thus welcoming the inductive research approach of sociology and social sciences—as the starting point of theologizing. In dealing with moral issues, this implies knowing first the empirical reality of moral situations before theological reflection or the application of moral principles to resolve them. Thus, a synodal understanding of GI should identify the empirical issues and basic areas of conflict, separating the sociological truth from moral panic.

A synodal-sociological investigation of GI is in line with Francis's latest Church reform project, called the SoS, which encourages dialogue and consultations with Catholics, the marginalized, and even such representatives of humanity as feminists, gender activists, LGBTQI people, and sociologists, whose voices are rarely heard in the RCC, to realize Francis's synodal church in contemporary times.

Inculturating Sociological Gender Perspectives in RCC

The RCC's evangelization mission is a process of inserting the Christian message into human cultures in accordance with the Vatican II document *Gaudium et Spes* [Joy and Hope] (1965), recognizing that evangelization is a living exchange between the Church and the various cultures around the globe. In accordance with the Vatican II *aggriornamento* [renewal], which the SoS aims to implement, the RCC needs to read the new signs of the times regarding gender, gender diversity, and LGBTQI inclusivity.

If the RCC is to inculturate the Gospel of love and social justice into the lives of gay and nonbinary people, it needs—in the spirit of Francis's synodality and inductive theology—to listen to the personal struggles, psychological traumas, and societal harassment that they have suffered through human history, rather than dismissing outright pro-gender advocacies, gender diversity and LGBTQI movements as part of GI.

Despite Pope Francis's welcoming attitude towards homosexuals and the LGBTQI in the Church and inductive synodal theology, the RCC has not undertaken the in-depth inquiry into gay culture that would enable it to inculturate the Gospel into the personal life and thought patterns of people of diverse genders and sexualities. In a spirit of synodal listening and inculturation, instead of vigorously opposing pro-gender movements and labeling them part of GI, Catholic bishops and moral theologians should be open to new perspectives and ways of understanding gender, gender diversity, and LGBTQI inclusivity beyond the philosophical approach to Catholic morality based on TNLT.

The social struggles and protests of gay and gender-diverse people against the heteronormativity that recognizes heterosexuality as the only gender standard in society have a long history. The growing visibility of LGBTQI in the broadcast and social media is a new sign of the times that needs synodal listening and dialogue between Catholic bishops, moralists, and representatives of the gay community. The SoS has attempted to dialogue with members of the LGBTQI community by appointing members of the gay community such as Fr James Martin, S.J. among the 365 Church representatives during the 2023 roundtable discussions in Rome. But this is not enough. At the plenary session that discussed homosexuality and

LGBTQI moral issues, the LGBTQI voice was overwhelmed by representatives of the African Church, who are mostly influenced by their anti-gay culture.

This book seeks to inculturate the sociological and social science perspectives on gender, gender diversity, and LGBTQI inclusivity into the RCC's moral teachings. It attempts to incorporate sociological and feminist approaches to gender in the traditional moral doctrines for a newer and nuanced perspective on gender and gender diversity in the contemporary Catholic Church. Without changing its core moral teachings, The RCC could not respond to gender challenge as a new sign of the times, where gender diversity or fluidity is sociologically connected with the growing "liquidity" of the contemporary world.

Gender identity, which is a person's intrinsic self-identification of personal femaleness and maleness, connected to but distinct from their biological sex (Scott 1999), has evolved in various forms in recent years; hence the rise of LGBTQI as distinct genders. This volume argues that today's growing voice of nonbinary people and the LGBTQI movement for public recognition of their rights and normalization of their gender constitute a new synodal call of the times for the RCC and not a mere imposition of liberal values on sexuality and GI by Western countries.

Since the concepts of gender, gender diversity, and GI are recent developments for the RCC, sociological literature and research inculturating scientific gender studies into Catholic morality appear to be lacking. Embracing the scientific approaches of sociology and feminism necessarily challenges the RCC's traditional and philosophical view on sexuality and gender. But the prophetic call to update the empirical foundations of some of the RCC's topical moral teachings to make the Church's mission responsive to the signs of the times is a Christian vocation. Thus, this volume seeks to achieve a nuanced understanding of gender, gender diversity, and LGBTQI inclusivity in the RCC that incorporates the sociological gender perspectives in the RCC's moral magisterium through Pope Francis's synodal way.

Conclusion

This chapter has provided an overview of the book in terms of its social background, the research gap and contribution to the literature, objectives, main arguments, methodology, and overall theoretical foundation. Applying Pope Francis's synodality and inductive synodal theology as well as sociological perspectives on gender, gender theory, gender diversity, and LGBTQI inclusivity, it has critically examined the nature of GI as a moral panic and its alleged threats to humanity, family, children's welfare, and human dignity. It has also explored the major areas of conflict between GI's proponents, led by bishops and moral theologians, and pro-gender sociologists, feminists, activists, and LGBTQI leaders in the search for a common ground for synodal dialogue and inculturation.

It is argued that the prescriptive understanding of morality and gender that is still based on the highly philosophical Thomistic natural law theory needs to be updated with scientific and sociological approaches to gender and sexuality for today's world. The chapter recommends inculturating sociological and social science gender perspectives into the RCC's traditional philosophical approach to achieve greater moral acceptability of gender diversity and inclusivity of the LGBTQI community in the contemporary Catholic Church.

References

Ballano V (2019) Catholic social teaching, theology, and sociology: exploring the common ground. Religions 10(10):1–16. https://doi.org/10.3390/rel10100557

Ballano VO (2020) Inculturation, anthropology, and the empirical dimension of evangelization. Religions 11(2):101. https://doi.org/10.3390/rel11020101

BBC News (2013) Pope Francis: who am i to judge gay people? BBC News Website (29 July 2013). https://www.bbc.com/news/world-europe-23489702#:~:text=%22If%20a%20person%20is%20gay,marginalised%20but%20integrated%20into%20society. accessed 30 April 2014

Bracke S, Paternotte D (eds) (2016) Habemus gender! The catholic church and 'Gender Ideology'. Special Issue Religion Gender 6(2)

Brickell C (2009) Sexuality and the dimensions of power. Sex Cult 13:57–74. https://doi.org/10.1007/s12119-008-9042-x

Case MA (2019) Trans formations in the Vatican's war on 'gender ideology'. Signs J Women Culture Soc 44(3):639–664

Cohen S (1972) Folk devils and moral panics. Paladin, Herts

Cole NL (2019) Definition of cultural relativism in sociology. ThoughtCo. Available online: https://www.thoughtco.com/cultural-relativism-definition-3026122

Crossman A (2020) A sociological understanding of moral panic. ThoughtCo, Dec. 18, 2020, thoughtco.com/moral-panic-3026420. https://www.thoughtco.com/moral-panic-3026420

DDF (Dicastery of the Doctrine of the Faith) (2023) Fiducia Supplicans: on the pastoral meaning of blessings. Vatican: The Roman Curia. Available at: https://www.vatican.va/roman_curia/congregations/cfaith/documents/rc_ddf_doc_20231218_fiducia-supplicans_en.html

DDF (Dicastery of the Doctrine of the Faith) (2024) Declaration Dignitas Infinita on human dignity. Vatican: The Roman Curia. https://www.vatican.va/roman_curia/congregations/cfaith/documents/rc_ddf_doc_20240402_dignitas-infinita_en.html

Fagbamigbe Sr MA, Synod in the teachings of church fathers: lessons for a Synodal church today. Catholic Voyage 20(1):17–37

Ford CJ (2018) Transgender bodies, catholic schools, and a queer natural law theology of exploration. J Moral Theol 7(1):70–98

Frodeman, 2013 Frodeman R (2013) Philosophy Dedisciplined. Synthese 190:1917–1936. https://doi.org/10.1007/s11229-012-0181-0

Garbagnoli S (2016) Against the heresy of immanence: Vatican's 'Gender' as a new rhetorical device against the denaturalization of the sexual order. Religion Gender 6(2):187–204. https://doi.org/10.18352/rg.10156

Garbagnoli S, Prearo M (2017) "La croisade 'anti-genre': Du Vatican aux manifs pour tous" [The 'antigender' crusade: From the Vatican to the Manifs pour Tous]. Petite encyclopédie critique, Paris

Gaudium et Spes [Joy and Hope] (1965) The pastoral constitution on the church in the modern world. Vatican: Vatican Archive. https://www.vatican.va/archive/hist_councils/ii_vatican_council/documents/vat-ii_cons_19651207_gaudium-et-spes_en.html

Gill R (2012) Theology in a social context: sociological theology, vol 1. Routledge, London

Graff A (2016) 'Gender ideology': weak concepts, powerful politics. Religion Gender 6(2):268–272. https://doi.org/10.18352/rg.10177

Greeley A (2012) Sociology and theology: some methodological questions. Proceedings of the catholic theological society of America. http://ejournals.bc.edu/ojs/index.php/article/view/2872/2497

Graff A, Korolczuk E (2018) Gender as 'Ebola from Brussels': the anticolonial frame and the rise of illiberal populism. Signs J Women Culture Soc 43(4):797–821

Gwiazda A (2020) Right-wing populism and feminist politics: the case of law and justice in Poland. Int Polit Sci Rev 42(5):1–16. https://doi.org/10.1177/0192512120948917

Hahnenberg EP (2007) A concise guide to the documents of Vatican II. St. Anthony Messenger Press, Cincinnati, Ohio

ITC (International Theological Commission) (2018) Synodality in the life and mission of the church. Vatican: The Roman Curia. Available at: https://www.vatican.va/roman_curia/congregations/cfaith/cti_documents/rc_cti_20180302_sinodalita_en.html

Jarvie I (2007) Relativism and historicism. In: Turner SP, Risjold MW (eds), Handbook of the philosophy of science, philosophy of anthropology and sociology. Amsterdam: North-Holland

Kováts E, Põim M (eds) (2015) Gender as Symbolic Glue: the position and role of conservative and far right parties in the anti-gender mobilization in Europe. Foundation for European Progressive Studies and Friedrich-Ebert-Stiftung Budapest, Brussels

Leal Filho W, Azul AM, Brandli L, Lange Salvia A, Wall T (eds) (2021) Gender equality. Encyclopedia of the UN sustainable development goals. Cham: Springer. https://doi.org/10.1007/978-3-319-70060-1_86-1

Luckman T (2022) The invisible religion: the problem of religion in modern society, 1st edn. Routledge, London

Mares C (2024) Pope Francis: gender ideology is 'one of the most dangerous ideological Colonizations' today. Catholic News Agency (March 11, 2023). https://www.catholicnewsagency.com/news/253845/pope-francis-gender-ideology-is-one-of-the-most-dangerous-ideological-colonizations-today

Mayer S, Sauer B (2017) 'Gender ideology' in Austria: coalitions around an empty signifier. In: Kuhar R, Paternotte D (eds), Anti-gender campaigns in Europe. Mobilizing against Equality. Lanham, MD Rowman & Littlefield

Paternotte D, Kuhar R (2017) 'Gender ideology' in movement: an introduction. In: Kuhar R, Paternotte D (eds) Anti-gender campaigns in Europe: mobilizing against equality, 1–22. New York, London: Rowman & Littlefield International

Paternotte D, Van Dusen S, Piette V (eds) (2016) Habemus gender! Deconstruction d'une riposte religieuse. Editions de l'Université de Bruxelles, Brussels

Pontifical Council for Justice and Peace (2005) Compendium of Social Doctrine of the Church.
Rome: Libreria Editrice Vaticana. http://www.vatican.va/roman_curia/pontifical_councils/justpeace/documents/rc_pc_justpeace_doc_20060526_compendiodott-soc_en.html.

Pope Francis (2015) Address during the ceremony commemorating the 50th anniversary of the institution of the Synod of Bishops. 17 October 2015. http://w2.vatican.va/content/francesco/en/speeches/2015/october/documents/papafrancesco_20151017_50-anniversario-sinodo.html

Pope Francis (2016a) Post-Synodal exhortation Amoris Laetitia. Vatican: Dicastero per la Comunicazione—Libreria Editrice Vaticana. https://www.vatican.va/content/francesco/en/apost_exhortations/documents/papa-francesco_esortazione-ap_20160319_amoris-laetitia.html

Pope Francis (2016b) Meeting with the polish bishops: address of his holiness pope Francis, 27 July 2016. Vatican: Dicastero per la Comunicazione--Libreria Editrice Vaticana https://www.vatican.va/content/francesco/en/speeches/2016/july/documents/papa-francesco_20160727_polonia-vescovi.html. Accessed 30Aoril 2024

Pope Francis (2023) Apostolic letter issued "Motu Proprio" Ad Theologiam Promovendam. Vatican. Available at: https://www.vatican.va/content/francesco/en/events/event.dir.html/content/vaticanevents/en/2023/11/1/ad-theologiam-promovendam.html

Pope Paul VI (1965) Apostolica Sollicitudo [Apostolic Letter]: Establishing the Synod of Bishops for the Universal Church. Vatican City: Dicastero per la Comunicazione—Libreria

Editrice Vaticana. https://www.vatican.va/content/paul-vi/en/motu_proprio/documents/hf_p-vi_motu-proprio_19650915_apostolica-sollicitudo.html
Pugh J (2009) Religionless Christianity: Dietrich Bonhoeffer in Troubled Times. Continuum, New York, NY
Scott JW (1999) Gender and the politics of history. Columbia University Press, New York
Synod of Bishops (2021) For a Synodal church: communion, participation, and mission. Preparatory Document. Synod of Bishops
Toldy T, Garraio J (2020) Gender ideology: a discourse that threatens gender equality. In: Leal Filho W, Azul A, Brandli L, Lange Salvia A, Wall T (eds), Gender equality. Encyclopedia of the UN Sustainable Development Goals. Cham: Springer. https://doi.org/10.1007/978-3-319-70060-1_86-1
Zengarini L (2024) Pope Francis: gender ideology is the ugliest danger of our time. Vatican News (March 1, 2024). https://www.vaticannews.va/en/pope/news/2024-03/pope-francis-gender-ideology-is-the-ugliest-danger-of-our-time.html

Chapter 2
Gender and "Gender Ideology" in the Catholic Church: A Synodal-Sociological Exploration

Abstract In applying the inductive synodal approach and sociological perspectives, this chapter aims to sociologically unpack so-called "gender ideology" in the Catholic Church, distinguishing the fundamental differences between the Church's philosophical–theological understanding of gender, sexuality, and gender theory and those of sociology and the social sciences. It aims to find common ground to understand gender between the Church's moral magisterium and the social sciences in an attempt to update the traditional moral approach in spirit of Pope Francis's synodality and inductive theology. It argues that the synodal-sociological approach offers new hope for the Church to achieve a more empirical, inculturated, and nuanced view of gender and sexuality in the contemporary world, despite Francis's strong opposition to "gender ideology."

Keywords Gender · Gender ideology · Gender complementarity · Synodality · Inductive Synodal theology · Sociology

Introduction

One of the most contentious concepts that has engulfed the Roman Catholic Church (RCC) in recent years is gender. The late Pope Benedict XVI predicted that gender would be the next great challenge for the RCC and the final rebellion against God (Caldwell 2023). In his Christmas 2012 address to the Roman Curia, less than two months before he resigned as Pope, Benedict XVI strongly opposed the new philosophy of gender, which for him questions "the very notion of being—of what being human really means as consisting only of biological male and female".

Quoting the feminist Simone de Beauvoir that "one is not born a woman, one becomes so" (*on ne naît pas femme, on le devient*), Benedict XVI condemned the social science perspective of gender as social and cultural experience. He declared that de Beauvoir's words constitute the philosophical foundation of today's conception of "gender" and sexuality:

V. O. Ballano, *Gender Ideology and the Contemporary Catholic Church*,
https://doi.org/10.1007/978-981-97-8124-9_2

> According to this philosophy, sex is no longer a given element of nature, that man has to accept and personally make sense of: it is a social role that we choose for ourselves, while in the past it was chosen for us by society. The profound falsehood of this theory and of the anthropological revolution contained within it is obvious. People dispute the idea that they have a nature, given by their bodily identity, that serves as a defining element of the human being. They deny their nature and decide that it is not something previously given to them, but that they make it for themselves. (Pope Benedict XVI 2012, para. 6)

Benedict XVI strongly upheld the traditional Church teaching on gender complementarity based on the Bible. To him "being created by God as male and female pertains to the essence of the human creature. This duality is an essential aspect of what being human is all about, as ordained by God" (Pope Benedict XVI 2012, para. 6). Benedict introduced the term "gender ideology" (GI) or "gender theory" (GT) in his pronouncements and writings to signify any gender theorizing that contravenes the Church's moral teaching on heterosexuality. Benedict was allegedly influenced by the anti-feminist pamphlet by the American pro-life journalist Dale O'Leary entitled "Gender: The Deconstruction of Women."

Without clearly defining GI, Benedict XVI played a key role in establishing and promoting it in the RCC. GI replaced Pope John Paul II's "culture of death" as the theological framework to explain the alleged dangers of contemporary gender theories (Vaggione 2020). Through Benedict's writings and homilies, the RCC has gradually incorporated this term in its official documents. GI became a label for prevailing feminist and social science gender theories and beliefs perceived to be inimical to ecclesiastical gender teachings, specifically any attack against the Church's doctrine on gender complementarity as immutable and ordained by God.

Influenced by Benedict XVI's understanding of GI, Pope Francis magnified the moral panic against gender in his address to the participants of a two-day conference in the Vatican to study gender entitled "Man-Woman Image of God: For an Anthropology of Vocations" (Zengarini 2024). Francis called GI the "greatest threat" to humanity because it erases the gender differences between a man and a woman, as well as endangering the moral foundations of the heterosexual family in society and children's welfare. He thus called on the participants to resist GI and promote the gender complementarity teaching of the Church.

Since Pope John Paul II, the RCC has vigorously defended the moral doctrine of gender complementarity against attacks by feminists, gender activists, sociologists, and LGBTQI leaders. The Congregation for Catholic Education's 2019 document "Male and Female He Created Them" strongly defended the biological complementary of the sexes and condemned GI for its alleged dangers to children's education. It specifically blamed gender for the current educational crisis in areas of affectivity and sexuality that cancels out the natural differences between men and women. According to the Congregation:

> It is becoming increasingly clear that we are now facing with what might accurately be called an educational crisis, especially in the field of affectivity and sexuality. In many places, curricula are being planned and implemented which "allegedly convey a neutral conception of the person and of life, yet in fact reflect an anthropology opposed to faith and to right reason". The disorientation regarding anthropology which is a widespread feature

> of our cultural landscape has undoubtedly helped to destabilize the family as an institution, bringing with it a tendency to cancel out the differences between men and women, presenting them instead as merely the product of historical and cultural conditioning. (Congregation for Catholic Education 2019, #1)

In all these ecclesiastical pronouncements against GI, it is apparent that the RCC is pursuing a deductive philosophical approach to understand gender and is characterizing GI as a new philosophy of sexuality that promotes the social and cultural nature of gender. Instead of first inquiring and accurately studying the nature of these gender theories and engaging in dialogue with gender sociologists and feminists to understand the bundle of issues contained in GI as a signifier, the RCC has already judged gender theories that oppose gender complementarity and heterosexuality as inimical to Church moral teachings. Pope Benedict XVI, for instance, has already judged the social science concept of gender, labeled as GI, as the final rebellion against God (Caldwell 2023).

This moral scare against GI further increased with Pope Francis's declaration that GI is the ugliest and most dangerous ideology to threaten the survival of humanity (Zengarini 2024). This declaration is consistent with his earlier attack against gender during the early part of his pontificate, which he characterized as an ideological colonization. To Francis, GI is "a neocolonial project through which Western activists and their governments try to export their decadent values and secularize non-Western societies" (Paternotte and Kuhar 2017, 8). To him, GI is trying to impose Western values about gender, gender diversity, transgender sexuality, non-traditional forms of family structure, and other perceived anti-Catholic moral values on developing and non-Western countries.

With all these accusations against GI in ecclesiastical and papal declarations, one wonders which of them are fully or partially empirical and fictional. The RCC's traditional philosophical and metaphysical approach to sex and gender does not prioritize social and cultural experiences in judging people's sexuality and gender identity in society. It uses logic and deductive reasoning as well as espousing the Thomistic natural law theory (TNLT) to assess the morality of sexuality and gender.

Natural law theory (NLT) asserts that there are naturally occurring fundamental and pre-existing rights conferred on everyone by "God, nature, or reason". These rules of right and wrong are inherent in people and cannot be created or changed by society or the courts" (Jagose 2023, 712). St. Thomas Aquinas made the most influential formulation of NLT in the RCC. To him, "natural law is the rule and measure of acts, and it induces the person to act or to refrain from acting by its appeal to the actor's reason (law is connected to reason, not to the will, so it is not coercive)" (Beckwith 2021, 1). The TNLT that uses deductive reasoning to assess the morality of human acts has become central to the RCC's moral magisterium (Long 2013).

The Philosophical and the Sociological Approaches to Moral Issues

Amid the media hype against the alleged "evils" and threats of GI expressed in papal pronouncements and ecclesiastical writings, it is notable that there are no clear conceptual and operational definitions of the real meaning of this signifier in behavioral terms. GI remains a complex and slippery term that has been invented by the RCC (Vaggione 2020). It is a mix of various social issues that need sociological and scientific clarification. What is clear is that in the RCC, GI serves as a signifier or unifying concept used by conservative Catholics to interpret the evils of liberalism in human sexuality (Graff 2016).

GI's conceptual framework remains in the philosophical and metaphysical realm. In sociology, gender ideology and gender are complex realities which cannot simply be categorized as GI. Unfortunately, the RCC evaluates the nature of gender and its ill-effects as GI in accordance with the TNLT philosophical moral framework that analyzes moral issues using deductive reasoning. This method disregards human experience and empirical gender relations in society as the starting point for moral analysis. TNLT views gender and sex as immutable, metaphysically inseparable and ordained by God, contrary to the sociological perspectives that understand them as social and cultural.

Thus, any attempt by sociologists and feminists to understand gender and gender theory from an inductive and scientific approach that starts with the lived and cultural experiences of people is inaccurately labeled by the RCC's moral watchdog as GI and a form of "scientism." The following characterization of gender by Bryan Cross' (2019), for instance, is indicative of the RCC's prevailing lack of sufficient understanding of the scientific reasoning of sociology and the social sciences:

> One of the most common sources of difficulty with the Church's teaching in this area is a failure to recognize its philosophical dimension. This domain is between that of the physical and social sciences and that of sacred theology. As inheritors of twentieth-century positivism, many people today assume that the quantitative sciences are the arbiters of truth, and that any other way of knowing, except that privileged and direct access to one's own internal subjectivity, can be no more than private opinion or pseudoscience. This diminished conception of the power of human reason is called scientism, and it is the philosophical air we breathe. (Cross 2019, paras 4–6)

Philosophy and theology generally employ the deductive approach when dealing with moral issues based on TNLT principles. This approach does not normally take human experience and data collection as the starting point to understand moral situations or ethical dilemmas. Philosophical moral reasoning is not obliged to provide empirical evidence to back up its theorizing. Thus, its assessment is largely conceptual rather than empirical, using logic and deductive reasoning to analyze the morality of human acts based on a set of metaphysical standards.

In contrast, sociological and social science reasoning combines both theory and research, and always requires data to support it as empirical and scientific. A sociological explanation of reality always entails reliable data, whether quantitative and/

or qualitative, to be scientifically acceptable. The theory serves as a framework to interpret data. And data confirm its applicability in society in a scientific study. Understanding gender and sexuality from a sociological perspective requires a fine blend of theory and data to scientifically assess gender relations and issues in society.

This blending of theory and data to explain empirical reality – the scientific method used by sociologists and social scientists – is often misunderstood by theologians in the RCC as "scientism." As Mooney (1991, 290) argues, "theologians do not yet know how to deal theologically with the findings of science." For theologians, nature is an object of faith and a way of discovering God. "Scientists, who usually maintain moral neutrality in judgment, fundamentally treat nature as an object of study to advance empirical knowledge, regardless of its supernatural origin. For many people, the naturalism of science is sometimes equated with 'materialism' and 'physicalism' and eventually atheism" (Ballano 2021, 42).

Doing scientific research to explain social reality does not necessarily mean scientism. Modern sciences apply methodological naturalism (MN) when doing scientific studies, which is different from deductive philosophical reasoning. In this method, to attain objective analysis scientists momentarily suspend their personal biases and even their belief in God to empirically analyze the world and people's behavior (Torrance 2017). This attitude is only temporary and does not necessarily imply atheism. The main purpose of MN in scientific research is to achieve value-free judgments that accurately describe the world of nature and people.

MN requires that scientists should only use natural causes and mechanisms to explain the world (Boudry et al. 2010). It implies bracketing out the creator of these phenomena to reach a scientific or empirical understanding of the world (Torrance 2017). "This rigorous attachment to 'natural' explanations is an essential attribute of science by definition and by convention" (Jones 2005, 66). As a rule, the scientist focuses their attention on the secondary causes of phenomena and life observed or explained in the physical or social world and not on the ultimate causes, or on the transcendental cause operating in the natural world (Torrance 2017).

Although some Catholic scholars misunderstand the sociological and social science approach to sex and gender as "scientism" and recent papal pronouncements have attacked it as GI, Pope Francis's latest ecclesiastical reform project, the Synod on Synodality (SoS) and inductive synodal theory push the boundaries of deductive reasoning in dealing with urgent pastoral and moral issues in the RCC. His synodal approach thus encourages openness to scientific methods, offering new hope for the adoption of modern sciences in Catholic moral theology.

Following the TNLT, the RCC's natural moral law approach, which disregards the scientific investigation of human behavior before moralizing, continues to dominate, even in evaluating contemporary moral issues such as gender and sexuality. As Trigilio (2004, 2–3) argues:

> The principles of the natural moral law are not options or suggestions, but they are to be dutifully obeyed...Augustine and especially Aquinas to develop the entire methodology of using logic and objective human reason to discern and interpret the constituent precepts of good behavior...The Natural law uses fundamental principles and when applied to everyday

situations, it is presumed that one can reason his or her way to know what is the morally right thing to do.

Under natural law morality, logic and deductive arguments based on metaphysical criteria are the primary tools for assessing morality, disregarding the real experiences of people such as the LGBTQI community in society. However, Francis's inductive theology requires listening and learning about people's aspirations and personal struggles before theological reflection and judgment. Thus, the sociological and inductive synodal approach is necessary for understanding the personal stories and motives of the LGBTQI group and unpacking the complex empirical nature of gender and gender diversity in contemporary society.

This approach can also separate fact from fiction in the papal declarations on GI. It can also provide a more balanced, realistic, and scientific assessment of gender, removing the polemics and animosities towards feminists and advocates of gender equality in society. The crux of the matter is to differentiate the RCC's philosophical and theological approach to gender and sexuality from the sociological and feminist approach, in order to unpack GI and find a common ground to improve the Church's moral teaching in spirit of Pope Francis's synodality and synodal church.

The current RCC natural law morality on gender needs to be updated to incorporate social science gender research to fully welcome nonbinary people and members of the LGBTQI community as "normal" persons in the Christian community, with moral and legal rights to marriage and family life like heterosexual Catholics. The Catholic hierarchy should also recognize the contribution of sociologists, feminists, and activists whose research agenda and advocacies can greatly assist the RCC to adapt Church teachings in the contemporary gender social structure, abandoning GI as a misleading signifier that discriminates against gender-diverse people.

Objectives, Major Sections, and Arguments

This chapter aims to sociologically unpack the RCC's GI in the Catholic Church by distinguishing the fundamental differences between the Church's philosophical–theological understanding of gender, sexuality, and gender theory, which is founded on natural moral law, and that of sociology and the social sciences, applying the inductive synodal approach and sociological perspectives. It also aims to find a common ground to enrich and inculturate traditional moral teachings with the current scientific and feminist approaches to sex and gender as an attempt to realize Pope Francis's vision of synodality and the inductive theological method.

Drawing on secondary scholarly literature, media reports, and church documents, it contends that the sociological-synodal approach offers a new way for the Church to achieve a more empirical and nuanced view of Catholic morality on gender and sexuality in the contemporary world, despite Francis's strong opposition to gender and GI. It recommends a synodal dialogue between the Catholic hierarchy and sociologists and gender studies scholars, to achieve a holistic and inculturated view of sex and gender in contemporary society for the full inclusion of the LGBTQI community in the RCC.

The chapter has four main sections. The first section discusses the theoretical orientation of the study. It elaborates Francis's inductive synodal theology as well as the sociological approach to sex and gender in contemporary society. It clarifies the limitations of the current deductive philosophical method of Catholic morality based on TNLT and calls for the incorporation of scientific gender theories and the adoption of a sub-discipline called "sociology of morality" in Catholic moral theology.

The second section discusses the RCC's traditional teaching on sex and gender based on the latest papal pronouncements on gender and TNLT. It briefly traces the origin of the TNLT in the RCC and explains its deductive philosophical approach in dealing with gender in contemporary world. It argues that this philosophical approach based on TNLT is inadequate for today's gender relations. It provides a sociological reappraisal of the empirical basis of gender complementarity in the Scriptures to point out the conceptual roots of this limitation.

The third section explores the common ground between the traditional moral approach to sex and gender based on TNLT and that of sociology and feminism. It contends that maintaining this traditional approach to understanding gender can alienate people with diverse sexualities such as members of the LGBTQI group in the Christian community. It thus recommends an inductive, interdisciplinary, and synodal approach and a healthy dialogue between Catholic theologians and sociologists to understand gender in a more empirical way and fully welcome nonbinary people in the RCC.

Theoretical Orientation

Gender Moral Issues and Inductive Synodal Investigation

Catholic moral teachings on topical ethical issues are fallible and always subject to revision, depending on assessment of the evolving moral situation in society. Unlike creedal doctrines and dogmas on the Christian faith, which are non-negotiable for Catholics, requiring only cognitive acceptance, moral teachings need an accurate evaluation of the empirical nature of moral cases before the Catholic moral principles can be appropriately applied in concrete situations in society. Moral dilemmas cannot be resolved by mere deductive philosophical reflection without inquiry into the empirical nature of moral situations.

The application of the RCC's moral principles needs inductive moral investigation. The late Pope John XXIII, for instance, recommends an inductive approach which begins with the accurate assessment of the moral situation before resolving moral issues. To him, the first step in applying the moral doctrines of the Church is reviewing the concrete situation before forming moral judgment and deciding "what the circumstances can and should be done to implement these principles" (*Mater et Magistra* [Mother and Teacher] 1961, para. 235).

Prioritizing the assessment of the moral situation before moral judgment and action to resolve moral issues is also the concern of the inductive synodal theology of Pope Francis, which emphasizes knowing people's lived experiences as the starting point for theological or moral reflection. The main objection of the LGBTQI community to the RCC's moral approach to sexuality, gender, and gender diversity is its deductive moral approach, which ignores their personal gender experiences and the personal struggles of nonbinary people in the Church and society.

Recently, an open letter was written by Catholic students, theologians, and ministers (National Catholic Reporter 2024) and addressed to Pope Francis and the Dicastery of the Doctrine of the Faith (DDF), expressing sadness and objecting to the Vatican's declaration known as *Dignitas Infinita* [Infinite Dignity] (*DI*) (DDF 2024), which condemned "gender ideology" and sex change by transgender individuals as violations of human dignity, without regard to the personal and gender experiences of nonbinary people in society. The petitioners feared that this declaration could cause future harm to transgender people:

> We are saddened, therefore, that the document fails to recognize the dignity of trans and gender-nonconforming people. In its condemnation of gender "ideology" and "sex change," the document marginalizes the infinite dignity in people of all genders and their authentic self-expression and inadvertently perpetuates the harm it aims to overcome....*Dignitas Infinita* shows no evidence that its authors were informed by true encounters with trans, nonbinary and intersex people ...a phantasm disconnected from actual lives. (*paras* 2–3)

Moral teachings cannot be applied by mere logic and reasoning, as *DI* seems to imply. Understanding real lives of LGBTQI people through scientific research and immersion in the actual moral situation is necessary before approving or condemning the morality of human acts. Thus, this letter opposes *DI*'s argument on human dignity, since it does consider the actual lives of the nonbinary community in society.

Contemporary gender moral issues are complex, since their social and cultural contexts are evolving and the application of Church teachings largely depends on scientific readings of these contexts. The recognition of infinite human dignity and the social struggle of nonbinary people against harassment, discrimination, and victimization, as well as their aspiration to be fully recognized and respected as having distinct gender identity in society, cannot be achieved by deductive philosophical analysis, as *DI* aims to achieve.

The crux of the matter is that the RCC's moral magisterium recognizes only heterosexuality as the standard sexual orientation in the Church and society. Homosexuality, transgenderism, and gender diversity are considered deviations from this moral norm, thus are judged as sinful and ethically unacceptable in the RCC. Those who condemn homosexual unions, homosexuality, and the inclusivity of the LGBTQI community are normally people who lack real encounters with trans people, sociological research, sociological and feminist gender theory studies, and a sense of history as to why and how the LGBTQI movement arose in contemporary society.

Living Church Tradition and Ad Theologiam Promovendam (ATP)

Those who immediately opposed Pope Francis's welcoming attitude towards homosexuals and LGBTQI in the Church in the declaration *Fiducia Supplicans* [Supplicating Trust] (DDF 2023) lacked an in-depth empirical understanding of current gender and sexual issues. It is easy to judge the morality of homosexuality, same-sex unions, and the inclusivity of LGBTQI using the deductive approach. But this judgment is prone to misunderstanding of the true moral situations behind these moral issues. Homosexuality and the rise of LGBTQI Catholics in the contemporary world are not as simple as they seem. To fully understand their empirical and historical contexts requires not only a deductive philosophical analysis but also an inductive sociological and synodal investigation of nonbinary people's actual lives, informed by current scientific gender studies of sociologists, feminists, and other social scientists.

If Church tradition is living, evolving and dynamic, its moral teachings – without abandoning their timeless divine message – should be constantly inculturated or adapted to the ever-changing social structure and cultural situation of society. Transgender sexuality, for instance, is a complex moral situation. Current technological and biomedical advances that allow people to change their biological sex in accordance with their gender identity and experience need an inductive synodal and sociological investigation before moral judgment on whether sex change is indeed a violation of human dignity.

Pope Francis's (2023) quest for a more inductive, inter-Christian theological, disciplinary, and sociological approach in his *Ad Theologiam Promovendam* (*ATP*) is attuned with the current trend. Recently, relating theologizing to the study of lived religion has been seen as "a quest of making life theologically meaningful and making theology meaningful in life" (Tveitereid 2022, 70). To explore theologizing as lived religion means approaching the creative processes of theological reflection as rooted in experience. Indeed, "[t]he experiences and the practices of people themselves are a *locus theologicus*, a place from which to theologize" (Dillen 2014, 226).

ATP encourages Catholic theologians to engage in this type of inductive theology, shifting the starting point from abstract formulas to the everyday lived experiences of people as the locus of the new Catholic synodal theology that Francis envisioned. Pope Francis's vision of synodality emphasizes that the RCC's tradition is a living one and not static. To Francis, ecclesiastical teachings and practices need to be inculturated, based on a sound and scientific understanding of people's religious experiences in today's world. Catholic theology should thus begin with accurate understanding of people's experiences before applying divine and Church teachings.

To Pope Francis, "[g]ood theologians, like good pastors, also smell of the people and the street and, by their reflection, pour oil and wine on the wounds of men." Openness to the world, to man in the concreteness of his existential situation, with its problems, wounds, challenges, and potential, cannot, however, be reduced to a "tactical" attitude, extrinsically adapting now-crystallized content to new situations, but must urge theology to an epistemological and methodological rethinking" (Pope Francis 2023, para.3). This implies a shifting of focus and method in theological reflection, one that begins with human experience and empirical reality before the application of biblical or Church teachings.

This paradigm shift in theologizing should also apply to Catholic moral theology. Instead of pursuing the old deductive method of moral assessment based on TNLT, moral theologians should try to engage in an inductive moral approach that is open to the inductive methods of sociology and the social sciences. Pope Francis (2023) thus urges theologians to develop an inductive method in their theological reflection, one "which starts from the different contexts and concrete situations in which peoples are inserted, allowing itself to be seriously challenged by reality, in order to become discernment of the 'signs of the times' in the proclamation of the salvific event of the God-agape, communicated in Jesus Christ" (Francis 2023, para. 8).

In *ATP*, Francis exhorts Catholic theologians and scholars to adopt a transdisciplinary approach in resolving ecclesiastical issues before theological reflection, that is, to "make use of new categories elaborated by other knowledges in order to penetrate and communicate the truths of faith and transmit the teaching of Jesus in today's languages" (Francis 2023, para. 5). This approach should then be utilized to understand and resolve moral issues on sexuality, GI, gender diversity, and LGBTQI inclusivity in today's world.

Gender Moral Issues and Limitation of Philosophical Theology

The current dilemma of the RCC is how to resolve the highly intricate, complex, and persistent moral issues such as gender and GI in the RCC with the current theological-philosophical approach, which still relies on reasoning and deductive theological reflection with an apparent lack of integration of social science research that deals with the empirical world. The current generation of Catholic clerics and theologians is still predominantly educated in the normative discipline of philosophical theology.

The contemporary world that supports these urgent controversial moral issues is vastly different from the medieval world in which St. Thomas Aquinas conceived philosophical theology, as well as from the modernizing world of the Second Vatican Council (Vatican II), a universal gathering of all bishops around the world led by the Pope in the early 1960s. Vatican II recognized the complexity of contemporary culture, recommending the assistance of exact sciences such as sociology in understanding it for evangelization purposes.

An accurate empirical understanding of society as well as people's behavior is beyond the scope of the philosophical theology synthesized by St. Thomas. Philosophy and theology, which ask ultimate questions about life and rely on a priori knowledge, cannot provide a scientific account of today's moral issues without the assistance of sociology and the social sciences. Philosophical theology can be appropriate for dealing with the metaphysical or dogmatic aspects of the Christian faith to rationally justify it, but inadequate for investigating its empirical and behavioral issues.

It is also limited when it comes to analyzing the social systems and societal structures that underpin the preaching of the Christian faith. Science, with its empirical and naturalistic methods of understanding the world and human behavior, has gradually become popular in centers of learning in Europe, and contemporary theology has started to utilize the scientific method of sociology and the social sciences in theological reflection to engage in inductive theology that begins with people's lived experiences.

Thus, the birth of new types of theology that engage with science, such as lived theology, critical theology, practical theology, empirical theology, and other forms of contemporary theology that use scientific and sociological methods in addition to the traditional theological tools. Sociology only aims to generate reliable and cumulative knowledge of the regular patterns of social phenomena in order to comprehend society scientifically (Ballano 2019). If sociology is seen more as a partner than an adversary in Catholic theology and the RCC's mission, it can be a potent tool for Pope Francis's synodality and for resolving persistent hotly debated moral issues in the RCC.

The Sociology of Morality

The revival of interest in the sociology of morality has returned morality to the center stage of the sociological enterprise. Indeed, sociology was once an integral component in the scientific study of morality in society. However, its explicit focus has waned over the past half-century (Hitlin and Vaisey 2013, 3). It is only in recent years that it has experienced a revival. The emerging field of the sociology of morality has made morality a central concern again in sociology (Abend 2010).

"Traditionally, as seen in the work of Durkheim, Goffman, and Collins, the sociology of morality emphasizes how morality binds people together through a common system of rules and expectations during interactions" (Stets and Carter 2012, 121). To these scholars, morality is inseparable from social life (Hitlin and Vaisey 2013). Because of the significance of morality in society, social scientists have started to investigate and recognize the social dimensions of morality in society. Unfortunately, after neglecting morality for decades, sociologists have little systematic guidance available to them (Hitlin and Vaisey 2013).

In the RCC, the anti-positivist and anti-science attitude of the 19th-century Catholic hierarchy prevented a science-engaged theology and sociological morality from flourishing in Catholic research and scholarship. The strong influence of scholastic philosophy and TNLT since the medieval period has stunted the growth of sociological and science-engaged research in the RCC. Seeing gender, gender theories, feminism, LGBTQI inclusivity and other complex contemporary moral issues, which are products of the evolving nature of society, using deductive as well as philosophical and theological reasoning is inadequate given the complex and constant evolution of moral situations.

In Catholic morality, the sociological voice has been weak owing to Catholic theologians' and bishops' fear of modern sociology's positivism and its main agenda in society. But this resistance to positivism and science gradually waned after Vatican II showed openness to the exact sciences as tools for evangelization. Realizing the complexity of the current global culture, which is beyond the expertise of philosophers and theologians, the RCC, after Vatican II, became receptive to the contribution of sociology and the social sciences to aid the Church in analyzing behavioral and moral issues.

Post-Vatican II papal documents have also acknowledged the great contribution of the social sciences to Catholic moral theology and church discipline. In the post-synodal exhortation entitled *Pastores Dabo Vobis* [I Shall Give you Shepherds], for instance, Pope John Paul II (1992) recognized the contribution of sociological research in the human formation of Catholic priests. Pope Francis's (2023) *ATP* further recommends applying other branches of knowledge such as the social sciences to understand the current cultural revolutions in society, update church teachings, and establish a synodal church.

Central to the concept of GI or GT is the proper understanding of the relationship of sex and gender in society to the issue of immutability in the RCC's teaching on gender complementarity. In TNLT and RCC's moral magisterium, it is always assumed that biological sex and gender are immutable, inseparable, and ordained by God, and that a man and a woman are natural complementary. Heterosexuality is regarded as the norm for a mature person. Homosexuality and other forms of transexual identity and homosexual unions are considered deviant and naturally disordered in the RCC.

GI as a Catholic invention condemns all forms of gender theories that view gender as social and cultural experience and other types of family structure that challenge the heterosexual union of a man and a woman. The traditional Catholic moral theology sees sex and gender as inseparable, while sociology and the social sciences view sex as biological and gender as social and cultural. In exploring the basic difference between RCC and sociological perspectives on gender and sexuality, this book seeks to help unpack the popular complex concept of GI in the RCC and, by using the inductive synodal and sociological approach, to reveal some of its misconceptions.

Inseparability of Sex and Gender in TNLT

"The theory of Natural Law had become in the sixteenth century, and continued to remain during the seventeenth and eighteenth, an independent and rationalist system, professed and expounded by philosophers of the secular school of natural law" (Porter 2005, 1). As it envisions a purely rational morality, the natural law theory does not accept investigating human experiences surrounding moral issues as a basis for resolving ethical dilemmas. Through St. Thomas Aquinas, the natural law theory, which originated from stoicism, became the theoretical and theological framework for analyzing moral issues.

"Natural law tradition continued to be preserved and developed by Roman Catholic moral theologians, with the results that it came to be associated with Catholic thought—an association that persists to this day. [It views] the natural law as a set of moral rules capable of being established by 'pure' reason" (Porter 2005, 32–33). As Russell Hittinger (2002, 61) explains, "St. Thomas himself makes it clear that the definition of natural law is not arrived at simply by examining the meaning or concept of law; it is defined in reference to what is absolutely first in the order of being." In short, natural law is a metaphysical law and not a human or societal product as conceived in the social sciences.

The universal catechism of the RCC (1993, #1956) explains, "The natural law, present in the heart of each man and established by reason, is universal in its precepts and its authority extends to all men." This implies that "morality is real, that it is natural and not a mere human artifice or construction" (Beckwith 2021, 1). To Aquinas, natural law is the "rule and measure of acts" and it induces the person to act or to refrain from acting by its appeal to the actor's reason (law is connected to reason, not to the will, so it is not coercive).

Under this purely philosophical construction of morality, the empirical reality and people's lived experiences are not the starting point in the application of the Church's moral principles. Thus, regardless of the human experience and cultural beliefs and practices, moral issues can be resolved deductively through human reason. Under the TNLT, sex, gender, homosexuality, and same-sex union are moral issues that can be resolved primarily through logic and deductive reasoning, without inquiring into and analyzing carefully the moral situations and sociological contingencies behind their emergence in society.

This deductive philosophical approach to resolving moral issues, rather than an inductive empirical one, became the dominant approach in Catholic moral theology. The traditional perspective of the RCC that views gender as ahistorical, immutable, and intrinsically linked to the person's sex and sexuality is an influence of the TNLT. The Congregation for the Doctrine of the Faith's letter on the Collaboration of Men and Women in the Church and in the World (2004, No. 2) does not see gender as distinct from sex. Thus, the RCC opposes modern sociology and social science perspectives that view sex as assigned at birth and referring only to the person's biological aspect based on genitalia, and gender as primarily referring to his or her social and cultural learning in society on how to express masculinity and femininity. Accordingly, the RCC has rejected several contemporary sociological and feminist gender theories. In the Church's view, "biological sex and the socio-cultural role of sex (gender) can be distinguished but not separated" (Pope Francis 2016, #56). Following the traditional biblical interpretation of gender complementarity and natural law theory, it sees sex and gender as metaphysically given by God. It rejects gender theories, often labeled by the RCC as "gender ideology," which minimize sex while the purely cultural element, termed gender, is emphasized to the maximum and held to be primary by social scientists and feminists.

In recent years, the Church has been opposing the emergence of GI or GT (Bracke and Paternotte 2016; Case 2016). It rejects perspectives that view gender differences as the result of historical and cultural forces (Congregation for Catholic Education 2019). The RCC fundamentally sees men and women as different and yet complementary and equal in both nature and social roles. It contends that denying the distinction and complementarity between a man and a woman can weaken the family as a vital institution in society (Congregation for Catholic Education 2019).

The newer teachings of the RCC on gender and sexuality, as well as Pope John Paul II's doctrine on the "theology of the body," have greatly shaped the conservative and rigid understanding of gender that has universally permeated the Church. In recent years, the RCC has espoused an "anti-gender" position in response to feminism, contraception, sexual liberation, and changes in gender beliefs in the Western world (Bracke and Paternotte 2016).

Although some Catholic theologians have attempted to assume a more positive view of sex, they remain within the parameters of the present doctrine and theology of the body of the RCC (Capecchi 2020). The traditional perspective of the RCC still views gender as transcendental and based on biological make-up. The traditional gender view of manhood in the RCC, for instance, contrasts with the contemporary inclusive masculinity view, which is based on an increasingly liberal perception and a rapid decline in homophobia, with men no longer required to display traditionally masculine behaviors in order to be accepted as men (Anderson 2009; Anderson and McCormack 2018; McCormack 2011).

The RCC's teachings on the body, gender, and sexuality as immutable, fixed since birth and not subject to historical change, and primarily based on the philosophical arguments of natural law, are empirically untenable and contrary to scientific research findings. For example, the emergence of "inclusive masculinity theory" in social science research has led to a rapid decline in homophobia and homohysteria – the cultural fear of being homosexualized – and enables contemporary men to no longer feel they need to perform hyper-masculine or traditionally masculine behaviors to be accepted as men (Anderson 2009; Anderson and McCormack 2018).

People are traditionally categorized in the RCC according to their sex organs; thus, heterosexuality became the only standard to become a normal human person in the eyes of the Church. How the person express their femininity and masculinity or sexual orientation, which is now in the realm of gender, may not necessarily be in accordance with their biological make-up (Blank 2012).

Reappraising Gender and Gender Complementarity

Recognizing that sex is distinct from gender, although constituting the same person, as well as acknowledging that homosexual identity and the LGBTQI are separate genders is the key to the full acceptance of transgender individuals in the Church and towards the dissolution of the complex and imprecise concept of GI in the RCC. A more scientific and empirical view of gender and sexuality, however, cannot be achieved in the absence of adequate education in sociology and the social sciences for clerics and healthy dialogue between Catholic theologians and sociologists. The RCC needs to re-examine the applicability of the TNTL and scholastic philosophy in dealing with the complex moral issues of gender and sexuality in the contemporary world.

Unlike the RCC's application of the TNLT, the application of gender theory to explain social reality in sociological sciences is not absolute. A theory aims to interpret data and human experience. But it is the data, not the theory, that is the determining factor. A theory cannot be absolutized to explain empirical realities in the social sciences. A different theory should be adopted if the data or moral situation requires a different theoretical approach. A fine blend of theory and data is the scientific method for explaining empirical reality of moral issues such as gender, homosexuality, or LGBTQI inclusivity. Scientific rationality is therefore vastly different from philosophical rationality, which is based on deductive reasoning that does not require empirical evidence to support its theoretical assertions.

In sociology, gender is socially and culturally conditioned. "Human beings make other human beings into specific male and female genders, and the family remains the main modeling for male heterosexuality" (Hopkins 2008, 576). To shape the individual's gender according to society's expectations, gender socialization is normally introduced in the family and continued as the person becomes more exposed to others in society. Being gay or lesbian is not intentional on the part of the person but acquired through the process of socialization and largely influenced by social interaction. Thus, gender is not immutable as assumed by the traditional Church teaching, which is highly influenced by a purely rational morality of natural law theory.

There are various ways of expressing one's gender in terms of femininity and masculinity, depending on one's culture. As Winkler (2021) argues, to be a "male" man implies following certain societal rules. There are various cultural expressions of masculinities, not just the one commonly interpreted by Catholic theologians to defend heterosexuality as the only way to be human.

The RCC's current sexual teaching on gender complementarity is based on a collection of homilies by Pope John Paull II that constituted the popular "theology of the body" and was affirmed by Pope Benedict XVI and Pope Francis. Under this theology, "sexual and [gender] identity is complementary [i.e., not at variance] because persons live in society according to the cultural aspects corresponding to their sex. Sex and gender are inseparable" (Ford 2018, 81).

The Church's moral magisterium on gender complementarity assumes that when a man and woman are together, "they produce a unified reality, forming a whole that neither of them could form alone: Masculinity and femininity express the twofold aspect of man's somatic constitution… [which] consists in reciprocal enrichment" (Ford 2018, 81). It upholds that the "biological sex and the socio-cultural role of sex (gender) can be distinguished but not separated" (Pope Francis 2016, #56). Relying fundamentally on the traditional TNLT and scholastic philosophy that view sex and gender as immutable and metaphysical, any form of homosexuality and homosexual union are considered "unnatural" and sinful; thus, they cannot be blessed by the Church.

The traditional model of categorizing people based on their biological make-up or sex without regard to their social and cultural experience in society needs a scientific sociological reappraisal. Pope Francis's approval of *Fiducia Supplicans* [Supplicating Trust] (FS) and blessings of homosexual couples is part of the vision of his latest ecclesiastical reform project, the SoS, and his intention of establishing a synodal church, that is, a church that welcomes the voiceless and marginalized groups in the RCC such as homosexuals and members of the LGBTQI community.

Although the RCC has strictly upheld the gender complementarity teaching as the moral basis for Christian Catholic marriage, social scientists, Bible scholars, and theologians continue to debate whether Genesis is really teaching gender complementarity as only referring to union between a biological man and a woman. The gender complementarity requirement of the doctrine on the sacrament of matrimony remains the fundamental hurdle for the complete moral and social acceptance of homosexual unions and transgender sexuality as well as the inclusion of the LGBTQI community in the Church.

The evolution of gender and sexuality is largely a result of the cultural change in society. Therefore, it is important to understand and translate the cultural context of the biblical message on gender complementarity and apply it in contemporary times without altering the basic divine message that God created humanity. If the creation story in which God created man and woman was based on the Jewish patriarchal culture at the time when it was written, what would the spiritual message that God created people in his image and likeness as male and female mean in today's global culture, where everything seems to be changing, including gender identity and sexuality, with the advancement of technology?

The empirical basis of the biblical teaching on gender complementarity, which is the cornerstone of the RCC's theology of the body, needs to be reappraised with the advent of the social sciences as a new method of acquiring knowledge in the modern world. The root cause of the RCC's hesitation to fully accept the LGBTQI group and its hostile attitude towards gender diversity is the insistence of Church doctrine on the complementarity of sexes based on some kind of rational morality founded on natural law that interprets Genesis as accepting heterosexual union between a man and a woman as the only divinely approved union.

Re-evaluating the empirical foundation of gender complementarity in biblical teaching in the light of the latest sociological research and method is necessary for the dissolution of GI in the RCC as an imprecise signifier that inaccurately labels all gender theories and issues as an ideology that contravenes orthodox Church moral teachings.

Re-evaluating Biblical Gender Complementarity

A closer inductive sociological analysis of the creation story of humans in Genesis 2 as "male and female" would most likely reveal a prototypical rather than archetypical approach. The story only explains how things came to be: that humanity, both male and female, was created by God. But it is not a timeless message. It does not teach that it is only heterosexuals, the ideal human beings, who are only allowed by God to enter marriage beyond the period of the story. What is timeless is that God created humanity. An archetypical interpretation of the biblical gender complementarity in Genesis that only male and female are the true genders is debatable and subject to scientific reappraisal.

Traditionalists tend to interpret the gender complementarity of Genesis in the literal sense as the basis for heterosexual marriage and rejection of homosexual union and other forms of non-heterosexual genders such as the LGBTQI categories. Thus, the traditional Catholic moral teaching that sex and gender are one inseparable reality, that one's sex determines one gender and sexuality in society, can have a rival empirical interpretation when Weber's "interpretive understanding" of the authors' real motives in Genesis is applied. To James Brownson (2013),

> God created males and females after God's image (Gen 1:27), which is "intended to convey the value, dominion, and relationality shared by both men and women, but not the idea that the gender complementarity is somehow necessary to fully express or embody the divine image." According to affirming scholars, the main thrust of Gen 2 is thus not on the complementarity of male and female, but the similarity of male and female. The interpretation of "one-flesh" in Gen 2:24 connotes the idea of kinship bonding through marriage, not to physical complementarity. (Sim, 2023, 8)

Gender as biological sex rather than a social experience and relationality was what the authors of Genesis probably had in mind in their gender complementarity message. As Stiebert and Walsh (2001, 121) explain, "It is important to note that the idea of sexuality necessarily entails an idea of relationality. A person may be gendered (i.e., male or female) without necessary reference to another, but a person is sexual only in relation to another person." Thus, a person's sex is biologically assigned during birth. However, how they actualize their gender to express their masculinity and femininity in society, is highly influenced by their relationality and socialization in society.

The traditional interpretation of gender complementarity in Genesis is cisgender, that is, the person's sex or genitalia determines their gender as a heterosexual. Transgenderism, where one's gender as a social experience differs from the sex assigned at birth, is seen by the RCC as abominable and deviant. In short, the traditional interpretation of gender complementarity regards heteronormativity as the only way to become a "normal human being," and that only a biological male and female can enter a moral marriage. Transgenders or people whose gender identity is different from their gender they were thought to be when they were born" (National Center for Transgender Equality 2023, para. 2), contradicting their sex, are "immature" and "unnatural" in the eyes of traditional Catholic moralists and thus ineligible for Christian marriage.

The problem is that "to the traditionalist/behavioralist, the question of same sex relationships appears decisively closed. This is because neither male-male nor female-female relationships can fully embody the complementarity nature of humanity intended by God in creation" (Henegar 2011, 4). However, this traditional view that rejects same-sex marriage has been increasingly challenged by contemporary social science scholars specializing in gender and sexuality. "What was previously relegated to the silence of 'the closet' and to euphemistic speech is now being discussed more directly and openly. And with this greater directness and openness of speech comes the need to face questions that the church has not faced so directly and explicitly before" (Henegar 2021).

The creation story of human beings in Genesis requires a scientific and sociological investigation to ascertain whether the categories of "man" and woman" in the text are really to be taken literally, whether God really intends only a heterosexual marriage at the beginning. James Brownson (2013), for instance, raises the exegetical question: what is the connection between the image of God and maleness and femaleness? Thus, he argues that God created males and females after God's image (Gen 1:27), which is "intended to convey the value, dominion, and relationality shared by both men and women, but not the idea that the gender complementarity is somehow necessary to fully express or embody the divine image."

Some scholars believe that "the main thrust of Gen 2 is thus not on the complementarity of male and female, but the similarity of male and female. Thus, the notion of 'one-flesh' in Gen 2:24 implies the idea of kinship bonding through marriage, not to physical complementarity" (Sim, 2023, 8). Other Bible scholars also doubt whether the interpretation of the biological and procreative complementarity of Genesis 2, which is the popular basis for rejecting homosexuality and homosexual marriage, is empirically acceptable (Sim 2023).

To Caleb Day (2016, 8), reading gender complementarity of these ancient texts without regard to their cultural context of patriarchy is anachronistic:

> The declaration that a man leaves his parents and "cleaves" to his wife, becoming "one flesh," because of God's creation of a "helper as [Adam's] partner," does not celebrate a system of gender roles so much as an intimate, even egalitarian, kinship bond between two human beings (2:18, 24-25)...This is not to say that gender is irrelevant to these discussions of the goodness of sex; they do arise from patriarchal contexts.

To traditionalists/behavioralists who believe in the complementarity of the sexes in Genesis, same-sex relationships are totally unacceptable. "This is because neither male-male nor female-female relationships can fully embody the complementarity nature of humanity intended by God in creation" (Brownson 2013). But one wonders whether the complementarity in Genesis is to be taken literally or to be understood in broader cultural and social contexts. Or whether complementarity is to be taken as a protype or archetype.

In her article, "The Role of the Popes in the Invention of Complementarity and the Vatican's Anathematization of Gender," Mary Anne Case (2016) contended that sexual complementarity is a twentieth-century theological innovation. Adherents of the papal teaching on the theology of the body popularized it in the RCC as the appropriate response to the sexual crises of late modernity. Gender complementarity is a doctrinal tool used by the RCC to resist feminism, women's reproductive rights, and gay rights as well as to defend the masculinity of Catholic priesthood (Beattie 2016).

As Joan Scott (2007, 71) contends, "the male/female opposition" serves to "vindicate political power" by making references to gendered, hierarchical relationships "seem sure and fixed, outside human construction, part of the natural or divine order." In this sense, the RCC has turned the gender complementarity issue into a "Catholic ideology" to resist feminism and other gender and reproductive rights issues. It upholds the heteronormativity that marginalizes transgender people and the LGBTQI in the Church. The traditional "Christian interpretations of Genesis continue to lend divine legitimation to a heterosexual social order predicated upon male authority and female subordination" (Beattie 2016).

Exploring a Common Ground Through Synodality

"The study of gender emerged as one of the most important trends in sociology in the twentieth century and that legacy continues today. The study and research associated with studying gender issues propelled the sociology gender from the margins to become a central feature of the discipline" (Lindsey 2021). No academic discipline gives more attention to gender issues than sociology. In fact, gender is one of the most widely researched areas in sociology (Connell 2014). Gender theories were conceived in sociology and the social sciences to take account of problematic gender relations in society. They are not constructed with the primary aim of attacking the doctrinal position of the RCC on gender and sexuality.

Modern sociology became the foundation for theoretical investigation of gender relations in society (Barrett 1980; Walby 2009, 2020) as "the injustice, violence and distress that unequal gender relations produced are widely recognized as key concerns for applied sociology" (Connell 2014, 552). Not all theory pertaining to gender is feminist, although all feminist theory centers much or all of its attention on gender. "Feminism is a theory and approach that supports economic, political and social equality, specifically valuing and advocating for the equal opportunities of women. It also provides frameworks and practices for bringing about the unfinished project of social change" (Fotaki and Pullen 2023, 1–2).

> The Church's theological position on women's "place" remained systemically unchecked until the late 19th and early 20th Centuries, and even then, the Church only adjusted slowly to demands of the broader women's movements, which were initially only seen as a threat to the patriarchal structure of Catholicism. When the Church did finally begin to make changes in its attitude toward women, the female gender slowly gained traction in moving toward equality in society. (Meyer 2017, 2–3)

Feminism and feminist movements have taken the lead in advocating gender equality in society, while the RCC remains preoccupied with TNLT and scholastic philosophy. The perceived attack of GI against the RCC's moral magisterium is only an unintended consequence of the RCC's slow response to gender inequality and oppression in the contemporary world, with poor social science education of clerics. Since several of the RCC's structures, religious practices, and moral doctrines are seen by feminists as patriarchal and oppressive to women, the Church has become vulnerable to the critical scientific investigations and advocacies of sociologists and feminists who generally seek equality and justice in gender relations.

It is indeed necessary to update the rigid moral position of the RCC on heteronormativity and natural law which results in an immutable and ontological view of gender and sexuality that overlooks the social and cultural experience of people in society. GI is a philosophical and theological construction, based on TNLT, that alienates people with diverse sexualities and LGBTQI members of the Christian community. The inductive synodal approach requires a healthy dialogue between Catholic theologians and sociologists to understand gender in a more empirical way. A productive dialogue between sociologists and social scientists specializing in gender and sexuality and the senior Catholic theologians who assist the Vatican's Dicastery of the Doctrine of the Faith (DDF), as well as members of the International Theological Commission, would help to update current Church teaching with the pastoral objective of fully accepting the LGBTQI community in the synodal church.

Aside from the prevailing distrust by several Catholic bishops of sociology's positivism, which they view as challenging Church teaching on human dignity and solidarity, the root cause of the lack of interdisciplinary approach to gender, homosexuality, and other moral issues in the RCC is the cool relationship between sociology and theology. Pickering (1980) calls this relationship one of conflict and alliance. Although both sociology and theology give an account of the human condition and include topics through which they can potentially find common ground, most sociologists and theologians have dismissed each other's views as irrelevant, creating the barrier that has marked much of their coexistence (Brewer 2007).

Both sociology and theology are sciences, but each in a different way. The priest-sociologist Greeley (2012) characterizes the root of the conflict between sociologists and theologians as one of respect: both claim to view their disciplines as a science with a distinct methodology. However, theology and sociology are interconnected and related disciplines, despite being methodologically distinct. All theology contains, implicitly, sociology and a sociological theory about the self and society.

Catholic theologians who advise the Pope on doctrinal and moral matters are predominantly educated under the traditional Thomistic ethical approach when dealing with gender and sexuality. Despite new efforts by Catholic feminist theologians to incorporate social science gender theories into the RCC's traditional moral teachings, these remain within the parameters of the philosophical natural law theory. Despite the RCC's teaching on inculturation, Catholic theology has not reached out to dialogue with professional sociologists and anthropologists, who specialize in the study of culture, to aid them in this endeavor.

The prevailing RCC view on gender, which has indiscriminately labeled gender theories or any opposition to the magisterium's teaching on gender and sexuality as GI and indicative of a lack of synodal dialogue, demonstrates the lack of an interdisciplinary approach to gender and sexuality in the RCC. The apparent absence of sociologists and social scientists in the current SoS is another indication that the RCC is continuing to disregard the contribution of modern sociology to Catholic theology, despite Vatican II's encouragement to use the exact sciences to understand the cultural revolution in society for evangelization.

An interdisciplinary approach that combines but distinctly recognizes disciplinal limits between sociology and Catholic theology is necessary to avoid misinterpretation of the true nature of gender and sexuality. The TNLT is not an absolute theoretical framework to interpret morality. In fact, before St. Thomas Aquinas's synthesis of Aristotelian philosophy and Catholic theology became widely accepted by the RCC from the medieval period up to the present, other theoretical frameworks were used to interpret moral issues. For instance, before Aquinas, the theological framework of St. Augustine's teaching on sexuality, influenced by Manicheanism, was adopted to frame Catholic teaching on marriage and sexuality.

Pope Francis's inductive synodal theology in his *ATP* calls for a paradigm shift in Catholic theology that requires the inductive approach – an accurate understanding of people's lived experiences as the starting point for theological reflection (Pope Francis 2023). This approach reflects the inductive approach of sociology and other social sciences, which typically begins with data collection and ends up applying an appropriate theory to interpret them. In the grounded theory approach, the theory may emanate from the patterns of the data collected by the investigator to understand the empirical reality. The Church should listen to people from below, especially to those in the peripheries such as sociologists, feminists, and gender advocates whose approach is often labeled as "scientism" and thus unheard and condemned in the RCC. Francis's SoS and process called synodality implies synodal consultation and listening to people behind GI and the Catholic hierarchy.

Conclusion

This chapter has distinguished the fundamental conflict of perspectives on gender, sexuality, and gender theory between the Catholic Church's philosophical–theological moral teachings and those of sociologists, feminists, and other gender specialists. It sociologically explored common ground to enrich the RCC's traditional moral teachings in the spirit of Pope Francis's synodality. It contended that the synodal-sociological approach could open up new hope and nuanced perspectives on gender and sexuality for the Church to achieve a more balanced and sociologically informed moral theology in the contemporary world. This chapter recommended a synodal dialogue, aiming to achieve an inclusive synodal church, between the Catholic hierarchy and gender sociologists, LGBTQI leaders, and feminists, as well as representatives of what the RCC has labeled the people behind GI.

References

Abend G (2010) What's new and what's old about the new sociology of morality. In: Hitlin S, Vaisey S (eds) Handbook of the sociology of morality. Springer, New York, pp 561–586

Anderson E (2009) Inclusive masculinity: the changing nature of masculinities. Routledge, London

Anderson E, McCormack M (2018) Inclusive masculinity theory: overview, reflection and refinement. J Gend Stud 27(5):547–561
Ballano V (2019) Catholic social teaching, theology, and sociology: exploring the common ground. Religions 10(557):1–16. https://doi.org/10.3390/rel10100557
Ballano VO (2021) Science, theology, methodological naturalism, and the Catholic Church's Inculturation. Int J Religion Spirituality Soc 11(2):41–52. https://doi.org/10.18848/2154-8633/CGP/v11i02/41-52
Barrett M (1980) Women's oppression today: problems in marxist feminist analysis. Verso, London
Beattie T (2016) Gendering genesis, engendering difference. A catholic theological quest. Svensk Teologisk Kvartalskrift 92(3–4):102–117
Beckwith F (2021) Catholicism, and the natural law: a response to four Misunderstandings. Religions 12(6):1–10. https://doi.org/10.3390/rel12060379
Blank H (2012) Straight: the surprisingly short history of heterosexuality. Beacon Press, Boston
Boudry M, Blancke S, Braeckman J (2010) How not to attack intelligent design creationism: philosophical misconceptions about methodological naturalism (Draft). https://biblio.ugent.be/publication/956838/file/6828796.pdf.
Bracke S, Paternotte D (eds) (2016) "Habemus Gender! The catholic church and 'gender ideology'." Special issue of religion and gender 6, no. 2
Brewer JD (2007) Sociology and theology reconsidered: religious sociology and the sociology of religion in Britain. Hist Hum Sci 20:7–28
Brownson JV (2013) Bible, gender, sexuality: reframing the Church's debate on same-sex relationships. Grand Rapids, MI: Eerdmans
Caldwell S (2023) Pope benedict predicted gender ideology would be final rebellion against god. Catholic Herald (May 18, 2023). https://catholicherald.co.uk/pope-benedict-predicted-gender-ideology-would-be-final-rebellion-against-god/
Capecchi C (2020) Christopher west rolls out his 2020 'made for more' tour." The catholic spirit. Available at: https://thecatholicspirit.com/news/local-news/christopher-west-rolls-out-his-2020-made-for-more-tour/
Case MA (2016) The role of the popes in the invention of complementarity and the Vatican's anathematization of gender. Religion Gender 6(2):155–172
Congregation for Catholic Education (2019) Male and female he created them. Vatican: Vatican Press. rc_con_ccatheduc_doc_20190202_maschio-e-femmina_en.pdf
Congregation for the Doctrine of the Faith (2004) Letter to the bishops of the catholic church on the collaboration between men and women in the church and in the world. Vatican: The Roman Curia. https://www.vatican.va/roman_curia/congregations/cfaith/documents/rc_con_cfaith_doc_20040731_collaboration_en.html
Connell R (2014) The sociology of gender in Southern perspective. Current Sociol Monograph 62(4):550–567.https://doi.org/10.1177/0011392114524510
Cross BR (2019) Gender ideology and the Catholic Church. Public Discourse J Witherspoon Inst. https://www.thepublicdiscourse.com/2019/06/53437/
Day CM (2016) An unsatisfactory trajectory: a critique of gender complementarianism. Available at: https://www.academia.edu/33865814/An_unsatisfactory_trajectory_a_critique_of_gender_complementarianism. Accessed 10 May 2024
DDF (Dicastery of the Doctrine of the Faith) (2023) On the pastoral meaning of blessings. Vatican: The Roman Curia. Available at: https://www.vatican.va/roman_curia/congregations/cfaith/documents/rc_ddf_doc_20231218_fiducia-supplicans_en.html
DDF (Dicastery of the Doctrine of the Faith) (2024) Declaration Dignitas Infinita on human dignity. Vatican: The Roman Curia. https://www.vatican.va/roman_curia/congregations/cfaith/documents/rc_ddf_doc_20240402_dignitas-infinita_en.html
Dillen A (2014) Power balances and bridges between church discourses, academic theological views and daily experiences and reflections on family life. In Intams Review 20(2):226–235
Ford CJ (2018) Transgender bodies, catholic schools, and a queer natural law theology of exploration. J Moral Theol 7(1):70–98

Fotaki M, Pullen A (2023) Feminist theories and activist practices in organization studies. Organization Studies, 1–24.https://doi.org/10.1177/01708406231209861
Graff A (2016). 'Gender ideology': weak concepts, powerful politics. Religion Gender 6(2):268–272. https://doi.org/10.18352/rg.10177
Greeley A (2012) Sociology and theology: some methodological questions. Proceedings of the catholic. Theological Society of America. Available online: http://ejournals.bc.edu/ojs/index.php/article/view/2872/2497
Henegar M (2011) Mid-day discussion guide for bible, gender, sexuality: reframing Church's debate on same-sex relationships by James V. Brownson. https://www.efaidnbmnnnibpcajpcglclefindmkaj/http://podcast.manhattanchurch.org/docs/coffee-stretch/Bible-Gender-Sexuality-Notes.pdf
Hitlin S, Vaisey S (2013) The new sociology of morality. Annual Rev Sociol 39(1):51–68
Hittinger R (2002) The first grace: rediscovering the natural law in the post-christian world. ISI Books, Wilmington, DE
Hopkins DN (2008) Toward a positive black male heterosexuality. Angl Theol Rev 90(3):575–581
Jones JE (2005) Kitzmiller v. Dover. In 400 F. Supp. 2nd 707 (M.D. Pa.)
Lindsey LL (2021) Gender: sociological perspectives, 7th edn. Routledge, New York
McCormack M (2011) Mapping the terrain of homosexually-themed language. J Homosex 58:664–679. https://doi.org/10.1080/00918369.2011.563665
Mater et Magistra [Mother and Teacher] (1961) Social encyclical of Pope John XXIII on christianity and social progress. Vatican: Libreria Editrice Vaticana, Available online: http://w2.vatican.va/content/john-xxiii/en/encyclicals/documents/hf_j-xxiii_enc_15051961_mater.html
Meyer AN (2017) Gender complementarity in the catholic church: origins & feminist response. Available at: Gender_Complementarity_in_Catholicism__Angela_Nevitt_Meyer-libre.pdf (d1wqtxts1xzle7.cloudfront.net)
Mooney CF (1991) Theology and science: a commitment to dialogue. Theological Studies 52:289–229. http://cdn.theologicalstudies.net/52/52.2/52.2.4.pdf.
National Catholic Reporter (2024) Catholic students, theologians, ministers write an open letter to pope Francis. National Catholic Reporter Website (25 April 2024). https://www.ncronline.org/opinion/guest-voices/catholic-students-theologians-ministers-write-open-letter-pope-francis
National Center for Transgender Equality (2023) Understanding transgender people: the basics. National Center for Transgender Equality Website (January 27, 2023). https://transequality.org/issues/resources/understanding-transgender-people-the-basics
Paternotte D, Kuhar R (2017) 'Gender ideology' in movement: an introduction. In Kuhar R, Paternotte D (eds) Anti-gender campaigns in Europe: mobilizing against equality, 1–22. New York, London: Rowman & Littlefield International
Pickering WSF (1980) Sociology and theology: alliance and conflict. Harvester Press, Hertfordshire
Pope Benedict XVI (2012) Address of his holiness benedict XVI on the occasion of Christmas greetings to the Roman Curia. Vatican: Libreria Editrice Vaticana. https://www.vatican.va/content/benedict-xvi/en/speeches/2012/december/documents/hf_ben-xvi_spe_20121221_auguri-curia.html
Pope Francis (2016) Post-Synodal exhortation Amoris Laetitia. Vatican: Dicastero per la Comunicazione—Libreria Editrice Vaticana. https://www.vatican.va/content/francesco/en/apost_exhortations/documents/papa-francesco_esortazione-ap_20160319_amoris-laetitia.html
Pope Francis (2023) Apostolic letter issued "Motu Proprio" Ad Theologiam Promovendam [To Promote Theology]." Unofficial full English translation available at: https://returntotradition.org/unofficial-full-english-translation-of-francis-revolutionary-motu-proprio-ad-theologiam-promovendam-plus-breaking-news-report-on-text/
Pope John Paul II (1992) Pastores Dabo Vobis [I Shall Give you Shepherds]: Pope John Paul's Post-Synodal Exhortation on the Formation of Priests in the Circumstances of the Present Day. Vatican: Libreria Editrice Vaticana. https://www.vatican.va/content/john-paul-ii/en/apost_exhortations/documents/hf_jp-ii_exh_25031992_pastores-dabo-vobis.html.

Porter J (2005) Nature as reason: a thomistic theory of natural law. William B. Eerdsmans Publishing Company, Grand Rapids, MI

Scott J (2007) Gender: a useful category of historical analysis. In: Parker R, Aggleton P (eds) Culture, society and sexuality: a reader, 2nd edn. Routledge, London, pp 61–81

Sim J (2023) What does the creation story tell about homosexuality? TheoRhēma 18(1):5–30

Stets JE, Carter MJ (2012) A theory of the self for the sociology of morality. Am Sociol Rev 77(1):120–140

Stiebert J, Walsh JT (2001) Does the hebrew bible have anything to say about homosexuality? Old Testament Essays 14(2001):119–152

Torrance AB (2017) Should a christian adopt methodological naturalism? Zygon 52(3):691–725. https://research-repository.st-andrews.ac.uk/bitstream/handle/10023/18330/Torrance_2017_Zygon_MethodologicalNaturalism_AAM.pdf?sequence=1&isAllowed=y

Trigilio Jr J (2004) Thomistic Renaissance—The natural moral law: the reawakening of scholasticism in catholic teaching as evidenced by Pope John Paul II in Veritatis Splendor. Irvine, CA: Universal Publishers.Com

Tveitereid K (2022) Lived theology and theology in the lived. In: Ward P, Tveitereid K (eds) The wiley blackwell companion to theology and qualitative research. Chichester, UK: John Wiley & Sons, Ltd., 66–77. https://doi.org/10.1002/9781119756927.ch8

Vaggione JM (2020) The conservative uses of law: the catholic mobilization against gender ideology. Soc Compass 67(2):252–266. https://doi.org/10.1177/0037768620907561 journals.sagepub.com/home/scp

Walby S (2009) Globalization and inequalities. Sage, London

Walby S (2020) Varieties of gender regimes. Soc Polit Int Stud Gend State Soc 27(3):414–431. https://doi.org/10.1093/sp/jxaa018

Winkler M (2021) The Ancestors' Masculinities in Genesis." J Study Old Testament 46(2):269–288.https://doi.org/10

Zengarini L (2024) Pope francis: gender ideology is the ugliest danger of our time. Vatican News. https://www.vaticannews.va/en/pope/news/2024-03/pope-francis-gender-ideology-is-the-ugliest-danger-of-our-time.html

Chapter 3
Separating the Wheat from the Chaff in the Catholic Church's "Gender Ideology": A Sociological-Synodal Analysis

Abstract Applying Pope Francis's synodal theological approach and sociological arguments, this chapter aims to unpack fact from fiction in the Catholic Church's concept of "gender ideology." It specifically clarifies the nature of gender, ideology, gender theory, and feminist gender theory in sociology. It argues that the Catholic Church's adoption of a strictly philosophical approach to morality is a primary factor in the misconception of the true nature of the sociological and feminist views on gender and gender theory that are present in gender ideology. It recommends a synodal dialogue between Catholic moral theologians and gender sociologists and feminists to reconcile conflicting views and achieve inculturated synodal moral teachings.

Keywords Synodality · Sociology · Gender · Gender ideology · Theology of the body · LGBTQI inclusivity · Natural law theory

Introduction

In the Gospel of Mathew (3:12), Jesus teaches us to winnow or separate the wheat from the chaff, the essential from the non-essential, the good from the bad, or the "truth" from "falsehood," so to speak: "His winnowing fork is in his hand, and he will clear his threshing floor, gathering his wheat into the barn and burning up the chaff with unquenchable fire" (NIV). This chapter aims to separate the "wheat" from "chaff," or the fact from fiction, of the Roman Catholic Church's (RCC) so-called "gender ideology" (GI) or "gender theory" (GT). It aims to unpack the concept of GI as understood by the Catholic hierarchy from sociological and feminist perspectives, using a sociological lens and Pope Francis's latest inductive synodal theology (Francis 2023).

In recent years, the RCC has increased its attacks against GI through papal homilies and pronouncements. Pope Benedict XVI was said to have coined the term (Vaggione 2020). His reading of the anti-feminist pamphlet "Gender: The Deconstruction of Women" by the American journalist-activist Dale O' Leary (1995) is

V. O. Ballano, *Gender Ideology and the Contemporary Catholic Church*,
https://doi.org/10.1007/978-981-97-8124-9_3

said to have influenced his negative attitude towards feminism and gender theories (Graff 2016). As the former Prefect of the Congregation for the Doctrine of the Faith, Pope Benedict XVI, who was Cardinal Joseph Ratzinger at that time, is said to have played a key role in the adoption, circulation, and legitimation of GI in the RCC (Vaggione 2020, 256).

GI is "a descendant of John Paul II's 'culture of death,' 'bad feminism' and a close companion of 'natural rights and 'complementarity'" (Graff 2016, 282). Since Benedict XVI, GI has been used by the RCC to understand and counter the influence of feminist and lesbian, gay, bisexual, transgender, queer, and intersexual (LGBTQI) movements that are popular in various countries, specifically in the United States, Europe, and Latin America. It became a political signifier by conservative Catholics to interpret the perceived evils of liberalism in human sexuality.

Through papal pronouncements, the RCC has gradually replaced Pope John Paul II's concept of "culture of death" with GI as the theological framework by which it understands the dangers of contemporary gender theories to society. Pope Benedict XVI warned the Catholic faithful of the dangers posed by GI to the traditional Christian notion of the family as derived from biological sex: "The integrity of the family, understood as both Christian and natural, was said to be imperiled by this gender ideology" (Butler 2019, 3). In 2012, he specifically attacked GI for promoting "ideologies" that rejected the Church's teachings on gender complementarity between a man and a woman and on the family as established by creation. To him, "those who seek to create themselves deny the creative power of God and are misled by an atheistic set of beliefs" (Butler 2019, 4).

The RCC opposes GI mainly because of its perceived threats to traditional moral doctrines on heterosexuality as the only standard for gender, marriage, and family life in the Church and society. Following Benedict XVI's understanding of GI, Catholic scholars also opposed GI and underscored the dangers of gender to the Church's traditional moral teachings. In Catholic Poland, for instance, GI dominated public discourse. It was named "Word of the Year" in 2013 by a committee of seven renowned Polish linguists affiliated to six Polish universities. GI was condemned as an enabler of violence against women and domestic violence. Thus, after various academic debates on GI at the Polish Episcopacy Conference, Catholic bishops condemned gender theories and issued a pastoral letter entitled "Threats to family resulting from gender ideology" (Sroczynski 2016).

The rise of GI in the RCC can also be attributed to increased pressure from the African church, whose culture is highly anti-homosexual and patriarchal. Bracke and Paternotte (2016), for instance, saw the emergence of GI as part of the "rise of a post-colonial Church" in which the "competitive religious market is characterized by an increased pressure on the African Catholic Church to position itself uncompromisingly when it comes to homosexuality, in response to Pentecostal and Charismatic denunciations of the Catholic Church as partaking in a global conspiracy promoting gay rights" (Bracke and Paternotte 2016, 150).

GI in the RCC is a complex and difficult concept that needs sociological and inductive synodal analysis to separate fact from fiction or exaggeration about the dangers of gender. A theory and an ideology are two separate things in the social sciences. To categorize and condemn all sociological and feminist theories, gender and LGBTQI social movements, and feminist advocacies under the umbrella term of GI, which is often seen by the Catholic hierarchy as attacking the Church's moral teachings, is highly inaccurate and misleading, and requires sociological analysis. There are varieties of gender regimes and theories that cannot be categorized under one label as an ideology such as GI (see Walby 2020).

Sociological and feminist gender theories, which are seen as GI, are not actually meant to directly attack the RCC's moral doctrines. They are generally intended to describe and explain gender dynamics and inequalities as well as women's insubordination in society. As gender theories, these conceptions and explanations by sociologists and feminists about gender and sexual relations and identities, as well as women's oppression in society, are generally tentative in nature, requiring data support and confirmation to consider them true or factual in certain research situations.

Although sociological and feminist theories also advocate societal change in gender relations, gender theories are generally morally neutral and inconclusive about gender realities in society when used in scientific research, unless confirmed by data. Because Catholic clerics and theologians are largely educated in the normative discipline of philosophical theology, sociological and feminist gender theories are often misunderstood as ideologies that attack the RCC's moral teachings on sex and gender. This chapter aims to unpack the RCC's GI for Catholics' synodal pastoral guidance by providing clarification on the distinction between a theory and an ideology in sociology, as well as the role of theory in understanding gender relations in society.

Pope Francis's Mixed Signals on Synodality and GI

No pope in recent RCC history other than Francis has shown a friendly and welcoming attitude to homosexuals and members of the LGBTQI community. In an interview with Associated Press, he criticized laws that criminalize homosexuality as unjust, declaring that God loves all his children just as they are. He called on Catholic bishops who support these laws to welcome LGBTQI people into the Church. To him, it is not a crime to be homosexual (Winfield 2023).

Francis spoke out against more than 70 countries which still criminalize homosexuality and encouraged other faith leaders around the globe to do the same. He also encouraged Catholic parents of queer children to love their children and condemned parents who exclude them from their homes (Knox 2023). He attributed discriminatory attitudes against gays to cultural backgrounds and exhorted bishops to undergo a process of conversion to recognize the dignity of everyone, including those with diverse sexualities and identities.

To date, Pope Francis's most aggressive action to assert the rights of the LGBTQI group and welcome nonbinary and transgender people into the RCC is his approval of the document *Fiducia Supplicans* [On the Pastoral Meaning of Blessing] (*FS*), a declaration released by the RCC's doctrinal watchdog the Dicastery of Doctrine of the

Faith, which allows informal and pastoral blessing to same-sex couples by Catholic priests as well as permitting adult homosexuals to act as godparents in baptism (DDF 2023). Going even further, he encouraged gay couples in homosexual union to seek legal protection in civil marriage. Despite stiff opposition from conservative bishops, priests, and Catholics, Francis stood his ground, declaring that God welcomes all in the Church regardless of sexual orientation: "If a person is gay and seeks God and has good will, who am I to judge?" (BBC 2013).

However, Francis's friendly attitude towards homosexuals and his advocacy for LGBTQI inclusion in the RCC and gay civil rights are accompanied by a strong opposition to gender diversity and GI that ironically includes respect for nonbinary gender identity and LGBTQI inclusion both in the Church and society. Like his predecessors Pope John Paul II and Pope Benedict XVI, Francis (2016) reiterated the theology of the body, which upholds gender complementarity that sees biological sex and the socio-cultural role of sex (gender) as distinguishable but metaphysically inseparable. Any attempt by feminists, activists, and sociologists to oppose this teaching through gender theories is generally termed GI by him without regard to its complexity as a concept.

Thus, Francis has sent mixed signals about gender and LGBTQI inclusivity. He welcomes homosexuals in the Church and respects people with diverse gender identities as they are, and yet vigorously opposes GI and gender diversity, subscribing to heterosexuality as the only gender standard in society as taught by Pope John Paul II's theology of the body, based on gender complementarity. How, therefore, can the LGBTQI with their diverse genders be fully accepted in the Christian community as children of God?

Francis's most recent attack against GI came during the Vatican gender conference of March 2, 2024, in which he called gender "the ugliest ideology" that threatens humanity's survival, cancelling the gender differences between a man and a woman as well as threatening the foundations of the family in society and children's welfare (Zengarini 2024). Unfortunately, despite the repeated use of this term by Pope Francis and the RCC, GI remains broad and imprecise, lacking in conceptual and operational definitions.

Owing to the dominance of philosophy and the marginalization of the social sciences in the RCC, complex behavioral terms such as gender, ideology, or feminism are often used by clerics without sociological and empirical definitions. Thus, the formulation of Church moral and gender concepts is largely philosophical and conceptual, lacking the behavioral and research indicators that would provide practical clarity to scholars and the Catholic faithful. The RCC's teaching on gender and sexuality needs to incorporate sociological and feminist theories on gender and find a common ground for mutual understanding between Catholic moral theologians and social scientists.

Pope Francis's synodal inductive theology is open to the contribution of other branches of knowledge such as sociology to an understanding of the cultural revolution of the current age. Thus, a nuanced and inculturated understanding of sex, gender, gender diversity, gender complementarity, and LGBTQI inclusivity between the RCC's moral teachings and sociological and social science perspectives is necessary to resolve GI. In his document *Ad Theologiam Promovendam* [To Promote Theology] (*ATP*), Pope Francis (2023) also exhorted Catholic theologians to be open to new branches of knowledge such as the social sciences to provide a scientific account of the complex ecclesiastical and moral issues caused by today's cultural revolution.

In order to unpack GI, separating the wheat from the chaff, as well as inculturating and updating the RCC's traditional philosophical approach to sexuality and gender, it is necessary to clarify the nature and sociological significance of gender, gender theory, gender diversity, and LBTQI inclusivity, using Pope Francis's inductive synodal approach.

Objectives, Major Parts, and Arguments

The primary aim of this chapter is to sociologically unpack and analyze the RCC's understanding of GI, sift its fact from fiction, and find a common ground to inculturate the social science gender perspectives in the Church's moral teaching, applying Pope Francis's inductive theological method. Specifically, it intends to clarify the meaning of gender, ideology, gender theory, and feminist gender theory in sociology.

It theorizes that the RCC's opposition to gender theories espoused by sociologists, feminists, activists, and other social scientists is largely a consequence of the adoption of a highly philosophical approach to Catholic morality based on TNLT, as well as the lack of an adequate empirical grasp of the nature of scientific and sociological reasoning to understand complex social and moral issues in GI. It attempts to find common ground between the RCC's traditional teaching on gender, and sociological and feminist gender theories, in order to advance Pope Francis's synodal church, a church that welcomes the marginalized in the Church such as the LGBTQI community.

There are four main sections in this chapter. The first section discusses the theoretical orientation of the study, which basically applies Pope Francis's inductive synodal theology and sociological approach to justify the importance of the use of scientific method such as the application of theory and method in resolving moral issues on gender and sexuality in the RCC.

The second section clarifies the nature of scientific reasoning and method and contrasts them to philosophical and theological reasoning. It argues that sociology and social sciences are necessary to Pope Francis' inductive synodal theology in the analysis of contemporary moral issues on gender and sexuality in society. The third section briefly surveys the major types of sociological and feminist theories and their usefulness for scientific research and social reforms for gender equality in society.

The last section sociologically examines the unintended negative effect of the highly prescriptive and philosophical education of clerics on the Catholic hierarchy's inaccurate and normative view on gender and sexuality. It recommends an intensive sociological training, a gender awareness program, and ongoing synodal dialogue between Catholic theologians, bishops, sociologists, feminists, and other experts on gender.

Overall, this chapter contends that categorizing gender theories and feminist perspectives that tend to contravene the RCC's official moral teachings as GI is sociologically inaccurate. Gender theories are diverse and their impact on society has been variable (Balme and Bulbeck 2008). Thus, labeling them under one category as gender ideology is highly inaccurate and misleading. Describing gender perspectives that oppose the TNLT as GI is also a misunderstanding of the true nature of scientific reasoning in sociology and the social sciences.

Gender theories do not directly aim to attack the RCC's moral doctrines. They are meant to explain gender inequalities but are still subject to confirmation by research and data. Although sociological and feminist theories can also advocate societal change in gender relations, gender theories are generally morally neutral and tentative assessments of gender realities in society when used in scientific research. The RCC's opposition to the gender theories espoused by sociologists, feminists, and other social scientists is largely a consequence of the lack of adequate grasp of the nature of scientific and sociological reasoning to explain social and moral issues.

Unlike philosophical and theological reasoning that do not require empirical data, sociological gender study necessitates the application of a theory and method, two major components of the scientific method. The conceptualization of GI is a negative unintended consequence of the lack of sociological and social science education as well as the dominance of scholastic philosophy and Thomistic natural law theory in clerical training that has largely conditioned the normative and philosophical mind of the Catholic hierarchy on gender, gender complementarity, and sexuality in society.

Theoretical Orientation

Pope Francis's Inductive Theological Approach

Pope Francis provides hope of an RCC more open to sociological and feminist gender theories that would minimize inaccurate characterization of complex sociological terms such as GI in the Church. His latest document, *Ad Theologiam Promovendam* [To Promote Theology] (*ATP*), demands a paradigm shift in Catholic theological investigation, which he insists should begin with empirical reality and the lived experiences of people in society (Francis 2023). Francis is opening new horizons in Catholic moral theology that encourages empirical and sociological research to first understand the lived experiences of Catholics in today's complex world before passing moral judgment.

To him, listening to and learning from people's experiences in today's society necessitates an accurate understanding of the empirical reality and the application of Christian discernment to find God's will in these experiences. Thus, he declares: "[T]he Mystery of God is always beyond us and that the lives of people and the world around us are, and will always remain, superior to ideas and theories. Life is always superior to ideas" (Francis 2023, para.9).

As of this writing, Pope Francis remains faithful to the RCC's traditional teaching on gender, gender complementarity, and the Christian concept of heterosexual marriage. He opposes GI and continues to affirm Pope John Paul II and Pope Benedict XVI's theology of the body to uphold the Church's moral teaching on the unity and metaphysical inseparability between sex and gender.

Despite this, Francis is open to new ideas and welcomes divergent views in the RCC to attain his vision of a synodal church. His latest ecclesiastical reforms in synodality exhort Catholic theologians to dialogue with social scientists and develop an interdisciplinary Catholic theology to address today's cultural revolution as well as calls for greater LGBTQI inclusion in the RCC. Francis's vision and innovation in synodality are pushing boundaries in encouraging scholars to explore new approaches to ecclesiastical and moral issues in contemporary society to achieve inculturation in moral teachings.

Furthermore, Francis's inductive synodal theology in *ATP* recommends that in resolving issues, accurate knowledge of the empirical life of people in contemporary society and the application of inductive scientific methods should come before theological reflection.

Theological and Sociological Methods and Morality

Unlike Catholic moral theologians who judge human behavior with a fixed set of metaphysical criteria such as the natural law theory, sociologists usually adopt an attitude of moral neutrality in judging people's action and social situations to attain scientific knowledge. To them, moral claims and truth claims are not self-evident or absolute but are relative to the cultural conventions in which those who utter them are embedded (Jarvie 2007).

Catholic moral theology, which primarily relies on philosophical reasoning, uses the absolutist approach to resolve moral issues. Moral absolutism holds that moral commands are always true, regardless of cultural context. Thus, moral theologians and moralists evaluate people's behavior and social phenomena according to whether they conform with or deviate from these ideal moral commands. This reasoning is based on the metaphysical rules of TNLT. St Thomas's natural law theory assumes that the divine law is implanted in human nature and reasoning which guide individuals on what is right or wrong in all circumstances.

Sociology of Gender and Misconceptions of GI

As Cardinal Joseph Ratzinger who headed the Congregation for the Doctrine of the Faith, Pope Benedict XVI defended the TNLT as the philosophical and theological foundation of Catholic morality, arguing that every human law is legitimate only if it conforms with the natural moral law. To him, "The secular law should not only reflect what is moral; it is in itself a moralizing instrument because the law play[s] a very important and sometimes decisive role in influencing patterns of thought and behavior" (Vaggione 2020, 254).

Following Benedict XVI and Church tradition, the RCC still maintains the philosophical approach to morality based on TNLT, disregarding most scientific research on complex moral issues such as gender, gender diversity, transgenderism, or LGBTQI inclusivity. Sociological and feminist gender theories that aim to give an account of gender relations and women's oppression in society, as well as the emergence of gender diversity in society, are often seen as opposing Church moral doctrines and labeled as GI.

Instead of understanding the true nature of these scientific and sociological theories as part of scientific rationality that applies both theory and method or data collection to explain the nature of gender and gender relations in the world, the RCC sees them as deviating from the philosophical reasoning of the TNLT and constituting an ideology. In sociology, a theory is still tentative and subject to data confirmation, thus not definitive; thus, labeling gender theories as GI and attacking Church teaching is a highly inaccurate conception that needs sociological clarification.

With the cultural revolution taking place in contemporary societies, gender and sexuality can become more complex for Catholic hierarchy and moral theologians to deal with without the assistance of sociologists and behavioral scientists. Gender research has emerged as a major field in sociology, with no other academic discipline giving more attention to current gender issues than sociology. Sociological research on gender has had a major impact in academic fields, specifically "in the education and health sectors, in violence prevention, antidiscrimination and equal opportunity policy" (Connell 2014, 550). Gender theories were conceived in sociology and the social sciences to give an account of problematic gender relations in society. They were not constructed with the primary aim of attacking the RCC's moral doctrines on gender and sexuality.

Modern sociology has become the foundation for theoretical investigation of gender relations in society (Barrett, 1980; Walby, 2009). "[T]he injustice, violence and distress that unequal gender relations produced is widely recognized as key concerns for applied sociology" (Connell 2014, 552). The RCC tends to attack gender theories as GI because they pertain to feminism. However, not all gender theories are feminist, although all feminist theories focus their attention on gender. "Feminism is a theory and approach that supports economic, political, and social equality, specifically valuing and advocating for the equal opportunities of women. It also provides frameworks and practices for bringing about the unfinished project of social change" (Fotaki and Pullen 2023, 1–2). Sociological and feminist theories do not generally aim to attack the RCC's moral teachings. Feminist opposition to the Church's moral doctrines on gender is largely an indirect consequence of their quest for social justice for women and gender-diverse people in the contemporary world. Some of the RCC's structures and practices are patriarchal and thus vulnerable to critical feminist analysis. A critical sociological analysis of GI to bring out some of its misconceptions on gender theories is necessary to establish a synodal dialogue between sociology and Catholic theology in the field of gender and sexuality.

The Difference Between Ideology and Theory

One serious problem associated with the use of GI as a signifier by the RCC is its lack of distinction between an ideology and a theory. In sociology, there is a big difference between these two terms. An ideology has a reformist normative stance of changing society according to a set of beliefs, whereas a sociological theory, which also consists of beliefs and a set of principles, intends to describe or explain a social phenomenon based on a set of quantitative and/or qualitative data.

The relationship between ideology and sociology is not an easy one. In sociology, ideology has an activist aspiration: it is generally seen as a set of beliefs that aim to explain and change social reality. It can be understood as "a relatively coherent body of beliefs about the various aspects of society, that is, as a cultural system and a guide for policy" (Ferrarotti). Marxist ideology, for instance, aims to achieve Karl Marx's revolutionary idea of a classless society.

When 80 French MPs of the Union for a Popular Movement opposed new biology textbooks that defined gender as a social construction rather than biologically given, they understood gender theory as an ideology. They perceived it as a "totalitarian ideology, more oppressive and pernicious than the Marxist ideology" and asserted that it "risks destabilizing young people and adolescents and altering their development" (Corredor 2019, 613).

Seeing gender theory as a form of ideology is sociologically inaccurate, since ideology is different from a theory, although there can be an overlap between them. Some who espouse gender, such as feminists, view their theories not only as instruments for the study of gender inequalities in society but also as serving to advance their social justice agenda. Some sociological gender theories, such as feminist theories, are used to advocate radical change in society, while others mainly aim to describe gender inequalities in scientific research. A gender theory could not be correctly labeled GI as understood in the RCC if it is merely used to scientifically describe a socio-cultural phenomenon.

A closer scrutiny of gender theory as a research theory and as an ideology reveals some overlapping concerns in gender studies. Feminist theories may be seen as conflict gender theories in sociology. But they are also conceived to respond to the existing injustices of certain social structures that oppress women in society. Feminism as a social justice reform movement calls for a sweeping change to systemic discrimination and associated acts of violence against women. It "works towards eradicating gender inequalities and associated violences arising from poverty, lack of opportunity and recognition, and sexual violence, which puts women's bodies at considerable risk globally, including at work and in organizations" (Fotaki and Pullen 2023, 2).

Thus, a gender theory for feminists can be a tool for both research and political change. It is not just "an abstract intellectual activity divorced from women's lives but seeks to explain the conditions under which those lives are lived" (Jackson and Jones 1998, 1). As Lindsey (2021, 21–22) contends:

> Feminist theory and its attention to intersectionality offers a framework for advocates addressing women's inferior social position and the social, political, and economic discrimination that perpetuates it. Many of these organizations form networks under the umbrella of **feminism**, an inclusive worldwide movement to end sexism and sexist oppression by empowering women. Although not identical, feminist movement(s) are largely interchangeable in the eyes of the public.

In feminist gender theory, there seems to be a difficulty distinguishing gender research from gender ideology, since many researchers relate to feminist organizations that also advocate social change. Despite this overlap, the RCC needs to distinguish the use of gender theory for research and for social justice. It cannot be lumped together under the banner of GI, which is seen by papal teachings as pronouncements directly attacking the Church's traditional moral teachings on gender, homosexuality, and other sexual issues.

Theory as Tentative in Sociology

Most people understand the word "theory" to refer to an idea or hunch that someone has. People do not normally search for evidence or data without a hunch or tentative theory. In science, theory refers to the way that people interpret facts. In contemporary sociology, theories are "overarching intellectual perspectives that sociologists use to explain, understand and, in some cases, transform the social world" (Stepnisky 2019, 295). A theory is a tentative explanation of reality that guides sociologists to interpret their collected data to confirm its validity.

Sociology as a social science has two major components: theory and method. A theory is used by sociologists to interpret scientific data in scientific research, while method refers to the data collection scheme researchers use to test the applicability of a theory in a particular research setting. When applying the sociological research method in a deductive research process, for instance, sociologists normally begin by adopting a theory in their research studies and proceed to gather data to test whether it is empirically correct or incorrect in a particular research setting. It is not yet a final description of social reality; it needs a set of data to confirm its applicability in certain research situations.

For example, a researcher might adopt a theory on social deprivation in religiosity research to explain why people become more prayerful during disasters. If the collected data confirm that disaster victims become more prayerful in a certain disaster, then the theory which assumes that material deprivation in life can lead to religiosity is correct for this specific disaster situation. The deprivation theory then appropriately explains scientifically why a group of disaster victims became more religious when faced with material deprivation during disasters.

Unlike philosophy and theology, which are not obliged to present empirical data to support theoretical explanation, such as the natural law theory that views homosexuality as "unnatural," sociology as a social science needs a theory to interpret data. However, the RCC tends to misinterpret gender theories as ideologies in its evaluation of the various sociological and feminist gender theories as "gender ideology." Gender theories that offer different views that tend to contradict the official church teaching are not definitive. As theories, they are not absolute explanation of gender relations in society. They are still subject to empirical support or data to confirm their validity.

The gender-essentialist view sees sexual and [gender] identity as "complementary [i.e., not at variance] because persons live in society according to the cultural aspects corresponding to their sex" (Ford 2018, 81). The conservative doctrine that influenced Catholic sexual teaching during Pope John Paul II's pontificate rejected the sociological and social science gender theories that aim to understand gender based on human experience and scientific method. John Paul II's doctrine on the theology of the body has shaped the conservative and rigid understanding of gender that permeates the entire Church. According to this doctrine, "masculinity and femininity express the twofold aspect of man's somatic constitution…[which] consists in reciprocal enrichment."

A gender theory differs from a gender ideology, although they may overlap. "Gender theory is the study of what is understood as masculine and/or feminine and/or queer behavior in any given context, community, society, or field of study (including, but not limited to, literature, history, sociology, education, applied linguistics, religion, health sciences, philosophy, cultural studies)" (Jule 2014, 2464).

Major Sociological Gender Theories

All social interactions, and the institutions in which the interactions occur, are gendered in some manner. Accounts of this gendering have reshaped the theoretical and empirical foundations of sociology. On the theoretical side, gender awareness has modified existing sociological theory and led to the creation of a new feminist paradigm" (Lindsey 2021, 4). Society is always changing and evolving. Thus, sociological gender theories also evolve to account for the changing gender relations in the social order. In sociology, gender theories are generally classified into functionalist, interactionist, and conflict.

Functionalist Gender Theory

Functionalism as a major sociological theory views society as consisting of interdependent parts that constitute the whole. Thus, gender under this theory is seen as a social function that divides work in society, or what is sociologically known as division of labor. The functionalist gender theory thus primarily sees gender inequalities in society as an effective means to establish the division of labor in society, that is, a social system where various social groups clearly perform certain type of tasks, such as homemaking for women, while other segments perform other acts of labor, such as breadwinning for men.

Under this theory, "gender is something efficient, in order to move society in proper way, by giving male and female some distinct roles. Also, gender builds social unity thanks to men and women get together for forming a family" (Macionis, 2010). Talcott Parsons, a classical theorist of structural functionalism, argues that acting according to proper gender roles for man and woman in the family also helps socialization and education of children (Parsons and Bales 1956).

Conflict Gender Theory

Inspired by Karl Marx's dialectical materialism, conflict theory in sociology views various social groups such as men and women as in constant struggle with one another, vying for control of the scarce resources in society. Marx views conflict in terms of economic production where the elite and dominant group controls the means of production and the working class as the subordinate group is exploited by the former in terms of low wages, inhumane working conditions, and alienation of their human nature as labor.

Karl Marx, the father of conflict theory, and his colleague Friederich Engels extended the idea of exploitation and applied it to the family structure. To them, the relationship between exploiter and exploited also exists in family households (Lindsey 2011). And the capitalist system plays an important role in the exploitation of women in the household in three ways:

> Firstly, capitalism provides power for men by giving them chance in order to have high income and private property. Secondly, women became the consumer part of society, because they do not produce, but get money from their husband and spend for satisfy their need or enjoy. Thirdly, capitalism divides men and women in working way. It puts men to factory and women to house, however, it does not pay for women's workings in the house, but pays for men for his working in factory, so it puts importance to male's job by paying money. (Baligar 2018, 617–618)

For conflict sociologists, social problems arise when dominant groups exploit the subordinate groups in society. When they study and analyze gender using the conflict perspective, they generally view men as the dominant group and women as the subordinate group. Since the husband earns income as the household's breadwinner, he becomes the dominant gender, while the wife, who is dependent on the husband for economic support, becomes the subordinate gender. In modern societies, women's unpaid household work is seen as unnecessary and unproductive, while husbands' jobs outside the home are considered productive (Lindsey, 2021). Husbands then become breadwinners and wives housekeepers in a capitalist system.

Symbolic Interactionist Gender Theory

The functionalist and conflict gender theories are usually applied in sociology for meso and macro studies. But studying gender at the micro level, especially in social interactions, requires another type of gender sociological theory. The symbolic interactionist gender theory is one of the most popular theories used by sociologists to analyze gender inequalities in people's daily interactions. Symbolic interactionism aims to understand human behavior by analyzing the critical role of symbols in human interaction.

Because the meanings attached to symbols are socially created and not natural, and fluid, not static, we act and react to symbols based on their current assigned meaning.

> According to symbolic interactionism, organized groups control the behavior of their members by serving as generalized others, which constitute a core element of the self. This general process of social control should be invariant across gender. (Bartusch and Matsueda 1996, 149)

A "symbolic interactionist approach, [which] posits that the multiple identities of an individual (i.e., the self) are manifested through behavioral, cognitive, and emotional responses to patterned societal symbols and language" (Blumer, 1969; Burke, 1980; 1991; Mead, 1934; Stryker, 1980). In this way, the self-forms through societal interaction, the responses of others in various situations, and ultimately reflects the perceived meanings of society" (Sartore and Cunningham 2007, 245).

In symbolic interactionist theory, both gender and sexuality are socially constructed. The social construction of sexuality refers to the way in which socially created definitions of the cultural appropriateness of sex-linked behavior shape the way people see and experience sexuality. "Females" or "males" as named by society are endowed with distinct character features defined as feminine or masculine. Gender does not exist by itself, but with the interaction among people in society. Erving Goffman's "Dramaturgy" study is an example of society "doing" gender (Lindsey, 2021). "To sum up, symbolic interaction theory handles that individuals create their social reality via daily interactions, therefore, they see gender as a component of personal performance. Gender plays a role in order to shape all relationship of people in daily life" (Baligar 2018, 618).

Feminist Gender Theories in Sociology

Feminist gender theories in sociology are a variant of conflict theory. They arise from women's movements under the umbrella term of feminism. The term "feminism" has various meanings and interpretations, depending on the social, political, religious, and cultural orientations of feminists. Thus, feminism is a diverse, rival and often opposing collection of social theories, political movements, and moral philosophies that broadly examines the social, political, and economic inequalities of women (Adawo et al. 2011).

Feminism aims to describe women's oppression as well as to seek strategies, causes, and consequences to remove gender inequalities in society (Mohajan 2022). It also "seeks to analyze the conditions which shape women's lives and to explore cultural understandings of what it means to be a woman. It was initially guided by the political aims of the Women's Movement the need to understand women's subordination" (Jackson and Jones 1998, 1).

In recent decades, feminism has become a major branch of sociological theory. As a gender theory, feminism seeks to investigate social inequalities in gender relations and to explain gender equality and oppression in society. It is a set of structural conflict approaches which view society as a conflict between men and women.

For a gender theory to be feminist, Chafetz (2006, 4) identifies three major characteristics, namely: "(1) a (not necessarily exclusive) focus on the inequities, strains, and contradictions inherent in gender arrangements; (2) an assumption that gender relations are not immutable but rather changeable social creations; and (3) a normative commitment that societies should develop equitable gender arrangements."

Although feminist theory is evolving owing to the constant change of gender relations in society, it is traditionally categorized into liberal, Marxist-socialist, and radical feminist theories. The liberal feminist theory is basically founded on "the general proposition that all people are created equal and should not be denied equality of opportunity because of gender. Rapidly ascending during the women's liberation movement in the 1960s, liberal feminism is associated with feminism's second wave" (Lindsey 2021, 22). It argues that "women are equal to men and works to obtain equal rights through political and economic action while basically accepting the capitalist organization of society" (Ritzer and Ryan 2011, 223).

The Marxist-socialist feminist theory "incorporates Marxist or socialist ideas and focuses on social production as the social process key to achieving equality" (Ritzer and Ryan 2011, 223). It applies "a Marx-Engels model linking women's inferior position to class-base capitalism and its alignment with the patriarchal family in capitalistic societies. Socialist feminism argues that sexism and capitalism are mutually supportive. Women's unpaid labor in the home and paid labor in reserve labor force to be called on and discarded as needed serve patriarchy and capitalism" (Lindsey 2021, 23).

Radical feminist theory is said to be the most radical theory on women's oppression in society. It fundamentally argues that all structures of society oppress women. It contends "that sexism is at the core of patriarchal society and that all social institutions reflect it…feminists focus on the patriarchal family as the key site of oppression" (Lindsey 2021, 24). This group of feminists is labeled radical, which they largely acknowledge, because of their assertion "that gender is the underlying form of oppression, cutting across race, class, and culture; today disability, age, and gender variant identity is added" (Lindsey 2021, 24).

Areas of Conflict Between the RCC and Feminism

In an article with the intriguing title "Catholic and Feminist: Can One Be Both?", Elizabeth Fox-Genovese (1999) argues that that there are such irreconcilable conflicts between Catholicism and feminism that most Catholics and most feminists would insist that such reconciliation is difficult if not impossible to achieve.

This argument assumes that there is a common strand that unites all feminist theories and that all feminist theories are attacking the Church's teaching that one cannot be a true Catholic and feminist at the same time. It reflects the RCC's concept of GI, which bundles together all gender theories as intrinsically irreconcilable with Catholic moral teachings. But, as already mentioned, feminism as both a theory and an ideology are diverse, and some feminists hold conflicting views which do not necessarily contradict the RCC's official moral teachings.

In fact, there are contemporary Catholic moral theologians who have started to reconcile feminist theories and Church moral doctrines. In her book *Sex, Gender, and Christian Ethics* (1996), Lisa Sowle Cahill, Professor of Social Ethics at Boston College and a Catholic feminist, attempted to reconcile feminist theories and the traditional Catholic Church teachings on sex, gender, and sexuality. "Cahill insists on both theological and philosophical sources of moral theology, but the theological is primary. Her philosophical notion of human flourishing is based on Thomism and feminism" (Curran 2022, 24).

Despite the attempts of the new breed of Catholic moral theologians to integrate feminism in Catholic teaching, the philosophical approach and the TNLT are still evident in the moral analysis that undermines the empirical and sociological aspects of gender. Although some contemporary Catholic moral theologians have started to take a more positive view of sex and incorporate some feminist theories, they still generally remain within the parameters of the present doctrine and theology of the body of the RCC (Capecchi 2020).

One significant area of conflict between feminists and traditional Catholic moral theologians is on understanding sex and gender. Following the RCC's traditional, TNLT-based approach to morality, Catholic moral theology views sex and gender as one and inseparable. The traditional theological perspective still views gender as immutable, ahistorical, and intrinsically connected with biological sex. It teaches that heterosexuality and cisgender – that one's masculinity and femininity should correspond to one's sex or biological make-up – remains the norm for Christian maturity and marital union. It still rejects transgenderism. It insists that transgender and LGBTQI people should receive the RCC's pastoral care in order to convert to heterosexuality.

Sociologists do not agree on the proper use of the terms "sex" and "gender" in their research and scholarship. As Wharton (2005, 18) contends,

> There is no firm consensus on the appropriate use of 'gender' and 'sex' among gender scholars. Some reject the term 'sex' altogether and refer only to 'gender.' Others use the terms almost interchangeably, while still others employ both concepts and recognize a clear distinction between them. These differences in usage are not merely semantic; rather, they reflect more fundamental differences in perspective and theoretical orientation.

To Jule (2014, 2464), *sex* refers to categories of the biologically observable human body, female and male or intersex (i.e., nature), while the term *gender* refers to the categories of social expectations, roles, and behaviors, feminine and masculine (i.e., what is nurtured). Feminists and sociologists fundamentally oppose the RCC's traditional views on sex and gender as one and inseparable. To them, sex and gender, although inseparable in the person, are distinct, and sex may not correspond to gender, which is socially and culturally acquired by the person through the process of socialization or social learning in society.

Thus, there is no one gender for feminists and sociologists since not all people follow the heterosexual gender. LGBTQI constitutes distinct genders that should be recognized and respected. Sociologists and feminists advocate gender diversity: "Gender Diversity refers to the different genders within the society. Every gender that exists within society should have equal rights" (Usman et al. 2023, 439). But this is opposed by the RCC and Catholic moral theologians. Following the philosophical approach to sex and gender, they reject any form of gender diversity in society, insisting on heterosexuality and cisgender as the only morally acceptable gender norms in the Church.

Aside from conflicting view on sex and gender, feminists and Catholic bishops and moralists also clash in some major areas, such as the root causes of women's oppression in society. Patriarchy as a social structure that generates gender inequality and oppression is one major area of conflict between them. The RCC is a highly patriarchal religious institution. It is governed by an all-male celibate group of ordained bishops and priests led by the Pope. Female ordination is forbidden.

The ideal Christian family as a domestic church (*domus ecclesia*) is also founded on patriarchy, where the husband is still recognized as the head of the household with the wife performing the traditional gender role of being the homemaker, domestic manager, and religious Christian educator for children at home. Since the RCC is a patriarchal religious institution, several feminists are critical of the Church's social structure and gender relations. Feminists are highly critical of patriarchy. Thus, the RCC finds itself the object of feminist attacks both in research and advocacy because of its patriarchal social and ecclesiastical system.

The RCC's moral teaching on heterosexuality, gender complementarity, and heterosexual marriage is also vulnerable to attacks by feminists as well as by those who advocate gender diversity and same-sex marriage, such as members of the LGBTQI.[1] The highly philosophical and deductive analysis of these moral issues is generally contrasted with the empirical and scientific approaches of sociological and feminist research. Pope John Paul II's writings on the theology of the body, using philosophical arguments and TNLT, traditionally view sex and gender as one and immutable and affirm the complementary gender roles of men and women, with the female role relegated to family affairs.

Sociologists and feminists, however, use scientific theory and method to back up their claims on gender, same-sex marriage, and gender diversity. The RCC's moral theologians, bishops, and moralists, who are not well-versed in social science research and feminism, tend to reject research-based empirical and scientific claims, labeling them all as GI, even though sociological and feminist theories and advocacies are very diverse and not all of them are directly attacking the Church.

Synodal Dialogue Between Feminists and Catholic Moralists

"Feminist theories help in empowering women to eliminate the social norms regarding gender inequality. These theories aim to understand the main reason for gender inequality to eliminate these issues from society" (Usman et al. 2023, 439). Although the RCC labels feminist gender theories GI, the concerns of feminists are very much in line with the Church's teachings on social justice and preferential options for the poor and the oppressed in society.

Some of these traits are based on scientific research and not on deductive philosophical reasoning. Since the RCC is slow to update its moral teachings for lack of exploration and incorporation of the social sciences in Catholic moral theology, these traditional moral teachings are now becoming the object of feminist attacks. The second feminist gender assumption above – that gender relations are not immutable – obviously contravenes the RCC's teaching on gender complementarity, which sees gender as immutable and inseparable from sex. Applying the natural law theory, the Church's moral magisterium opposes any attempt to conceptualize other forms of gender such as LGBTQI. Only heterosexuality is recognized as the standard morally accepted gender.

[1] For a more detailed discussion on the RCC's doctrines on heteronormativity, gender complementarity, and heterosexual marriage, please refer to Chapters 2 and 4 of this book.

Feminist theories in the sociological research and literature have various research and political agendas. Thus, they cannot be categorized together as GI if some of them happen to oppose the traditional Church teaching on gender. In the editorial "Feminism from the Perspective of Catholic Theology," Tracy Rowland (2020, 1) cautions Catholic theologians not to treat feminism as one unified movement:

> Unlike the Catholic Church, which does have an internal organ dedicated to doctrinal oversight—the Congregation for the Doctrine of the Faith—as well as various documents of popes and Church Councils described as being of "magisterial" standing that clarify teachings on different topics, feminism is a much more centrifugal force. There are many different "species" of feminist scholars such as first wave, second wave, third wave and fourth wave, essentialist, and constructivist and radical, to name just some of the most prominent of the sub-divisions. This means that when one seeks to examine the movement from the perspective of Catholic theology one has to be careful of making generalizations.

Thus, categorizing feminist theories that oppose the Church's moral teachings as GI is a sweeping generalization that needs sociological clarification. Feminists sometimes espouse opposing views: "Something that might be held as a doctrinal position by one group of feminists may be hotly disputed by another group. There are also numerous different foci to be chosen" (Rowland 2020, 1).

As a gender theory, feminism is primarily meant to explain the empirical realities of gender inequalities and injustices in society, although some feminist gender theories have linked sociological research to their advocacies, making it difficult to distinguish research from advocacy. But in general, feminist research tends to be critical of the RCC's gender and social structure only as an unintended consequence that aims to provide an empirical picture of gender relations in the highly patriarchal structure of the Church. It would seem inaccurate to judge these theories as GI aiming to directly attack Church doctrines.

Indeed, the RCC's position against women's ordination and on upholding patriarchy in the all-male priesthood, for instance, can be susceptible to feminist attacks when their gender theories are applied to an analysis of Catholic priesthood. Feminism advocates gender equality and opposes sexism and patriarchy. This movement was born in the United States in the 1840s to protest the suffering of women and African Americans, resulting in the recognition of women's voting rights in 1920 (Macionis 2010). Feminists continue to theorize gender relations to pursue their agenda of gender equality and the liberation of women from social injustices in society.

Although it opposes some theoretical feminist positions, the RCC's Catholic social teaching on social justice is sympathetic to feminism's quest for justice in society. "Feminists believe that women's subordination in society is a form of social injustice against women. It is social in origin. It is "not given by nature nor an accidental feature of relations between men and women" (Jackson 1998, 13). Catholic social teaching that denounces structural injustice to protect the common good also re-echoes the feminist social justice agenda.

Thus, instead of condemning sociological and feminist theories on gender as GI, the RCC should be open to the concerns of feminists and sociologists of gender and start finding a common ground in spirit of Pope Francis's synodal process. Catholic moral theologians should start a dialogue with sociologists, feminists, and other experts who advocate gender equality to identify how the Church's mission and moral magisterium are reflected in the feminist gender reform agenda.

In spirit of Pope Francis's synodality, the RCC, led by bishops and Catholic theologians and moralists, should dialogue and hold synodal consultations with sociologists and feminists who are experts on gender theories to reconcile their differences and find a common ground with the purpose of updating Church moral teachings on gender and removing the GI tag for gender theories that only aim to provide an empirical assessment of gender relations in society and promote social justice for women and all other forms of gender identity.

Conclusion

This chapter has clarified the meaning of gender, ideology, gender theory, and feminist gender theory in sociological literature to inductively separate fact from fiction or misconception in the complex concept of GI in the RCC's teachings. It contended that the Church's adoption of a strictly philosophical and metaphysical approach to morality based on natural law theory is a primary factor in the Church's misconception of the true nature and role of gender and gender theory in sociological and feminist research and literature. It recommends an interdisciplinary synodal conference between Catholic moral theologians and gender scientists and advocates to reconcile conflicting views on gender and gender theory in order to realize Francis's synodal church.

References

Adawo L, Gikonyo L, Kudu R, Olga M (2011) History of Feminism in Kenya. Spanish Agency for International Development Cooperation (AECID)

Baligar MP (2018) Gender theories in sociology. Int J Res Analyt Rev 5(3):617–619

Balme J, Bulbeck (2008) Engendering origins: theories of gender in sociology and archaeology. Australian Archeology 67:1–12

Bartusch DJ, Matsueda RL (1996) Gender, reflected appraisals, and labeling: a cross-group test of an interactionist theory of delinquency. Soc Forces 75(1):145–176

Bracke S, Paternotte D (eds) (2016) Habemus gender! The catholic church and "gender ideology." Special issue of Religion and Gender 6, no. 2

Butler J (2019) What threat? The campaign against 'gender ideology'. Globalism: J Culture Politics Innov

Chafetz JS (2006) The varieties of gender theory in sociology. In: Handbook of the sociology of gender. handbooks of sociology and social research. Springer, Boston, MA. https://doi.org/10.1007/0-387-36218-5_1

Congregation for Catholic Education (2005) Instruction concerning the criteria for the discernment of vocations with regard to persons with homosexual tendencies in view of their admission to the seminary and to holy orders. L'Osservatore Romano Weekly Edition in English, p 3., December 7
Connell R (2014) The sociology of gender in southern perspective. Current Sociol Monogr 62(4):550–567. https://doi.org/10.1177/0011392114524510
Corredor ES (2019) Unpacking "Gender Ideology" and the global right's anti-gender counter movement. Signs J Women Culture Society 44(3):613–638
Curran C (2022) Lisa Sowle Cahill: five significant contributions to reimagining Christian ethics. J Moral Theology 11(1):23–36
DDF (Dicastery of the Doctrine of the Faith) (2023) Fiducia Supplicans: on the pastoral meaning of blessings. Vatican: The Roman Curia. Available at: https://www.vatican.va/roman_curia/congregations/cfaith/documents/rc_ddf_doc_20231218_fiducia-supplicans_en.html
Ford CJ (2018) Transgender bodies, catholic schools, and a queer natural law theology of exploration. J Moral Theol 7(1):70–98
Fotaki M, Pullen A (2023) Feminist theories and activist practices in organization studies. Organ Stud 1–24. https://doi.org/10.1177/01708406231209861
Fox-Genovese E (1999) Catholic and feminist: can one be both? Logos J Catholic Thought Culture 2(4):11–26. https://doi.org/10.1353/log.1999.0023
Graff A (2016) 'Gender Ideology': weak concepts, powerful politics. Religion Gender 6(2):268–272. https://doi.org/10.18352/rg.10177
Jackson S (1998) Chapter 2: feminist social theory. In: Jackson S (ed) Contemporary feminist theories. Edinburgh University Press, Edinburgh, pp 1–11
Jackson S, Jones J (1998) Thinking for ourselves: an introduction to feminist theorising. In: Jackson S (ed) Contemporary feminist theories. Edinburgh University Press, Edinburgh, pp 12–33
Jarvie I (2007) Relativism and historicism. In: Turner SP, Risjold MW (eds) Handbook of the philosophy of science, philosophy of anthropology and sociology. Amsterdam: North-Holland
Jule A (2014) Gender theory. In: Michalos AC (ed), Encyclopedia of quality of life and well-being research. Springer, Dordrecht. https://doi.org/10.1007/978-94-007-0753-5_1137
Lindsey LL (2021) Gender: sociological perspectives, 7th edn. Routledge, New York
Macionis JJ (2010) Sociology, 13th edn. Pearson, London
Mohajan H (2022) An overview on the feminism and its categories. Res Adv Educ 1(3):11–26
O'Leary D (1995) Gender: the deconstruction of women. Analysis of the gender perspective in preparation for the fourth world conference on women, Beijing, China
Pontifical Council for Justice and Peace (2005) Compendium of social doctrine of the church. Rome: Libreria Editrice Vaticana, Available online: http://www.vatican.va/roman_curia/pontifical_councils/justpeace/documents/rc_pc_justpeace_doc_20060526_compendio-dott-soc_en.html
Pope Francis (2023) Apostolic letter issued "Motu Proprio" Ad Theologiam Promovendam [To Promote Theology]. Unofficial full English translation available at: https://returntotradition.org/unofficial-full-english-translation-of-francis-revolutionary-motu-proprio-ad-theologiam-promovendam-plus-breaking-news-report-on-text/
Rowland T (2020) Feminism from the perspective of catholic theology. Religions 11(578):1–4. https://doi.org/10.3390/rel11110578
Sartore M, Cunningham GB (2007) Explaining the under-representation of women in leadership positions of sport organizations: a symbolic interactionist perspective. Quest 59:244–265
Sroczynski M (2016) A year of conflict—the "war on gender ideology" discourse of the polish catholic church, and the Liberal Backlash. AG about gender. Int J Gender Studies 5(10):75–106
Stepnisky J (2019) Sociological theory. In: Michael Ryan J (ed), Core concepts in sociology, pp 295–301. Hoboken: Wiley Blackwell

Ritzer G, Ryan MJ (2011) The concise encyclopedia of sociology. Malden: Wiley-Blackwell
Vaggione JM (2020) The conservative uses of law: the catholic mobilization against gender ideology. Social Compass 67(2):252–266. https://doi.org/10.1177/0037768620907561journals.sagepub.com/home/scp
Wharton AS (2005) The sociology of gender: an introduction to theory and research. Blackwell Publishing, Oxford, UK

Part II
Gender Ideology's Alleged Threats to Humanity, Family, and Children's Welfare

Chapter 4
"Gender Ideology's" Alleged Threat to Humanity: A Critical Sociological-Synodal Analysis

Abstract This chapter sociologically unpacks the Catholic Church's concept of "gender ideology" and its alleged imminent threat to humanity's survival in light of Pope Francis's latest ecclesiastical reform project, the Synod on Synodality, and his inductive synodal theology. It argues that the concept of gender as espoused by sociologists, feminists, LGBTQI leaders, and gender activists does not inflict actual and imminent harm on humanity, but poses a serious epistemological challenge to the Church's traditional, metaphysical, and philosophical view of sex, gender, and gender complementarity, which is based on the Thomistic natural law theory, resulting in strong moral panic among members of the Catholic hierarchy against sociological and feminist gender perspectives and their labelling of gender theory as "gender ideology."

Keywords Synodality · Synodal theology · Gender · Gender ideology · Sociology · Feminism

Introduction

Background

The aim of the Synod on Synodality (SoS), the ecclesiastical reform project convened by Pope Francis in October 2021, was to listen to divergent and peripheral voices in the Roman Catholic Church (RCC) and society. He also introduced a paradigm shift in Catholic theology in his *motu propio* document *Ad Theologiam Promovendam* [To Promote Theology], which recommends an inductive consultative theology, one that begins with understanding people's lived experiences before synodal theological reflection. The term "synodality," which originated from the word "synod," is a theological concept coined by Pope Francis. It broadly refers to the process of consultation and the common responsibility of all the members of the People of God for the life of the Church and to preach the Gospel (Pope Francis 2015).

V. O. Ballano, *Gender Ideology and the Contemporary Catholic Church*,
https://doi.org/10.1007/978-981-97-8124-9_4

Synodality implies an inductive approach. It begins by consulting people, especially those on the peripheries of the Church and society. The paradigm shift of *ATP* also implies applying other branches of knowledge in theological research and reflection to understand the cultural revolution of the current age. *ATP* was published by Pope Francis after the SoS's first roundtable discussions in Rome in October 2023. In this document, Francis (2023) specifically discourages theologians from adopting the traditional deductive theological method based on formulas from the past. Instead, he encourages them to explore the inductive interdisciplinary theological approach and to try theologies that engage with science to provide an accurate account of human experience before passing theological or moral judgment.

Francis's inductive theology and synodal approach to resolving urgent moral issues in the RCC implies prioritizing the empirical analysis of moral actions and situations before the application of the Church's ethical doctrines. Rather than using the traditional deductive philosophical approach to settle moral issues through logic and reasoning, Francis seems more inclined to popularize the inductive synodal approach in moral theology, one that is rooted in people's ordinary moral experiences, to decide pressing moral dilemmas of our age.

One of the most urgent moral issues that continues to hound the RCC today is the so-called "gender ideology" (GI). GI is said to have replaced Pope John Paul II's "culture of death" in the RCC. John Paul II saw the contemporary concept of gender as threatening to erase biological differences between a man and a woman in society. Today's RCC regards GI as the greatest danger to the Church and the public good of society, threatening to cancel humanity, erode the foundations of the family, and undermine children's welfare. Subscribing to Benedict XVI's conception of GI, Pope Francis has also warned the public against the alleged moral danger of gender, as conceived and propagated by sociologists, feminists, and gender activists, as a new form of colonization in the postmodern world.

To Pope Francis, GI is a "a neocolonial project through which Western activists and their governments try to export their decadent values and secularize non-Western societies" (Patternote and Kuhar 2017, 8) on gender, gender diversity, transgender sexuality, non-traditional forms of family structure, and other perceived anti-Catholic moral values. In a meeting with Polish bishops ahead of World Youth Day in July 2016, Francis (2016b) also deplored the global threat of GI to the values of children in schools:

> In Europe, America, Latin America, Africa, and in some countries of Asia, there are genuine forms of ideological colonization taking place. And one of these – I will call it clearly by its name – is [the ideology of] gender. Today children – children! – are taught in school that everyone can choose his or her sex.

As of this writing, Francis's latest attacks against GI occurred during his address to the participants at a Vatican conference on gender entitled "Man-Woman Image of God: For an Anthropology of Vocations" on March 1, 2024. Here, he called GI the "ugliest danger" to society because it cancels out all the differences between a man and a woman that make up humanity (Zengarini 2024). Pope Francis has indeed provided GI with new "tactics and strategies…with his rhetoric of anticolonialism and his combination of warm receptivity to individuals with continuing opposition to their rights" (Case 2019, 659).

Since the 1990s, the RCC has felt threatened by feminist and LGBTQI movements that espoused abortion, gender diversity, and reproductive rights during a series of United Nations (UN) World Conferences that challenged the Church's moral teachings. "Amid intensified ecclesiastical opposition, anti-gender ideology rhetoric emerged for the first time" (Case 2016: 157). At the International Conference on Population and Development in Cairo in 1994, the RCC was joined by other conservative actors who were against "issues challenging the structure of gender relations, particularly as they are manifest in family arrangements and control over women's sexuality and role in reproduction" (Friedman 2003: 314).

Pope Benedict XVI invented, legitimated, and circulated the term GI to resist feminist and gender movements, which he perceived to be attacking the RCC's moral doctrine on heterosexuality as the only gender standard ordained by God in society. He became critical of feminism and gender theories after reading "Gender: The Deconstruction of Women," the antifeminist pamphlet by American journalist-activist Dale O' Leary (Graff 2016). The RCC has been using the term GI to counter the growing influence of feminist as well as lesbian, gay, bisexual, transgender, queer, and intersexual (LGBTQI) movements, which have become popular in the United States, Europe, and Latin America. GI is "a concept—a signifier for what conservative Catholics construe as the evils of liberalism in the realm of human sexuality" (Graff 2016: 282). It is "a reaction to the feminist and LGBTQI agenda mobilized in international human rights spaces in the mid-1990s" (Faúndes 2019, 403).

In recent years, the RCC has assumed an "anti-gender" position against feminism, contraception, sexual liberation, and progressive gender belief in the Western world (Bracke and Paternotte 2016). It strongly adheres to Pope John Paul II's "theology of the body," which upholds traditional Church teaching on the natural complementarity of sexes as ordained by God. To John Paul II, "When considered together [as man and woman], they produce a unified reality, forming a whole that neither of them could form alone: Masculinity and femininity express the twofold aspect of man's somatic constitution" (Ford 2018, 81).

The doctrine of gender complementarity sees the person's biological sex and its socio-cultural role or gender as mutually inseparable realities. To John Paul II's successors Pope Benedict XVI and Pope Francis, who affirmed this doctrine, GI threatens humanity's survival by attacking the natural complementarity of the sexes (Francis 2016a).

GI as a Moral Panic

Despite the repeated attacks of Popes Benedict VXI and Francis on GI, sociologists and feminists have generally remained skeptical of the alleged serious threats posed by gender to humanity's survival. There appears no clear and convincing proof that allowing gender diversity and sex change can lead to the annihilation of humanity. Recognizing and normalizing the long-suppressed nonbinary sexuality and diverse gender identities of the LGBTQI group in society does not necessarily lead to the elimination of heterosexuality and the destruction of humanity. Homosexuality and transgenderism have long existed in human history and yet no empirical evidence exists that humanity is on the brink of extinction because of nonbinary gender identities.

If the RCC is magnifying the evils of gender rather than reflecting its true empirical nature in society, then GI is an exaggeration of an imagined social threat of gender diversity to humanity's existence. Sociologists call this exaggeration of or over-reaction to an alleged danger of something to society's values a moral panic. To the sociologist Stanley Cohen (1972), a moral panic magnifies a perceived threat to societal values by authorities or media practitioners to generate urgent mass support for political action. GI in the RCC as a moral panic is purely an over-reaction by Church authorities to an unfounded belief that allowing gender diversity and transgenderism can erase heterosexuality and distinctions between men and women. Following Stanley's concept of moral panics and "folk devils," Eric Goode and Nachman Ben-Yehuda (2009, 2) characterize a moral panic as:

> a scare about a threat or supposed threat from deviants of "folk devils," a category of people who, presumably engaged in evil practices and are blamed for menacing society's culture, way of life, and central values. The word "scare" implies the concern over, fear of, or hostility toward the folk devil is *out of proportion* to the actual threat that is claimed.

Thus, if GI in the RCC inaccurately describes the nature of gender relations and makes exaggerated claims about the alleged threats of gender to humanity, then it only serves as a moral panic in the Church. As a moral panic, GI can instill fear among Catholics to make them resist feminism and gender diversity. It can also resist any empirical and scientific approaches to sex and gender to protect the philosophical natural law moral framework of the RCC. Owing to the lack of sociology and social science education in seminary training, Catholic clerics and moral guardians often misunderstand the true nature of gender and gender theory in society espoused by sociologists, feminists, and LGBTQI leaders.

In Poland, for instance, Catholic bishops inaccurately perceived GI as directly attacking the Church's traditional teachings on gender, gender complementarity, heterosexual marriage, and Christian family life without clear empirical evidence. In a pastoral letter, they erroneously blamed gender theory "as responsible for low birth rates, the collapse of traditional family models, the breakdown of marriages, abortion, homosexuality, sexual freedom due to contraception, the early sexualization of children and many other...negative phenomenon that are a threat to family, society and the whole of humanity" (Odrowąż-Coates 2015, 28).

Thus, one wonders to what extent GI's claim of the alleged threats of gender to humanity are sociologically or scientifically correct. Recent papal teachings tend to portray sociologists, feminists, and LGBTQI leaders who espouse gender diversity in society as promoters of GI—the "folk devils" in Cohen's concept of moral panics. Catholic bishops oppose the conceptualization of sexuality and gender as cultural and social products. They resist the sociological and feminist views that understand gender as culturally learned by people in society, contrary to the traditional Church concept that sees sex and gender as immutable and God-given realities based on natural law. For the RCC, GI seeks "to redefine, not only secular laws governing the sexes, sexuality, reproduction, and the family, but human nature itself" (Case 2016: 156). It thus poses a grave threat to humanity's survival.

This purely philosophical construction—without empirical foundation—of sex and gender and GI's alleged threat to humanity's survival has bred skepticism among sociologists, feminists, and LGBTQI leaders. Does the belief in gender and gender diversity in the sociological sense really pose a serious threat to humanity's survival? Or is this belief, labeled GI by the RCC, only an exaggeration or what sociologists call a moral panic? Which part of GI is fact and which a myth?

To Graeme Reid (2018, paras. 2–3), the Director of the Lesbian, Gay, Bisexual, and Transgender Rights Program, GI is a myth, "a catch-all phrase and short-hand for various anxieties about social change—a Hydra-like global conspiracy myth that, despite being mildly ridiculous and readily exposed, has significant traction." To him, GI is a dangerous term "adopted by the Holy See decades ago to refer to a supposed gay and feminist-led movement to subvert traditional families and social values, a reaction against the rights of women and expanding protections for sexual and gender minorities."

Aims, Main Sections, and Arguments

This chapter aims to sociologically unpack GI's alleged threat to humanity's survival as promoted in the RCC, identifying its exaggeration or moral panic in light of Pope Francis's synodality. It specifically examines the claim that gender and gender diversity really threaten human anthropology by cancelling gender complementarity in society. It also intends to sociologically identify the true "folk devils" or promoters of GI, clarifying whether sociologists, feminists, and LGBTQI leaders of gender movements are among them.

Applying sociological analysis and the inductive synodal theological approach of Pope Francis, this chapter investigates the real cause of this moral panic or over-reaction by Catholic leaders, led by recent popes, against the postmodern sociological and feminist concept of gender that is seen as destroying humanity. Francis's synodal theological approach in his *ATP* has opened new spaces for divergent views and marginal voices in the Church and society to achieve an interdisciplinary and scientific approach to gender issues, in order to realize an inclusive synodal church today.

There are three main parts to this chapter. The first provides the general theoretical direction of the chapter. The second part unpacks the moral panic claiming that gender diversity erases humanity, and dissolves gender complementarity and distinction between males and females. The final part attempts to find common ground and recommends some ways of improving the RCC's teaching on sex and gender through synodal dialogue between the Catholic hierarchy, together with Catholic moral theologians, and sociologists, feminists, and other social scientists specializing in sexuality and gender diversity in society.

Although the concept of moral panics has some theoretical limitations, it can nevertheless capture the exaggeration and fictional aspects of GI. There is a paucity of sociological literature in the RCC directly characterizing major pronouncements such as GI as moral panics. Although a few recent studies have started to interpret GI as a moral panic, their focus is not on a direct critiquing of natural law theory (NLT) as a moral framework but on gender social movements, especially its relation to Latin American gender movements, without reference to Pope Francis's new inductive synodal approach vis-à-vis the current gender issues on homosexuality and LGBTQI inclusivity in the RCC.

This chapter aims to address this research gap, arguing that GI's warning through papal pronouncements that gender is the greatest threat to humanity and gravest sin against God contains the elements of a moral panic in the sociological sense. Overall, it contends that the alleged threats of GI to humanity's survival are exaggerations caused by a moral panic promoted by papal media declarations and policies. It sees GI as an over-reaction that hides the RCC's fear of the conceptual challenge posed by sociologists, social scientists, feminists, and gender advocates to the traditional NLT moral framework that views sex and gender as immutable and divinely ordained.

There is no clear and convincing scientific proof that gender diversity and the growing recognition of LGBTQI as separate categories of gender can erase humanity's heterosexuality. The panic of the RCC over GI's moral threat to humanity, led by recent popes, is largely conceptual and fictional in nature and merely an over-reaction to the feminist and sociological challenge to the Church's traditional view of sex and gender and gender complementarity teaching as the foundation of humanity.

Theoretical Foundation

Pope Francis's concepts of GI and synodality provide two opposing theoretical directions on how to deal with gender, sexuality, and gender diversity in today's world. In GI, Francis is maintaining the traditional philosophical concept of sex and gender of the RCC's moral magisterium, while, in his view on synodality and synodal theology, advocating an inductive investigation of empirical human experience before theologizing and moralizing. He is also encouraging, in his inductive theology, the application of other branches of knowledge such as the social sciences as tools to understand human behavior and social issues in society before passing theological or moral judgment (Francis 2023).

In GI, Francis strictly aims to follow the RCC's NLT moral framework on sex, gender, and gender complementarity, and yet in his synodality he intends to be open to divergent views and empirical assessments of people's lived experiences in society, implying a disciplinal dialogue between Catholic theology and the social sciences to achieve synodal inclusive views on gender. This openness to divergent views suggests openness to what is known as normative pluralism in society, which acknowledges that there are various normative standards for judging sex, gender, and gender identity aside from Catholic doctrines and norms.

Thus, the RCC's teaching on GI pursues what anthropologists call ethnocentrism, or the cultural attitude that one's own culture is the best culture and others are inferior. It also promotes moral panics in the Church and society in the realm of gender, denying normative pluralism and respect for diversity. Ironically, GI opposes Francis's inductive synodal theology, which requires an accurate account of human experience, and his vision of a synodal church, a church that is open to marginalized people with divergent views. It also resists the inculturation of moral doctrines in contemporary times.

Pope Francis's Inductive Synodal Theology

This chapter aims to reconcile the seemingly contrasting cultural tendencies and attitudes between the ethnocentrism of the traditional Catholic moral teachings and Francis's "cultural relativism" or openness to cultural diversity in his synodality and inductive theology. In his *ATP*, which was issued just after the first assembly of his most recent synod of bishops, the Synod on Synodality (SoS), Pope Francis calls for reforms in modern Catholic theology according to his vision of synodality. He encourages Catholic theologians to undertake inductive interdisciplinary theologizing to pursue a synodal theology. To Francis, the old deductive method of Catholic theology is inappropriate for achieving the synodal consultative goals needed in today's world. He admonishes theologians who repeat the "abstract formulas of the past" in theologizing, given the cultural revolution of today. Francis says,

> There can be no going back to the days of theology engaging in lifeless and overly rationalistic deductive methods that begin with the truths of Revelation and then work their way down to concrete conclusions. Rather, theology must work inductively and begin with concrete experiences of believers and even nonbelievers. (Chapp 2023)

For him, a synodal theology should begin with knowing people's lived experiences in society. The study of ecclesiastical and moral issues must commence with empirical reality rather than with the deductive philosophical and theological reasoning that characterizes most of the theological processes in the RCC. This inductive synodal way of doing Catholic theology is manifested in the various consultations of the SoS, starting with the initial two-year Church-wide consultations in 2021 and culminating in roundtable discussions in Rome in October 2024.

Francis's call for an inductive theological approach to resolving ecclesiastical and moral issues requires the application of scientific methods. It also needs an ongoing dialogue between Catholic theologians and professional sociologists to achieve a Catholic synodal theology that engages with science, one that applies sociological research methods to understand people's lived experience before theological reflection. It demands the use of other branches of knowledge such as sociology and other behavioral sciences to accurately understands people's ordinary experiences in today's cultural revolution (Francis 2023).

ATP insinuates that this theology commences with scientific and accurate readings of human and ecclesiastical experiences before assessing them in the light of ecclesiastical teachings, specifically those of the Second Vatican Council (Vatican II) on the Church as People of God and on *aggriornamento*, i.e., bringing the Church's mission up to date with the current world.

Francis's inductive synodal approach also tolerates cultural diversity and openness to opposing views. Cultural diversity is the recognition that there are various cultural normative standards for judging human action and behavior in society. Informed by cultural diversity, sociologists and anthropologists generally assume a relativist rather than ethnocentric attitude to understand the diverse cultural and social standards in society, such as the morality of sex and gender.

In contrast, Catholic moral theologians who follow the RCC's philosophical approach to sex and gender, which is founded on natural law theory, still assume an ethnocentric attitude that recognizes Catholic moral standards as the only cultural norms in society. An "ethnocentric sense of superiority is a conscious, arrogant attitude with respect to 'foreign' and 'strange' customs, norms, beliefs, values, and ideas—a self-righteous conviction that one's cultural way of seeing and doing is the only way and the best way" (Santillan 2011, 198–199). One wonders whether this prevailing ethnocentric cultural attitude towards sex and gender sits well with Francis's new synodal approach.

Sociological Concept of Moral Panics and GI

Rohloff and Wright (2010, 2) explain moral panic as a sociological concept that aims to:

> explain a particular type of over-reaction to a perceived social problem. Developed in the turbulent political and intellectual context of the late 1960s, its principal aim was to expose the processes involved in creating concern about a social problem; concern that bore little relationship to the reality of the problem, but nevertheless provided the basis for a shift in social or legal codes.

The term moral panic was initially coined by Jock Young in Stanley Cohen's *Images of Deviance* (1971). Cohen later used it in his study of two 1960s British youth movements in his book *Folk Devils and Moral Panics* (1972). He defined a moral panic as a group or condition that is a response to a threat to established values or interests. The central actors in moral panics include the media, the public, law enforcement agencies, political officials, and action groups. The targets of moral panics are the so-called "folk devils," that is, individuals or groups who personify evil in society by engaging in harmful behavior that needs to be stopped.

The most systematic theoretical formulation of moral panic as a concept is developed by Erich Goode and Nachman Ben-Yehuda in their volume *Moral Panics:*

The Social Construction of Deviance (1994). They identified indicators of a moral panic in a group as heightened concern, increased hostility, consensus about the threat, disproportionality of the threat, and episode volatility. Despite the popularity of moral panic in sociology, some scholars remained skeptical of its accuracy as a concept. Other scholars continue to debate whether moral panic constitutes a discrete, meaningful category of sociological analysis. For them, the several theoretical and methodological issues of moral panics need to first be resolved (Bromley 2011).

Contemporary scholars also believe that the concept of moral panics is declining in contemporary society (e.g., Best 2008, 2013; Waiton 2008). To Joel Best (2012), the concept of moral panic has been adopted excessively as a casual analytic standard that lacks a clear and coherent definition. To Munchie (1987) and Hier (2003), moral panic as a theory per se cannot succeed since it lacks theoretical grounding and is characteristically circular rather than explanatory. Despite all these criticisms, prominent proponents of this concept such as Goode and Ben-Yehuda (2009) have defended moral panic as a sound sociological concept. To them, moral panic is both the most illuminating and fascinating of the sociologist's concepts.

In the RCC, understanding gender as GI is an exaggeration or moral panic by the RCC and popes in response to the threat of the feminist and sociological view of gender as diverse or fluid, which directly contravenes the Church's moral doctrines on the immutability and inseparability of sex and gender and gender complementarity. GI is also "a reaction to the feminist and LGBTQI agenda mobilized in international human rights spaces in the mid-1990s" (Faúndes 2019, 403). It is seen as the "folk devil" or the embodiment of evil promoted by gender feminists, activists, social scientists, and LBGTQI leaders, erroneously perceived as destroying the foundations of heterosexual humanity and children's welfare in same-sex families.

Despite its popularity in recent papal statements, GI has not been fully analyzed using a sociological lens and applying the sociological theory of moral panics in relation to Catholic moral issues such as threats to humanity's survival and children's welfare, although a few Catholic scholars have started to apply it in specific Catholic settings (e.g., Da Silva Pereira 2023). In addition, there is a need for a specialized literature on GI that uses the concept of moral panics in relation to Pope Francis's latest synodal and inductive theological approach in the RCC. This chapter aims to address this research gap and specifically debunk the GI moral panics or exaggeration over the alleged threat of gender, as perceived by sociologists and feminists, to humanity's survival.

Debunking GI's Alleged Threat to Humanity

Inculturation and Ethnocentric View of Gender in GI

Following Christ's command to preach the Good News to all people around the globe, the RCC aims to convert all people to the Christian faith and evangelize human cultures through the process of inculturation, that is, adapting the Gospel message to the specific way of life of people in society, and transforming secular values into Christian Catholic values. In this sense, the RCC takes its worldview and teachings as the standard or criterion for analyzing and judging moral values and actions in society.

The process of inculturating or inserting the Church's teachings in society requires discernment as well as interaction with human cultures and socio-cultural agents to identify and separate cultural traits that are compatible or incompatible with Christian values. Bosch (1991, 454) defines inculturation as "a process whereby cultural values can be transformed through their exposure to the Christian message and the insertion of Christianity into indigenous cultures." To him, inculturation is a double movement of adapting Christianity to culture and the Christianization of culture. This process can only be achieved if there is already an understanding of the local culture "as it relates to world views, ways of thinking, group solidarity, understanding of history and of modernity and its impact" (Duncan 2014, 2).

Thus, the inculturation of the Christian message implies an inductive understanding of the local culture and people's cultural experience as its first step. This process of knowing first the cultural and social experience of people before the application of Christian moral teachings in society accords with Pope Francis's synodal approach. Synodality and synodal theology prioritize listening, consultation, and empathizing with people's cultural experiences in daily life.

Despite this synodal emphasis in the RCC, the current direction in moral theology and ecclesiastical perspectives on sex, gender, and GI seem contrary to Francis's inductive approach. Synodal moral theology implies openness to scientific research on moral situations and inquiring into people's moral motives before passing moral judgment. With the anti-modernist stance of popes in the late 19th and early twentieth century led by Pope Pius X, the RCC's moral magisterium rejected the incorporation of the social sciences in the Catholic moral framework to update its moral doctrines on sex and gender in response to the evolving moral situation and the advance of gender studies in the modern world. It still strongly upholds the philosophical and metaphysical view of gender based on natural law, which opposes the empirical and scientific method of sociologists and feminists.

Instead of applying Pope Francis's synodal listening and availing itself of social science gender studies to enrich its moral doctrines on gender, the Catholic hierarchy and moral theologians still uphold the rigid view of gender as GI based on natural law arguments. This traditional moral stance resists inculturation and Francis's synodal theology, implying ethnocentrism, a concept conceived by William Graham Sumner (1906). "Ethnocentrism is a type of bias that results from viewing one's own ethnic group and culture as superior to others" (Santillan 2011, 198). The inability to appreciate the culture of the other implied by ethnocentrism can lead to hostility to "out-groups."

Vatican II encourages ecumenical views owing to the plurality of cultures and religions in the world. While the RCC's mission aims to convert all to the Christian faith for the sake of Christ, this does not mean coercing people with different beliefs and cultural orientations to accept Catholicism. After Vatican II, the RCC became open to cultural diversity with its concept of *aggriornamento* [renewal]. Pope Francis's concept of a synodal church also welcomes the marginalized and those with divergent views that oppose ethnocentrism and individualism. However, recent papal declarations on gender that largely refuse to integrate the divergent scientific views and research of sociology, feminism, and social science can be considered a form of ethnocentrism that is contrary to the spirit of Vatican II, and Francis's synodality and inductive theology.

In the RCC, gender is understood as a single "ideology" that refutes the reality of sexual difference and that seeks to appropriate the divine power of creation for those who wish to create their own genders" (Butler 2019, 1). A closer sociological investigation of GI reveals that strong ecclesiastical resistance to gender is primarily caused by a lack of sociological and social science education, especially on gender studies, in clerical training, as well as a lack of active dialogue between Catholic moral theologians and sociologists of gender and morality. The lack of sociological and anthropological research and knowledge on culture could result in ethnocentric views and intolerance of cultural diversity, such as gender diversity in the contemporary world.

No Empirical Proof of Gender's Threat to Humanity

Moral teachings in the RCC are generally non-dogmatic and non-infallible in nature. Resolving gender moral issues is always dependent on accurate evaluation of the behavioral and societal situation before the application of the RCC's ethical principles. In deciding moral dilemmas, the RCC emphasizes the review of the moral situation as the first stage for moral analysis:

> There are three stages which should normally be followed in the reduction of social principles into practice. First, one reviews the concrete situation; secondly, one forms a judgment on it in the light of these same principles; thirdly, one decides what the circumstances can and should be done to implement these principles. (*Mater et Magistra* [Mother and Teacher] 1961, para. 235)

Although these stages are primarily meant for Catholic social doctrines, they are nevertheless relevant to the resolution of moral issues pertaining to gender. These three stages are traditionally summarized by three keywords: see, judge, and act:

> The first (see) is observing and assessing the concrete social situation as accurately as possible. The second stage (judge) is passing moral judgment on the situation, whether it is

> immoral or moral or deviating from or conforming with CST principle. The last stage (act) is doing based on one's moral judgment to change or reform the concrete human situation. The first step is crucial, because the second and third stages are dependent on it. (Ballano 2019, 5–6)

Therefore, the first necessary step is to review concrete and empirical situations surrounding the moral panic and exaggerated claim of GI that gender is causing the imminent demise of humanity. In the absence of scientific proof, this claim remains unverified information, exaggeration, or essentially a moral panic. Social scientists agree that the key feature of moral panics is distortion. This occurs when media sources "exaggerate, grossly, the seriousness of events" (Cohen, 1972:31; Hall et al., 1978; Goode and Ben-Yehuda, 1994). Cohen (1972, 31) explains that such distortions can involve "…sensational headlines, the melodramatic vocabulary and the deliberate heightening of those elements in the story considered as news."

The RCC has strongly warned Catholics that GI is the greatest threat to humanity's survival. Recent papal homilies and media briefings have instilled fear among Catholics of the alleged evils of gender and gender theory espoused by feminists, sociologists, and social scientists. Pope Benedict XVI even predicted that GI would be the next great challenge to the Church and the final rebellion against God the Creator (Caldwell 2023). Recent papal pronouncements on GI as the ugliest form of colonization and the greatest sin against God because it annihilates humanity need sociological and empirical verification.

Because the RCC highlights the imminent threat of GI to humanity without scientific evidence, the feminist Agnieszka Graff (2016) claims that there is something "delightfully demonic about GI" that tends to magnify the negative impact of gender on people, such as its threat to children, the danger of "collapsing" differences between men and women, and the prophesied end of civilization. To her, GI only serves as a magnet for the "various fears, anxieties, and obsessions of cultural conservatism" rather than reflecting real gender relations in the world.

An inductive synodal and sociological analysis of the contemporary view on gender theory would reveal that gender does not inflict actual harm to humanity, as alleged by GI. It only proposes a social reconstruction or paradigm shift in the understanding of sex, sexuality, and gender identity in society, based on current sociological and scientific research. Sociologically speaking, GI is a fictional threat with no sound scientific basis in human experience. We have yet to see proof or social patterns, for instance, that humanity is on the brink of destruction because of the existence of the LGBTQI community or homosexual couples who challenge gender complementarity and heterosexual marriage as taught by the Church. The absence of scientific research showing a direct link between gender and humanity's imminent destruction indicates that GI is an over-reaction to gender research that challenges the philosophical construction of sex and gender in society. It is a conceptual construct rather than a factual signifier in the RCC.

Social Construction of Gendered Humanity Under Natural Law

The notion of natural law theory (NLT) in the RCC is a scholastic concept that was "developed by canon lawyers and theologians in the twelfth and thirteenth centuries" (Porter 2005, ix). "The natural law is usually regarded as a universal morality, accessible to all rational persons whatever their particular metaphysical or religious commitments (if any), and therefore most appropriately studied through philosophical analysis" (Porter 2005, 1). NLT is a school of jurisprudential thought that acknowledges the existence of naturally occurring fundamental and pre-existing rights given by God, nature, and reason to all people. And "these rules of right and wrong are inherent in people and cannot be created or changed by society or the courts" (Jagose 2023, 712).

St. Thomas Aquinas, who popularized NLT in the RCC, did not invent it but inherited it from the patristic traditions of both East and West, which originated from Stoicism and Greek and Roman legal traditions (Gallaher 2018). Aquinas's version of the NLT, which eventually became known in the RCC as Thomistic natural law theory (TNLT), became the dominant moral framework in Catholic morality. TNLT offers a moral worldview that sees a gendered humanity based on the biological complementarity of sexes. It laid the philosophical foundation that sees sex and gender as immutable, metaphysical, and ordained by God. To the Catholic hierarchy, "transgressing the assigned identities means denial of the 'natural' role, that is, given by God" (Szwed and Zielińska 2017, 121). One of the reasons why the RCC resists gender and labels it GI is precisely its challenge to biblical authority on gender complementarity (Butler 2016). The divine origin of gender and gender complementarity has influenced papal teachings on sex and gender, magnifying the sociological idea of gender as GI threatening humanity's existence with its promotion of gender diversity and fluidity which, allegedly, will dissolve society's gender complementarity.

According to Hayle (2013, 1125), the "folk devil" personifies negation, fear, and danger to human virtue and reality:

> He is the reverse image, the alternative to all we know: *the negation*. He is the fear of failure that is secreted at the heart of success, the danger that lurks inside security, the profligate figure by whom Virtue is constantly tempted, the tiny, seductive voice inside inviting us to feed rations. [p.16]

In the RCC's exaggeration of gender as GI, the "folk devil" is the empirical, inductive, and scientific approach of sociology, feminism, and social sciences to sex and gender that seriously pose the greatest threat to the TNLT's moral framework on the immutability and inseparability of sex and gender as ordained by God and gender complementarity. GI's threat is not empirical but conceptual. To the RCC, the natural complementarity of sexes is the immutable and non-negotiable foundation of humanity. Gender diversity and the social and cultural nature of gender as espoused by social scientists, feminists, and LGBTQI leaders remain morally unacceptable.

In his address to participants at a gender conference at the Vatican in May 2024, Pope Francis sounded the alarm that GI is the greatest threat to humanity because it destroys the gender differences between a male and a female (Zengarini 2024). Following Benedict XVI's warning on GI's destruction of man as created by God, Francis argue "that proponents of gender are like those who support or deploy nuclear arms and that their target is creation itself. This suggests that whatever gender is, it carries enormous destructive power in the minds of those who oppose it—indeed, an unfathomable and terrifying destructiveness" (Butler 2016, 4). Despite GI's destructive power, the RCC has not shown scientific and empirical evidence to back up its claim and moral panic on the dangers of gender to society.

Panic Reaction to Sociological and Feminist Challenges to TNLT

The RCC's moral panic on GI's destruction of humanity appears more fictional than factual. Sociologically speaking, gender as understood by social science and feminism poses no real threat to humanity's survival. There is no convincing empirical proof that the rise of gender diversity and LGBTQI as separate genders can lead to the cancellation of humanity and total disregard of heterosexuality in society. Nonbinary people and same-sex relationships have existed since ancient times and are not a mere product of contemporary gender social construction.

The RCC's panic response to gender as GI is ultimately a fear of the epistemological challenge posed by the sociological, feminist, and scientific conception of sex and gender as historical and cultural and thus subject to societal change, rather than metaphysical and immutable based on the NLT moral framework. The moral panic of GI appears to be a strong unfounded negative conceptual reaction to the current scientific and social construction of gender that promotes individuality and freedom to determine one's gender away from God's plan as envisioned in TNLT. To Judith Butler (2016, 2),

> It appears that the proposition that gender is a social construction can lead to a conviction that individuals could choose their gender or live in ways that are unconstrained by marriage and heterosexuality. That inference, however, assimilated the doctrine of social construction to an unbridled view of personal liberty, and there are many reasons to be suspicious of that reduction.

Unrestrained individuals who can determine how they live their life and actualize their gender outside the divine plan are morally alarming for the RCC and a deviation from the TNLT's purely philosophical approach to morality. Carl Trueman's characterization of GI generally reflects the RCC's broader fear of the postmodern anthropological revolution that encourages individual freedom and the power of society to determine gender rather than the divine authority envisioned by the RCC's TNLT. To him, GI is:

> a function of a far more comprehensive anthropological revolution than the narrow issues of sex and even gender would suggest. It is, at its core, part of a fundamental reimagination of what it means to be human. As such, it should be understood with reference not simply to the sexual revolution, but also to deeper understandings of selfhood, to gender theory, to feminist politics, and to technology. Not all of these influences point in the same direction: The modern notion of selfhood is that of the free, autonomous, self-defining individual; gender theory underscores the power of wider society to shape the social performances that are regarded as constitutive of what it means to be masculine or feminine. (Trueman 2023, 2)

The RCC sees gender as "a single 'ideology' that refutes the reality of sexual difference and that seeks to appropriate the divine power of creation for those who wish to create their own genders. Personal choice is understood to have taken the place of divine creativity" (Butler 2016, 2). This argument is largely philosophical and has no scientific support. Gender theory for sociological research is morally neutral and does not aim to attack Church teachings. Thus, it is ethnocentric and contrary to Pope Francis's synodality and inductive theology to disregard and disrespect people's divergent views on sex and gender, especially in scientific and feminist gender research studies by sociologists and social scientists. As Naudi and Azzopardi Lane (2020, 13) argue:

> As a whole, the fight against a supposed "gender ideology" demands in the first instance the "renaturalisation of the body, sex and desire", appealing to an imagined unified Other that, in its claimed antagonism to the laws of nature, composes a dire danger to society as a whole. Reoccurring tokens elected for protection are above all "the children" and "the family", along with "culture" and including human life itself. The same anti-community identified with a "gender ideology" is therefore considered the source of a "culture of death" and legitimately subject to elimination.

A closer sociological investigation of the contemporary view on gender reveals no imminent threat to the survival of humanity as imagined and taught by recent popes as GI. The perspectival challenges posed by sociologists, feminists, and gender activists to the gender complementarity teaching of the RCC do not constitute actual harm and annihilation of humanity as conceived by GI advocates, but an exaggerated fear of the reversal of the Church's traditional moral framework on sex and gender based on natural law.

Instead of seeing gender as metaphysical and divinely ordained, sociologists and feminists, following the methodological naturalism of science and the scientific method, view it inductively as a product of human and cultural experience. The RCC needs to recognize that there is a big difference between the philosophical and theological approach and the sociological and feminist method of seeing sex and gender. The primary harm posed by gender in the so-called GI is only theoretical, that is, at the level of conceptualization rather than at the physical and social level.

Resolving the Conceptual Conflict Through Synodality

Conflict of Fundamental Perspectives

The RCC is fundamentally philosophical and absolutist rather than empirical and culturally relativist in its understanding and resolution of doctrinal and moral issues. Clerics tend to reject divergent views that are considered contrary to the Christian faith. In adapting Christian teaching in society, however, the RCC's teaching on inculturation requires discernment of cultural traits, separating what is contrary to from what conforms with the normative ecclesiastical standards. It maintains that there are some things are always "morally right" or "wrong," regardless of the cultural context. It teaches that there is only one normative standard for judging the moral truth in society, that is, one that is based on the RCC's moral magisterium or teaching office.

For NLT moral theologians, the divine law that guides people on what is right and good is implanted by God through human nature and reason. This rigid and absolutist metaphysical and philosophical view of morality contrasts with the sociological and social science approaches to human behavior that view moral behavior as social. Applying cultural relativism, sociologists and feminists generally look at a diversity of normative standards for judging what is morally right or wrong in society. Relativism views the truth as constructed in society, relative to cultures, times, places, or individuals. "Relativists deny that there is a knowable, static reality and, consequently, they deny the possibility of absolute, universal truth" (Bleasby 2011, 455).

In Catholic moral teaching, gender is immutable and fixed at birth. Thus, it cannot be changed by society. This deductive and absolutist view of gender conflicts with sociological and scientific view, which considers gender, although related to sex, as a distinct experience conditioned by social and cultural influences through the process of gender socialization or social learning. Scholars and theologians who defend the RCC's GI specifically oppose current gender theorizing that distinguishes biological sex from gender as a social experience. With their normative training in philosophy and theology, Catholic anti-GI intellectuals and theologians cannot help the RCC and popes to unpack and debunk GI as a moral panic and an exaggeration with no empirical foundation in cultural and social reality.

In sociology and behavioral sciences, gender can be defined as "a socially constructed feminine or masculine identity of an individual, enforced through socialization processes, which becomes a basis of social division and a set of everyday social practices" (Odrowąż-Coates 2015, 28). Professor John Money is credited with inventing the term "gender" and distinguishing "sex" from "gender" (Goldie 2014). The term was later developed and theorized by Robert Stoller (1968), Ann Oakley (1972), Connell (1987), Laqueur (1990), and Fausto-Sterling (1992, 2000), to name a few. In its early application, the term "gender" was utilized for the study of women, sex roles, or both (Acker 1992). In recent decades, "'gender' has become a part of the everyday language of social science" (Odrowąż-Coates 2015, 28).

Contrary to the social sciences' empirical and scientific approaches to sex and gender, the RCC views sex and gender as ahistorical and not subject to societal change, rejecting sociological perspectives that view gender differences as the result of historical and cultural forces (Congregation for Catholic Education 2019). It basically understands men and women as different but complementary and equal in both nature and social roles as ordained by God. It argues that rejecting the difference and complementarity between man and a woman can weaken the family as a vital institution in society (Congregation for Catholic Education 2019). However, its deductive philosophical approach fails to take account of gender as a human experience.

Resolving Conceptual Conflict Through Synodality

A number of studies have characterized GI as a moral panic. However, their focus tends to be particular and micro such as GI's impact on children's learning in the classroom (e.g., Da Silva Pereira 2023). Investigating GI as a form of moral panic in relation to Pope Francis's new synodal theological approach has escaped the attention of Catholic sociologists. No sociological studies have critically analyzed the alleged grave threats of GI to society at the macro level—such as its dangers to humanity's survival, the moral foundations of the family, children's welfare, and human dignity—through the lens of Pope Francis's inductive synodal theology and the sociology of gender and morality.

One important aspect of synodality is recognizing and respecting the diversity of people's views and listening to marginalized people in the Church and society. Sociologists, feminists, and gender activists are among the marginalized people in the RCC. To welcome gender-diverse and discriminated individuals in society into the Christian community, Pope Francis envisioned a synodal church to embrace all in the Church. Despite his strong resistance to gender and GI, Francis's latest ecclesiastical reform project on synodality and inductive synodal theology encourages listening, consultation, and assimilation of the scientific methods in moral theologizing. Synodality promises a new inculturation process that incorporates sociological and research findings on sex and gender in contemporary society. Francis's inductive theological method insists that Catholic theology should begin with people's daily experiences in society. This implies that understanding sex and gender should commence first with the social and cultural experiences of people in dealing with their gender identity. An open letter from a group of Catholic students, theologians, and ministers to Pope Francis and the Dicastery on the Doctrine of the Faith, protesting the declaration of ecclesial document *Dignitas Infinita* [Infinite Dignity] (*DI*) for not including the gender experience of transgender and nonbinary people in characterizing human dignity, is an indication that the traditional deductive philosophical approach to gender is no longer adequate (National Catholic Register 2024). Scientific research has shown that people's biological sex assigned at birth may not necessarily reflect their gender identity and their personal expressions of masculinity and femininity in society.

Thus, the sociological realization that people's gender may not reflect their genitalia and biological make-up is empirically correct. The rise of transgender sexuality and LGBTQI as genders distinct from heterosexuality is a social reality that the RCC needs to recognize as a sign of the new times. Transgender individuals are people whose "gender identity is different from their gender they were thought to be when they were born" (National Center for Transgender Equality 2023, para. 2). One main reason why transgender identity is rejected in society is the resistance of traditionalists and conservatives to any same-sex relationship: "This is because neither male male nor female-female relationships can fully embody the complementarity nature of humanity intended by God in creation" (Henegar 2011, 4). Transgender people and members of the LGBTQI could be categorized under the gender category of heterosexuality.

To Calib Day (2016), gender complementarianism based on the creation account is an inappropriate trajectory to characterize the gender experience of gay and transgender people. In sociology, gender is socially and culturally conditioned. "Human beings make other human beings into specific male and female genders" (Hopkins 2008, 576). The processes of social learning and gender socialization determine people's gender identity and sexual orientation, which may not necessarily correspond to their biological sex.

A major obstacle to a synodal understanding of sex and gender that is open to the divergent views of people behind GI, such as sociologists and feminists, is the lack of social science training and gender awareness of many Catholic clerics and moral theologians. The dominance of scholastic philosophy and philosophical theology in priestly education and theological studies promote prescriptive rather than descriptive and scientific thinking. It hinders Catholic leaders' and moral guardians' ability to appreciate the positive elements of the sociology of gender and feminist gender studies, and to understand the real moral intention of transgender and nonbinary people in altering their sex and gender in the postmodern world of today.

The lack of familiarity with the nature and scientific method of sociology and the social sciences regarding gender and gender fluidity in society breeds contempt, moral panic, and the inaccurate labelling of gender theories as GI. An important area of Pope Francis's inductive synodal approach is to sharpen the empirical thinking of clerics and moral theologians in order to accurately assess the evolving moral situations of gender in contemporary society. Culture and society have greatly changed since the medieval period when St Thomas Aquinas synthesized Aristotelian philosophy and Catholic theology and popularized the natural law morality in the RCC.

In today's contemporary culture and global society, people, technology, and material things are undergoing constant change or growing "liquidity" (Bauman 2000; Ritzer and Dean 2015). The RCC's main concern is thus becoming an empirical one, that is, how to accurately review the rapidly evolving facts of moral cases before applying the Church's moral principles. The scholastic philosophy and theology taught to Catholic clerics and moral theologians are normative disciplines that cannot provide social contexts and scientific assessment of complex moral issues such as gender, gender diversity, LGBTQI inclusivity, and GI in our contemporary age.

Thus, with Francis's synodality and inductive theology, the time is ripe for the RCC to shift its moral framework from a deductive philosophical moral framework founded on NLT to an inductive sociological moral framework that utilizes social science and feminist research and perspectives on sex and gender to fully understand transgenderism and the dynamics of gender in today's world. Under this new and inculturated moral framework, living a homosexual and transgender life becomes more humanely and morally acceptable in the Church and society as a distinct and legitimate gender lifestyle like heterosexuality. GI as a moral panic that threatens the binary understanding of humanity will fade, preparing the way for the full acceptance of gender-diverse members of the LGBTQI community in the RCC.

Conclusion

Employing the sociological theory on moral panics, inductive sociological analysis, and Pope Francis's synodal theological approach, this chapter has unpacked the nature of the RCC's concept of GI as a moral panic, specifically its alleged grave threat to humanity's survival. It has illustrated that GI is an exaggeration and distortion of the true nature of sexuality and gender in society. GI is a political signifier a political signifier rather than a scientific concept describing gender diversity in society.

The chapter contended that the contemporary social science view of gender espoused by sociologists, feminists, activists, and LGBTQI reformers cannot inflict actual and imminent harm on humanity's survival. It also argued that the greatest threat of gender to the Church and society is not empirical but conceptual. The sociological concept of gender labeled GI by Pope Benedict XVI posed a serious and radical epistemological challenge to the RCC's traditional, metaphysical, and philosophical approach to sex, gender, and gender complementarity that is based on the natural law theory, resulting in moral panics among Catholic bishops and moral theologians.

This chapter recommends intensive clerical education in the social sciences and gender studies as well as synodal dialogue between Catholic bishops and moral theologians, and people behind GI such as sociologists, feminists, and LGBTQI leaders. Francis's synodality and inductive synodal theology encourage the incorporation of other fields of knowledge such as sociology and feminism for understanding the cultural revolution of the current age and for evangelization and inculturation of Church moral doctrines in society.

References

Acker J (1992) From sex roles to gendered institutions. Contemp Sociol 21(5):565–569. https://doi.org/10.2307/2075528

Ballano VO (2019) Catholic social teaching, theology, and sociology: exploring the common ground. Religions 10(557):1–16. https://doi.org/10.3390/rel10100557
Bauman Z (2000) Liquid modernity. Polity Press, Cambridge
Best J (2011) Locating moral panics within the sociology of social problems. In: Heir S (ed) Moral panic and the sociology of anxiety, 1st edn. Routledge, London, pp 37–52
Best J (2013) The problems with moral panic: the concept's limitations. In: Krinsky C (ed), The Ashgate research companion to moral panics. First Edition. London: Routledge
Bleasby J (2011) Overcoming relativism and absolutism: Dewey's ideals of truth and meaning in philosophy for children. Educ Philos Theory 43:453–466
Bosch DJ (1991) Transforming mission: paradigm shifts in theology of mission (American Society of Missiology Series). Orbis Books, Maryknoll, New York
Bracke S, Paternotte D (2016) Unpacking the sin of gender. Religion and Gender 6(2):143–154
Bromley DG (2011) Moral panics. Ritzer G, Michael Ryan J (eds), The concise Encyclopedia of sociology, pp 198–199. Malden, MA: Blackwell Publishing Ltd, 412–413
Butler J (2019) What threat? The campaign against 'gender ideology.' Glocalism J Culture Politics Innov 3:1–12. https://doi.org/10.12893/gjcpi.2019.3.1
Caldwell S (2023) Pope benedict predicted gender ideology would be final rebellion against god. Catholic Herald. https://catholicherald.co.uk/pope-benedict-predicted-gender-ideology-would-be-final-rebellion-against-god/
Case MA (2016) The role of the popes in the invention of complementarity and the Vatican's anathematization of gender. Religion Gender 6(2):155–172
Case MA (2019) Trans formations in the Vatican's war on "gender ideology. Signs J Women Culture Soc 44(3):639664
Cohen S (1972) Folk devils and moral panics. Paladin, Herts
Congregation for Catholic Education (2019) Male and female he created them: towards a path of dialogue on the question of gender theory in education. Vatican City. https://www.efaidnbmnnnibpcajpcglclefindmkaj/, https://www.newwaysministry.org/wp-content/uploads/2019/06/Male-and-Female-Document-June-10-2019.pdf
Connell RW (1987) Gender and power: society, the person, and sexual politics. Stanford University Press
Da Silva Pereira R (2023) Protect the children, save the family: 'Gender Ideology' in the classroom: a case study of moral panic in Brazil. MA Thesis submitted to the faculty of graduate and postdoctoral studies, University of British Columbia, Vancouver
Day CM (2016) An unsatisfactory trajectory: a critique of gender complementarianism. Available at: https://www.academia.edu/33865814/An_unsatisfactory_trajectory_a_critique_of_gender_complementarianism. Accessed May 10, 2024
Duncan GA (2014) Inculturation: adaptation, innovation and reflexivity. an african christian perspective. HTS Teologiese Studies/theological Studies 70(1):1–11. https://doi.org/10.4102/hts.v70i1.2669
Faúndes JMM (2019) The geopolitics of moral panic: the influence of argentinian neo-conservatism in the genesis of the discourse of 'Gender Ideology.' Int Sociol 34(4):402 –417.https://doi.org/10.1177/0268580919856488
Fausto-Sterling A (1992) Myths of gender: biological theories about women and men, 2nd edn. Basic Books, New York
Fausto-Sterling A (2000) Sexing the body: gender politics and the construction of sexuality. Basic Books, New York
Ford CJ (2018) Transgender bodies, catholic schools, and a queer natural law theology of exploration. J Moral Theol 7(1):70–98
Gallaher B (2018) Tangling with orthodox tradition in the modern west: natural law, homosexuality, and living tradition. The Wheel 13(14):50–63
Goldie T (2014) The man who invented gender: engaging the ideas of john money. UBC Press, Vancouver

Goode E, Ben-Yehuda N (1994) Moral panics: the social construction of deviance. Blackwell, Oxford

Goode E, Ben-Yehuda N (2009) Moral panics: the social construction of deviance, 2nd edn. Wiley-Blackwell, Malden, MA

Graff A (2016) 'Gender Ideology': weak concepts, powerful politics. Religion Gender 6(2):268–272. https://doi.org/10.18352/rg.10177

Hall S, Critcher C, Jefferson T, Clarke J, Roberts B (1978) Policing the crisis. Mugging, the State, and Law and Order. London: Macmillan

Hayle SJ (2013) Folk devils without moral panics: discovering concepts in the sociology of evil. Int J Criminol Sociol Theory 6(2):1125–1137

Hier SP (2003) Risk and panic in late modernity: implications of the converging sites of social anxiety. Br J Sociol 54(1):3–20. https://doi.org/10.1080/0007131032000045879

Henegar M (2011) Mid-day discussion guide for bible, gender, sexuality: reframing Church's debate on same-sex relationships by JamesV. Brownson. https://www.efaidnbmnnnibpcajpcglclefindmkaj/http://podcast.manhattanchurch.org/docs/coffee-stretch/Bible-Gender-Sexuality-Notes.pdf

Hopkins DN (2008) Toward a positive black male heterosexuality. Angl Theol Rev 90(3):575–581

Jagose R (2023) Catholic canon law and homosexuality: an assessment of the natural law justification for homosexual intolerance. Victoria Univ Wellington Law Rev 54(3):709–738. https://doi.org/10.26686/vuwlr.v54i3.8788

Jay Friedman E (2003) Gendering the agenda: the impact of the transnational women's rights movement at the UN conferences of the 1990s. Women's Studies Int Forum 26(4):313–331.https://doi.org/10.1016/S0277-5395(03)00077-3

Laqueur T (1990) Making sex: body and gender from the greeks to freud. Harvard University Press, Cambridge, MA.

Mater et Magistra [Mother and Teacher] (1961) Social encyclical of Pope John XXIII on christianity and social progress. Vatican: Libreria Editrice Vaticana, Available online: http://w2.vatican.va/content/john-xxiii/en/encyclicals/documents/hf_j-xxiii_enc_15051961_mater.html

National Catholic Reporter (2024) Catholic students, theologians, ministers write an open letter to pope Francis. National Catholic Reporter Website (25 April 2024). https://www.ncronline.org/opinion/guest-voices/catholic-students-theologians-ministers-write-open-letter-pope-francis

National Center for Transgender Equality (2023) Understanding transgender people: the basics. National Center for Transgender Equality Website (January 27, 2023). https://transequality.org/issues/resources/understanding-transgender-people-the-basics

Naudi, Marceline and Azzopardi Lane, Claire (eds) (2020) Mapping the rainbow: researching the diverse colours of the LGBTQ community. Malta: MJEG

Oakley A (1972) Sex, gender, and society. Temple Smith, London

Odrowaz-Coates A (2015) Is Gender neutrality a post-human phenomenon? The concept of 'gender neutral' in Swedish education. J Gender Power 3(1):113–133

Paternotte D, Kuhar R (2017) Chapter 1: 'Gender Ideology' in movement: an introduction." In: Kuhar R, Paternotte D (eds) Anti-gender campaigns in Europe: mobilizing against equality, 1–22. New York, London: Rowman & Littlefield International

Pope Francis (2015) Address during the ceremony commemorating the 50th anniversary of the institution of the Synod of Bishops. 17 October 2015. http://w2.vatican.va/content/francesco/en/speeches/2015/october/documents/papafrancesco_20151017_50-anniversario-sinodo.html

Pope Francis (2016a) Post-Synodal exhortation Amoris Laetitia. Vatican: Dicastero per la Comunicazione—Libreria Editrice Vaticana. https://www.vatican.va/content/francesco/en/apost_exhortations/documents/papa-francesco_esortazione-ap_20160319_amoris-laetitia.html

Pope Francis (2016b) Meeting with the polish bishops: address of his holiness pope francis, 27 July 2016. Vatican: Dicastero per la Comunicazione--Libreria Editrice Vaticana https://www.vatican.va/content/francesco/en/speeches/2016/july/documents/papa-francesco_20160727_polonia-vescovi.html. Accessed 30Aoril 2024

Pope Francis (2023) Apostolic letter issued "Motu Proprio" Ad Theologiam Promovendam [To Promote Theology]. Unofficial full English translation available at: https://returntotradition.org/unofficial-full-english-translation-of-francis-revolutionary-motu-proprio-ad-theologiam-promovendam-plus-breaking-news-report-on-text/

Porter J (2005) Nature as reason: a thomistic theory of natural law. William B. Eerdsmans Publishing Company, Grand Rapids, Michigan

Reid G (2018) Breaking the buzzword: fighting the 'Gender Ideology' Myth. Human Rights Watch (10 December 2018). https://www.hrw.org/news/2018/12/10/breaking-buzzword-fighting-gender-ideology-myth

Ritzer G, Dean P (2015) Globalization: a basic text, 2nd edn. John Wiley & Sons, Hoboken, NJ

Sumner WG (1906) Folkways: a study of the sociological importance of usages, manners, customs, mores, and morals. Ginn, Boston, MA

Santillian D (2011) Ethnocentrism. In: Ritzer G, Michael Ryan J (eds), The concise Encyclopedia of sociology, pp 198–199. Malden, MA: Blackwell Publishing Ltd.

Szwed A, Zielińska K (2017) A war on gender? The Roman catholic Church's discourse on gender in Poland. In: Ramet S, Borowik I, (eds), Religion, politics, and values in Poland. Palgrave Studies in Religion, Politics, and Policy. Palgrave Macmillan, New York. https://doi.org/10.1057/978-1-137-43751-8_6

Stoller R (1968) Sex and gender: on the development of masculinity and femininity. Science House, New York

Trueman CR (2023) Gender ideology and the future of the human person. Frist Principles No. 89. The Heritage Foundation Report, Gender. March 20,2023. https://www.heritage.org/gender/report/gender-ideology-and-the-future-the-human-person

Waiton S (2008) The politics of antisocial behavior: amoral panics. Routledge, London/Abingdon

Zengarini L (2024) Pope francis: gender ideology is the ugliest danger of our time. Vatican News (March 1, 2024). https://www.vaticannews.va/en/pope/news/2024-03/pope-francis-gender-ideology-is-the-ugliest-danger-of-our-time.html

Chapter 5
Gender Ideology's Alleged Danger to the Family in Society: A Synodal-Sociological Appraisal

Abstract This chapter critically examines the alleged threat of the Roman Catholic Church's concept of "gender ideology" to the family as the basic social unit in society, using sociological perspectives and Pope Francis's inductive synodal approach. It argues that the Catholic Church has gravely misunderstood gender in the sociological and feminist research literature and that its allegation of a threat to the family is conceptual rather than actual, constituting a moral panic or exaggeration rather than a real danger. It contends that the real cause or "folk devil" is not gender but the epistemological threat posed by the sociological and feminist concept of gender and gender diversity to the natural law moral framework of the Catholic Church. It recommends inculturation and the adoption of a sociological moral framework to dissolve the alleged threat.

Keywords Gender · Sexuality · Gender ideology · Moral Panic · Family · Synodality · Sociology

Introduction

Background

Does the concept of "gender ideology" as conceived by recent popes constitute a serious imminent threat to the existence of the family as the basic social unit of society?

In recent years, the RCC has stepped up its attacks on the contemporary concept of "gender" as propagated by sociologists, feminists, activists, and LGBTQI leaders, labeling it "gender ideology" (GI). Recent popes and bishops have regarded GI as striking at the very heart of the family as the basic social unit of society. Invented and propagated by Pope Benedict XVI, GI emerged in the 1990s when the Roman Catholic Family Council warned against the idea of "gender" as a threat to the family unit and to Biblical authority (Butler 2019). To recent popes of the RCC, the concept of "gender" is

V. O. Ballano, *Gender Ideology and the Contemporary Catholic Church*,
https://doi.org/10.1007/978-981-97-8124-9_5

> a threat to the family, the distinct values of masculinity and femininity, society, the Church, and civilization itself. It appears that the proposition that gender is a social construction that leads to a conviction that individuals could choose their gender or live in ways that are unconstrained by marriage and heterosexuality. (Butler 2019, 2)

Despite the diversity of gender theories, the Church continues to label "gender" as "a single 'ideology' that refutes the reality of sexual difference and that seeks to appropriate the divine power of creation for those who wish to create their own genders" (Butler 2019, 2). Traditional Church teaching maintains that biological sex and the socio-cultural role of sex (gender) are mutually inseparable (Francis 2016). It teaches that gender complementarity is the foundation of a Christian family: only a male and a female can become legitimate and morally accepted parents in the family as the basic social unit of society. Same-sex family structures are therefore considered morally "abnormal" and constitute a serious threat to the Christian heterosexual family unit.

In a collection of homilies, later called the "Theology of the Body," Pope John Paul II defended the heterosexual family, reiterating the inseparability of sex and gender based on natural law theory. To him, "Masculinity and femininity express the twofold aspect of man's somatic constitution...[which] consists in reciprocal enrichment. Refracting this theological perspective into the natural law tradition, this gender essentialism paired with gender complementarity is understood to be a natural complementarity between the genders" (Ford 2018, 81).

Pope Benedict XVI, who succeeded John Paul II, continued the moral tradition of the theology of the body and warned the Catholic faithful about the dangers inherent in GI that question the traditional notion of the family as derived from biological sex. He claimed that the integrity of the family as both Christian and natural was endangered by GI (Butler 2019). In his view, GI rejects the pre-ordained duality of man and woman and "the family" as established by the creation story in the Scriptures: "[T]hose who seek to create themselves deny the creative power of God and are misled by an atheistic set of beliefs" (Butler 2019, 4).

Following the lead of his predecessors, Pope Francis also condemned GI, which for him undermines the Christian understanding of marriage and human sexuality. To him, GI is "demonic," which is comparable to the policies of Adolf Hitler that rejected Biblical teaching of creation (Pentin 2015). Francis thus warned Catholics about the dangers of GI, which he likened it to an atomic bomb that is ready to explode and annihilate the human family and humanity.

Aside from Catholic popes, conservative scholars and theologians in the RCC also underscore the threats posed by GI to the traditional concept of a family—that a family should consist only of a man and a woman as parents to their biological or adopted children. In Poland, Catholic scholars defended the natural foundations of the family as taught in the Scriptures. At an episcopal conference in 2013, they condemned GI as a threat to the Christian family, resulting in the issuance of a pastoral letter by Catholic bishops of the Polish Episcopacy Conference entitled "Threats to family resulting from gender ideology." This letter was read out in all churches to warn the Catholic faithful about the serious threats of GI to the moral foundations of the family in society (Sroczynski 2016).

Popular Catholic authors have also denounced GI and defended the RCC's traditional heterosexual model of the family. In her book *The Global Sexual Revolution: The Destruction of Freedom in the Name of Freedom,* German Catholic author and staunch defender of the RCC's gender complementarity doctrine Gabriele Kuby (2015) condemned GI for rejecting the RCC's traditional teaching on gender complementary which unites people in marriage. She denounced GI and the teaching of children that there are different kinds of sexual orientation and family structure as "completely a mad attack" against the family and society. In her subsequent book, *The Abandoned Generation,* Kuby (2022) reiterated her warning to Catholics, claiming that GI and gender theories are a threat to the family.

Sociological Foundation of GI as Moral Panic

Despite the repeated attacks on GI by recent popes and Catholic academics, critical scholars remain unconvinced. Agnieszka Graff (2016), for instance, claimed that there is something "demonic" in RCC's GI that magnifies the perceived dangers of gender to the welfare of the family and humanity. To José Manuel Faúndes (2019, 403), GI is a mere "reaction to the feminist and LGBTQI agenda mobilized in international human rights spaces in the mid-1990s." To other scholars, GI is an empty signifier aimed only at creating a common enemy (e.g., Graff 2016; Garbagnoli 2016; Kováts and Põim 2015).

Gender sociologists are also skeptical of GI's alleged threat to the family. Modern sociology is at the forefront of theoretical investigations of gender relations in society (Barrett 1980; Walby 2020). Gender is seen as one of the key concerns of applied sociology in its investigations of "the injustice, violence and distress that unequal gender relations" in society" (Connell 2014, 552).

A theory in sociology is a tentative explanation of social reality and thus always subject to data confirmation. The RCC's popes, bishops, and scholars, however, regard its moral teaching as definitive or absolute and blame gender theory as GI for the imminent destruction of the family without convincing scientific data to back this up. Viewing gender and the gender theory espoused by sociologists, feminists, and LGBTQI leaders as GI and inimical to the family without convincing empirical evidence is merely a moral panic. It implies lack of knowledge of the empirical nature of gender and gender diversity as understood in sociological gender theories and research.

A moral panic is an exaggeration of an alleged threat to a societal value by authorities and the media. It is a sociological concept popularized by Stanley Cohen (1972) to understand a specific form of distortion to a perceived social problem. "Developed in the turbulent political and intellectual context of the late 1960s, its principal aim was to expose the processes involved in creating concern about a social problem; concern that bore little relationship to the reality of the problem" (Rohloff and Wright 2010, 2). In the opening chapter of his classic book, *Folk Devils and Moral Panics,* Cohen (1972) defines a moral panic as a situation where "a condition, episode or group of persons becomes defined as a threat to societal values and interests; its nature is presented in a stylized and stereotypical fashion by the mass media" (Cohen 1972, 9).

After Cohen, several scholars offered similar characterization of moral panics. To Hall et al. (1978, 16), moral panics represent the "official" reactions to events that are "out of all proportion to the actual threat offered." Goode and Ben-Yehuda (1994, 11) characterize them as periods of "strong, widespread (although not necessarily universal) fear or concern that evil doings are afoot, that certain enemies of society are trying to harm some or all of the rest of us." Social scientists agree that a key feature of moral panics is distortion of social reality, exaggerated grossly by media sources (Cohen 1972; Hall et al., 1978; Goode and Ben-Yehuda 1994).

Cohen (1972, 31) explains that distortions in moral panics can involve "…sensational headlines, the melodramatic vocabulary and the deliberate heightening of those elements in the story considered as news." In more recent years, the moral panic concept has undergone rigorous critique (Waddington 1986; Ungar 1992, 2003; McRobbie and Thornton 1995). Despite considerable interest in the merits and viability of Cohen's (1972) moral panic model, surprisingly little attention has been paid, exclusively, to his *folk devil* concept.

Cohen (1972, 10) defines *folk devils* as "social types" that serve as "visible reminders of what we should not be." Hall and his associates (1978) define the "folk devil" as the

> reverse image, the alternative to all we know: *the negation.* He is the fear of failure that is secreted at the heart of success, the danger that lurks inside security, the profligate figure by whom Virtue is constantly tempted, the tiny, seductive voice inside inviting us to feed rations [p.16]. (Hayle 2013, 1125)

If the RCC is magnifying the evils of gender to the foundation of the family in society rather than describing its true empirical nature in society, then GI is merely a signifier, exaggeration, and a moral panic. Case (2016: 157) explains how GI rhetoric emerged in the RCC:

> Feminist and LGBTQ+ movements mobilized for abortion liberalization, gender mainstreaming, and sexual diversity, and their gains, concretized in the agendas of the series of United Nations World Conferences in the first half of the 1990s, presented a growing challenge to the Catholic Church's natural law-based doctrine. Amid intensified ecclesiastical opposition, anti-gender ideology rhetoric emerged for the first time.

By promoting GI discourses as causing harm to the family and humanity, the RCC was able to establish the idea that feminist and LGBTQI gender agendas are based on ideological constructions that are contrary to objective reality (Diniz Junqueira 2017). The anti-gender movements under the banner of GI in the RCC have been largely driven by theological developments specifically on gender complementarity (Carnac 2014; Case 2011; Fillod 2014; Garbagnoli 2014; Kuhar 2015; Paternotte 2015). Currently, conservative and religious people and organizations that resist GI, LGBTQI rights, and gender diversity continue to guard the ideology of the healthy and traditional heterosexual family. This group assumes that if sexuality is not controlled, society will disintegrate, and that the only way to maintain social order is to preserve the traditional heterosexual family and promote sexual practices according to the conservative concept of a "natural" sexual order (Baird 2007). At the International Conference on Population and Development in Cairo in 1994, the Vatican joined other conservative actors in organizing vocal opposition to "issues challenging the structure of gender relations, particularly as they are manifest in family arrangements and control over women's sexuality and role in reproduction" (Friedman 2003: 314).

GI also aims to counter the influence of feminist and LGBTQI movements that are popular in the United States, Europe, and Latin America. It has therefore become "a concept—a signifier for what conservative Catholics construe as the evils of liberalism in the realm of human sexuality, ... 'bad feminism' and a close companion of 'natural rights and 'complementarity'" (Graff 2016, 282). Specially, GI is the rallying cry against the perceived destruction of the family by gender.

Aims, Major Sections, and Arguments

This chapter aims to sociologically analyze the alleged threat of gender and GI to the very foundations of the family as claimed by the Catholic hierarchy and proponents of the anti-gender movement in the RCC, applying Pope Francis's inductive synodal theology. Francis may not be aware of the implications of his latest ecclesiastical and theological reforms in his SoS, but his synodality and inductive theology are pushing boundaries that can challenge the deductive philosophical approach to gender and moral issues. Synodality implies inviting the marginalized "other" in the RCC with divergent views to a synodal dialogue in the hope of establishing a synodal church, one that welcomes the voiceless and those at the peripheries of the Church, which may include sociologists, feminists, and gender activists.

Specifically, this chapter intends to sociologically establish that GI's threat to the family is only a moral panic, rather than a scientific description of the gender diversity and cultural diversity of family structures in the world. It contends that the alleged threat of gender to the family is only conceptual rather than actual and empirical. GI's alleged threat to the family is only a theoretical panic by the RCC in response to the conceptual challenge posed by the scientific approach to sex and gender promoted by gender sociologists, feminists, and LGBTQI leaders to the purely philosophical natural law moral framework that only recognizes the heterosexual model of the family based on biological complementary of the sexes.

It further argues that nonbinary families have long existed in human culture with, thus far, no serious harm reported to the foundations of the heterosexual family in society. Instead, same-sex families only add to the diversity of family structures in the world. Growing media coverage and gender activism have provided greater visibility to other forms of family long established in various societies. One has yet to see credible scientific studies that consistently show that the rise of non-heterosexual families has resulted in the disintegration of society and humanity.

In pursuit of this argument, this chapter is divided into four major sections. The first section explains the relevance of modern sociology and Pope Francis's synodality and inductive theology to a critical assessment of urgent moral issues in the RCC such as GI that seeks to achieve a synodal church and provide pastoral guidance to Catholics on the true impact of gender on the family in today's global society.

The second section unpacks the moral panic of GI over the serious threat of gender to the foundations of the family in the Church and society. It argues that the danger of gender to family structure as perceived by the RCC is only a moral panic, an overreaction to the scientific approaches of sociology and feminism that are inappropriately seen as a direct challenge to the Church's purely philosophical natural law morality, which only recognizes the moral doctrine of the heterosexual family based on gender complementarity.

The third section identifies the real "folk devil" of GI's alleged threat to the family. It contends that the real panic of the RCC about the danger of gender, specifically of its threat to the family as the basic unity of society, is not empirical but conceptual—gender theory as conceived in the social sciences and feminism constitutes a serious threat to the philosophical and heterosexual view of the family-based natural law morality that disregards same-sex families and their capacity to beget children through reproductive technology and raise them like children of heterosexual families in society.

The last section provides an alternative synodal and sociological approach to gender and family structure to resolve GI's alleged threat to the family. It contends that the Church's natural law moral network needs to be updated to recognize the diversity of family structures in the world and to overcome its ethnocentric view on the family. The RCC also needs to recognize cultural relativism as well as to inculturate sociological and scientific theories on gender and the family in its moral teachings in light of Francis's inductive synodal theology.

Theoretical Foundation

Resolving Moral Panic Through Synodality

Pope Francis's vision of synodality adopts a contextual Catholic theology that begins with people's ordinary and faith experiences, emphasizing that the RCC's tradition is a living, not a static one. To Francis, ecclesiastical teachings and practices need to be adapted based on a sound and scientific understanding of people's religious experiences in contemporary society. Catholic theology should thus begin with an accurate understanding of people's behavior before Church doctrinal and moral teachings are applied.

In recent years, theologizing the lived experiences of people has been seen as "a quest of making life theologically meaningful and making theology meaningful in life" (Tveitereid 2022, 70). This theology implies approaching the creative processes of theological reflection based on ordinary human experiences. Indeed, "[t]he experiences and the practices of people themselves are a *locus theologicus*, a place from which to theologize" (Dillen 2014, 226). Pope Francis's *motu propio* document known as *Ad Theologiam Promovendam* [To Promote Theology] (*ATP*) (Francis 2023) encourages Catholic theologians to engage in this type of inductive theology, shifting the starting point of theological reflection from "abstract formulas" to the daily experiences of people as the focus of his new Catholic synodal theology.

If GI is a moral panic and a distortion of social reality, then the inductive synodal approach of Pope Francis and the sociological inductive research approach can both be appropriate conceptual tools to unpack its claim about gender's threat to the family: "The Magisterium has not shied away from utilizing sociological research and scientific data to inform its positions, teachings, and responses to various social, political, cultural, and religious issues" (Roy-Steier 2021, 1). The issues of sex, gender, and transgender sexuality in society are complex, requiring an accurate understanding of people's behavioral patterns—especially on gender relations and their societal contexts—with the aid of sociology and the social sciences.

The perceived attack of GI against the Church's moral magisterium is only an unintended consequence, since several of the RCC's ecclesiastical structures, policies, and religious practices are patriarchal, thus vulnerable to the critical scientific investigations of sociologists and feminists. Feminists and gender scientists generally seek to give an empirical account of gender relations in society, including those in religious institutions, through the sociological lens of various gender theories. These gender theories per se do not generally aim to attack the Church's moral teachings and gender essentialism.

Opposition to the RCC's moral doctrines is largely an indirect consequence of the sociological and feminist search for scientific knowledge on gender relations in society and the quest for social justice for women and gender-diverse individuals such as the LGBTQI community. Thus, a critical sociological analysis of GI to bring out some of its misconceptions on gender theories is necessary to establish a synodal dialogue between sociology and Catholic theology in the field of gender and sexuality.

Cultural Relativism and Francis's Synodality

The only way for the RCC to overcome its ethnocentrism on the concept of the family and become open to cultural diversity and various forms of family structure is to incorporate modern sociological theory and research on gender and family life. Allowing dialogue between Catholic moral theologians and sociologists of gender and morality can also minimize the misunderstanding of gender theory and the nature of sex and gender in society that have resulted in the moral panic of GI. Enhancing the social science education of future RCC leaders would further broaden clerical perspectives on cultural relativism and help overcome ethnocentric views on the family.

> The concept of cultural relativism refers to the idea that one needs to understand all cultures within the context of their own terms (i.e., values, norms, standards, customs, knowledges, lifeways, worldviews, etc.) rather than judge them from the perspective of one's own culture. This ideal of cross-cultural understanding requires an epistemological 'suspension' of one's own cultural biases in order to comprehend an unfamiliar cultural world. (Santillian 2011, 109)

Social scientists acknowledge that understanding cultural diversity can provide "an antidote to ethnocentrism (the biased tendency to consider one's own culture as the universal standard from which to judge all other cultures) and reveals the complexity of human existence in all its variations and manifestations, giving insight into one's own particular culture as an invention of human intention and social construction" (Santillian 2011, 110). Sociologists, as social scientists, assume a culturally relativist attitude to understanding society and human behavior. As relativists, they "deny that there is a knowable, static reality and, consequently, they deny the possibility of absolute, universal truth" (Bleasby 2011, p. 455).

Cultural relativism understands the truthfulness of moral values and norms as entirely dependent on society's cultural contexts. A moral value may be right in one culture but wrong in others. Sociologists usually adopt an attitude of moral neutrality in judging people's action and social situations. A culturally relativist approach is the best way to overcome the moral panic and ethnocentric views on sex, gender, and the family in the RCC's GI. This is not to disregard the Church's official teaching but only to recognize the diversity of cultural views on the family and the diversity of family structures in the world—and that the Catholic heterosexual family model is only one of the several and growing forms of the family structure in the ever-evolving contemporary society.

Recognizing and respecting the divergent views of people at the peripheries of the Church and society is acknowledged by Pope Francis in his synodality and inductive synodal theology. Openness to cultural diversity, such as seeing the existence of several family structures and synodal consultations to resolve cultural conflicts, are among the hallmarks of Francis's papacy. His approval of Catholic priests giving pastoral blessings to homosexual couples in his *Fiducia Supplicans* [Supplicating Trust] (DDF 2023) and encouraging them to seek civil union to protect their rights are important signs of Francis's openness to cultural diversity.

Synodal-Sociological Unpacking of GI's Threat to the Family

Conflicting Theological and Sociological Foundation of Gender

In his document *Fides et Ratio* [Faith and Reason, #83), Pope John Paul II argues the need for a philosophical and metaphysical method in Catholic morality. He contends that there is a "need of a philosophy of genuinely metaphysical range, capable, that is, of transcending empirical data in order to attain something absolute, ultimate and foundational in its search for truth… for adequate understanding of the moral good" (Long 2013, 110). In his document *Veritatis Splendor*, John Paul II in essence reaffirmed the centrality of the natural law theory (NLT) in Catholic moral tradition and "canonized" it as the only valid means to do good moral theology and to shepherd the RCC in terms of morality, faith, and reason (Trigilio Jr. 2004).

The opposition of both John Paul II and Pope Benedict XVI to homosexuality is well known. "John Paul II's theology left no room to account for same-sex attraction or the emotional and psychological needs of gay and lesbian persons who needed human companionship" Reid (2020, 233). In his theology of the body, John Paul II judged homosexuality as a condition "which is disordered, unnatural and with a limited role in the overall purpose of God" (Curran 1996, 141–142). Pope Benedict XVI, who succeeded John Paul II, reiterated this hostile view of homosexuality, following the NLT moral framework and gender complementarity teaching. In an interview published in the book *Light of the World* (Ignatius Press), Benedict affirmed John Paul II's biological complementarity of sexes as the only foundation of sexuality.

Homosexuality and homosexual sexual relations and unions can never be morally acceptable under the NLT morality, since they are contrary to the divine plan, enshrined in natural law and human reason, that only allows sexuality within the context of marriage and heterosexual vaginal intercourse. Homosexuality is always unnatural and unethical because it contravenes natural law. Same-sex families and parenthood are also deemed unnatural and unethical since they contravene the NLT morality that only permits a biological male and female to establish a family and exercise Christian parenthood.

Although there are attempts by some Catholic moral theologians to adopt a more positive approach to gender, these efforts remain within the context of the RCC's philosophical NLT moral framework and Pope John Paul II's theology of the body (Barnes 2022). The RCC still dismisses social science perspectives that view gender and gender differences as products of historical and cultural forces (Congregation for Catholic Education 2019). Catholic popes and bishops still see sex–gender unity and difference as something immutable and ahistorical following the NLT framework. As Szwed and Zielińska (2016, 120–121) explain,

> The Church also very seldom refers to the cultural or historical transformations of gender constructions…The Roman Catholic Church condemns the very notion of gender as ontologically impossible. The bishops reject the cultural fabric of gender because they perceive it predominantly in terms of the categories of nature and biology. They declare an "integral" approach to gender, encompassing carnality, spirituality, and psyche, and emphasize that "man's sexuality determines human identity and shapes the whole of man's life."

At present, the RCC still follows the traditional binary gender socialization and rejects the emerging feminist theories on gender in contemporary society (Bracke and Paternotte 2016; Case 2016). It continues to uphold the Catholic traditional doctrine on gender and sexuality that reflect 19th-century views of the biological complementarity of the sexes (Ruether 2008). The Church's moral magisterium teaches gender equality but relates it to the gender complementarity of men and women. To the Catholic hierarchy, "transgressing the assigned identities means denial of the 'natural' role, that is, given by God" (Szwed and Zielińska 2016, 121). It views heterosexuality as natural and closely related to male and female bodies.

Seeing gender strictly as "natural," immutable, complementary, and metaphysical is contrary to the empirical and scientific approaches of sociology, feminism, and the social sciences to gender as social and cultural. For sociologists, gender differs from sex. Sex refers to the biological aspect of the person, which is determined by their genitalia, while gender refers to their manifestations of masculinity or femininity, which is determined by society and culture (Blank 2012). "By expecting different behaviors from people because they are male or female, society nudges boys and girls in separate directions from an early age, and this foundation carries over into adulthood" (Cooley et al. 2010, 4).

Sociologists and social scientists who generally follow the empirical and scientific method rather than philosophical reflection thus view gender as socially and culturally learned in society through the social process called gender socialization—thus not divinely ordained (Blank 2012; Cooley et al. 2010; Rohlinger 2007). Socialization refers to "the process whereby individuals learn and internalize the attitudes, values, and behaviors appropriate to people living in any given society" (Wunder 2007, 589). And gender socialization specifically refers to "the process through which boys and girls learn sex appropriate behavior, dress, personality characteristics, and demeanor" (Rohlinger 2007, 590). Males and females learn what it means to be boys and girls and, later, men and women through socialization. This sociological view is radically different from the RCC's philosophical approach to gender under the NLT moral framework, which sees sex and gender as immutable, inseparable, assigned at birth, and ordained by God. Following heteronormativity, the Church expects people's gender to correspond to their assigned biological sex since birth, or what is called cisgender. Unlike sociology, which views gender as fluid and subject to social and cultural change through socialization, Catholic moral theology sees it as fixed under the NLT moral framework.

But human experience shows otherwise. A person's gender or expression of how to be masculine or feminine sometimes deviates from their biological sex assigned during birth, thus deviating from the RCC's cisgender norm. The correspondence between sex and gender does not always happen, due to a variety of causes during the gender socialization process and in the social environment that are beyond the individual's control. Thus, some people's gender identity becomes nonbinary or transgender. Sociologists believe that human action is conditioned by social structure just as it influences action. The RCC continues to teach—inappropriately—that homosexuality and homosexual identity is intentional and a sign of immaturity on the part of the person, an assessment that is empirically and sociologically contrary to human experience. Insisting on the immutability of gender based on natural law, the RCC refuses to see the empirical reality that members of the LGBTQI community exist in the Church and society and should be treated as normal human beings who are created in the image of God with legal and moral rights like heterosexuals.

"Transgender individuals have a gender identity that differs from their sex at the time of birth. To address this incongruence, many transgender patients may seek gender-affirming interventions to achieve concordance between self-identified gender, physical appearance, and function" (Canner et al. 2018, 609). The RCC declares that any sociological and feminist perspective on gender fluidity and sex change is part of GI, which threatens the survival of humanity and the family founded on heterosexuality and gender complementarity.

No Real Harm of Gender to the Family as Portrayed by GI

"The family is a basic unit of study in many social science disciplines, such as sociology, psychology, economics, anthropology, social psychiatry, and social work" (Sharma 2013, 306). The family is considered by anthropologists as one of the few cultural universals in the world. However, it has various cultural forms and structures that cannot be categorized solely in accordance with the Catholic concept of a heterosexual family. "Families can be classified in several different dimensions, for example, by marriage type (monogamous, polygamous), by location (patrilocal, matrilocal, and avunculocal), authority (patriarchy, matriarchy), and by kin composition (nuclear, joint)" (Sharma 2013, 306). Census definitions of family also reveal a variety of cultural understandings of the family "from country to country and also from census to census within country" (Sharma 2013, 306). Desai (1994) attempted to provide a universal definition of the family as "a unit of two or more persons united by marriage, blood, adoption, or consensual union, in general consulting a single household, interacting and communicating with each other." Although this definition is acceptable, the interaction and communication in the family under this description can be problematic to determine (Sharma 2013, 306).

The rise of same-sex families only adds to this growing cultural diversity and variety of family structures as a basic social unit in contemporary society. Same-sex family structure constitutes a minority, "a subgroup in society, and particularly a subpopulation of sexual minorities" (Haag 2016, 3). To the Catholic hierarchy, the advent of non-heterosexual families is the negative consequence of the contemporary GI that promotes gender diversity and the LGBTQI group, and the RCC opposes same-sex families as unnatural.

Homosexual families have long existed in society but were sidelined and ostracized in the Christian community:

> In the past, homosexual women and men who became parents often decided to marry and have children within a heterosexual union, because they did not see any other way of being a parent; others even gave up on the idea until they were convinced at a later time in their life courses that homosexuals could in fact become parents. (Haag 2016, 3)

In the eyes of the RCC, the normative definition of the family is the heterosexual family, a group of people consisting of a man and a woman as spouses and parents for their biological or adopted children. Under this normative criterion, homosexual couples with children either through their former heterosexual partners or adopted, as well as same-sex families, are deviating from this normative standard and thus immoral and dangerous to the welfare of society. The NLT moral framework and the institutional homophobia in the RCC play an important role in why homosexuality and homosexual families are considered unnatural, deviant, and immoral. As Haag (2016, 3) explains:

> Same-sex couples pursued parenthood in the past and they still do. Research can investigate the practices of a societal subgroup. Concerning same-sex parenting, there are two types of families that can be distinguished regarding their family formation: (1) same-sex couples with children from a previous (heterosexual) relationship (such as a marriage), and (2) couples who make the transition to parenthood within the context of a homosexual relationship.

The rise of the same-sex family does not constitute an imminent threat to the existence of the traditional heterosexual family in society; it merely adds to the cultural variety and complexity of the family as a basic unit of society, recognizing cultural diversity in the world. Cultural diversity implies that no group or institution can claim that there is only one normative definition of a normal family in the world. And the RCC's standard cannot claim to be only family model across the globe, despite its universal mission of evangelizing all cultures for Christ. Vatican II recognizes that cultural diversity must be respected in preaching the Gospel.

The Real "Folk Devil" and Reproductive Technology

In the sociological theory of moral panics, Stanley Cohen conceptualized "folk devils" as the cause of the exaggeration of the threat to society's values. In the RCC's GI, the real "folk devils" to the imminent destruction of the family in society are not the actual harm caused by gender, but the serious conceptual challenge posed by sociological and feminist theories of gender to the rigid philosophical NLT moral framework that defines the family based on gender complementarity.

A specific cause of moral panic against same-sex families is the use of reproductive technology to beget children, which the RCC interprets as bypassing the natural process of procreation. As Haag (2016, 4–5) explains,

> Same-sex couples face severe challenges on the way towards parenthood. The pathways they choose could also be an alternative for other individuals in the pursuit of parenthood ... There are similarities between couples in fertility treatment and same-sex couples who plan to become parents. Some of the pathways and methods used or deliberated by same-sex couples are from the catalogue of assisted reproductive techniques and are thus similar or identical to those used by heterosexual couples suffering from sub- or infertility.

The RCC strongly opposes alternative and assisted reproductive techniques because they run directly counter to the traditional biological reproductive process as framed by the NLT moral framework. Catholic moralists and ethicists also tend to see the morality of the external act rather than understanding the motives and good intentions of homosexual couples who want to be parents for their children in a same-sex family. Traditional Catholic morality recognizes the intention of the person doing the act as crucial in judging morality. Although the use of reproductive technology to beget children for same-sex couples can be complicated, understanding moral motives is crucial to judge the morality of the act rather than merely analyzing it through logic and deductive reasoning of natural law.[1]

The RCC needs to recognize that same-sex families with homosexual parents do exist in society, and do not constitute real harm to humanity as portrayed by GI. Whilst the blessing of homosexual couples is a major step towards the recognition of same-sex unions and families, there is a need to update the RCC's NLT moral framework and come up with a more sociological moral framework to accurately and scientifically understand the nature of gender, gender diversity, and same-sex families in society and apply the Church's moral doctrines appropriately in the contemporary world. The time is ripe, with Pope Francis's vision of an inclusive synodal church that welcomes the marginalized, the voiceless, and those at the peripheries of society. And this includes homosexual couples and their children in same-sex families.

Ethnocentrism, Cultural Relativism, and Synodality

The constant development and evolution of society play a crucial role in all aspects of people's changing behavioral patterns, including the formation of the family as a basic social unit. In post-modernity, important social changes are taking place: traditional patterns of everyday life, while trying to resist these changes, are giving way to new modes of living, new lifestyles and—perhaps most importantly—new identities (Giddens 1991, 1992; Bauman 2000). Plummer (1995) contends that the rise of new identities and lifestyles in the contemporary world implies moral and political changes.

Ethnocentrism, or seeing one's own culture as the best culture while others are inferior, is contrary to Pope Francis's synodality, which implies openness and dialogue with marginalized groups in society with divergent views such as those of same-sex couples and families. It is ethnocentric to confine the definition of family to the RCC's heterosexual family and to attribute the breakdown of heterosexual families to non-heterosexual models such as the same-sex family, or "folk devils" to use Cohen's term. Francis's inductive synodal theology encourages theologians and scholars to first understand the diversity of people's cultural experiences before theological reflection or moral judgment. He also welcomes interdisciplinary research, encouraging sociologists and social scientists to assist Catholic theologians to accurately understand people's moral lives in today's cultural revolution.

The RCC's institutionalized homophobia sees anything associated with homosexuality such as homosexual union, homosexual family, and same-sex parenthood as abominable and challenging the natural order ordained by God. The growing visibility of same-sex couples and their same-sex families caused by the increasing

[1] For a more detailed discussion by the author on the need to reappraise the empirical basis of gender complementarity teaching for marriage in Genesis, please consult Chapter 4 of his 2024 book entitled *LGBTQI Inclusivity, Homosexuality, and Same-Sex Marriage: Pope Francis's Synodal Theology, Sociology, and Moral Issues*. Singapore: Springer Nature.

LGBTQI activism and media exposure that directly challenge heteronormativity in gender identity and family structure is what causes the moral panic of conservative clerics and Catholics. If it is to overcome the moral panic caused by the alleged threat of gender to the family, the RCC needs to utilize Pope Francis's inductive theological method and adopt the sociological moral approach to gender and family structure and recognize gender diversity as well as cultural relativism:

> Cultural relativism understands the truthfulness of moral values and norms as entirely dependent on society's cultural contexts. A moral value may be right in one culture but wrong in other cultures. Therefore, whether an action is right or wrong would depend on the cultural meaning and context where the action takes place and on the type of normative cultural standard used by the local inhabitants to judge it. (Ballano 2019, 8–9)

Sociologists recognize cultural diversity and various normative standards in judging what is right or wrong. Sociology is a descriptive rather than a prescriptive discipline such as theology. As such, it aims to be value-free in its judgments about the world and human behavior. It only describes behavior and the various cultural practices and traits in the world using the scientific method. It respects same-sex union and family due to gender diversity in the world.

In his *ATP*, Pope Francis encourages Catholic theologians and scholars to use the inductive method and the social sciences to understand people's diverse cultural experience in the world before moral judgment and action. The traditional method of "see-judge-act" also acknowledges empirical evaluation or "to see" as the first step in resolving moral issues (Ballano 2019). And in this case, the scientific research of sociology and the social sciences can greatly assist moral theologians to correctly appreciate behavioral and cultural patterns in family relations.

Instead of immediately condemning "gender" under the banner of GI as causing the destruction of the family, the RCC should encourage Catholic moral theologians and scholars to avail themselves of sociological research on the family and become open to cultural diversity. "In post-modernity important social changes are taking place: traditional patterns of everyday life, while trying to resist these changes, are giving way to new modes of living, new lifestyles and—maybe most importantly—new identities" (Kuhar 2007, 35).

Conclusion

This chapter has analyzed the RCC's moral panic over the negative impact of "gender" on the existence of the family in society, using the synodal-sociological approach, and concluding that the alleged threat to the family is a distortion rather than a reflection of the cultural diversity of family structures and relations in the world. The emergence of newer forms of families is largely a product of societal influence rather than a consequence of gender as promoted by feminists and social scientists to directly attack the sacredness of the heterosexual Catholic model of the family.

Sociologists believe that there have been various forms of human family that deviate from the Catholic notion of a Christian family based on heterosexual standards, long before the advent of GI as first conceived by Pope Benedict XVI. The real moral panic of the RCC on GI is not empirical but conceptual. It greatly fears the conceptual challenge posed by gender sociologists and feminists to the natural law moral framework that metaphysically sees sex and gender as immutable and ordained by God and the heterosexual family based on gender complementary of sexes as the only model for society.

This chapter recommends resolving the moral panic by adopting the sociological-synodal approach and culturally relativist attitude towards gender and family structures. The RCC also needs to inculturate the sociological and feminist perspectives in its moral teachings on gender and the family to dissolve the concept of GI and its serious threat to the family in Church declarations.

References

Baird V (2007) The no-nonsense guide to sexual diversity (No-Nonsense Guides). New Internationalist, Oxford, UK

Ballano VO (2019) Catholic social teaching, theology, and sociology: exploring the common ground. Religions 10(557):1–16. https://doi.org/10.3390/rel10100557

Barnes MW (2022) Catholic seminarians on 'real men', sexuality, and essential male inclusivity. Religions 13(352):1–14. https://doi.org/10.3390/rel13040352

Barrett M (1980) Women's oppression today: problems in marxist feminist analysis. Verso, London

Bauman Z (2000) Liquid modernity. Polity Press, Cambridge

Blank H (2012) Straight: the surprisingly short history of heterosexuality. Beacon Press, Boston

Butler J (2019) What threat? The campaign against 'gender ideology'. Glocalism J Culture Politics Innov 3:1–12. https://doi.org/10.12893/gjcpi.2019.3.1

Canner JK, Harfouch O, Kodadek LM, Pelaez D, Coon D, Offodile AC 2nd, Haider AH, Lau BD (2018) Temporal trends in gender-affirming surgery among transgender patients in the United States. JAMA Surg 153(7):609–616. https://doi.org/10.1001/jamasurg.2017.6231.PMID:29490365;PMCID:PMC5875299

Case MA (2011) After gender the destruction of man? The vatican's nightmare vision of the 'gender agenda' for law. Pace Law Rev 31(3):802–817

Cohen S (1972) Folk devils and moral panics. Paladin, Herts

Connell R (2014) The sociology of gender in southern perspective. Current Sociol Monogr 62(4):550–567.https://doi.org/10.1177/0011392114524510

Cooley CH, Mead GH, Piaget J, Kohlberg L, Gilligan C (2010) Socialization. In: Cooley studies the development of the self, coining the term "the Looking-Glass Self", 2–39. Available at: http://www.csun.edu/~hbsoc126/soc1/chapter%203%20outline.pdf

DDF (Dicastery of the Doctrine of the Faith) (2023) Fiducia Supplicans: on the pastoral meaning of blessings. Vatican: The Roman Curia. Available at: https://www.vatican.va/roman_curia/congregations/cfaith/documents/rc_ddf_doc_20231218_fiducia-supplicans_en.html

Desai M (1994) Concept and conceptual frameworks for understanding family. Enhancing the role of the family as an agency for social and economic development. Unit for Family Studies Report, pp 16–41. Bombay, India: TISS

Diniz Junqueira R (2017) 'Ideologia de genero': a genese de uma categoria politica reacionaria ou: a promocao dos direitos humanos se tornou uma 'ameaca a familia natural'? In: Costa Ribeiro

PR, Corpes Magalhaes J (eds), Debates contemporâneos sobre Educação para a sexualidade. Rio Grande: Ed. da FURG, pp 25–52

Faúndes JMM (2019) The geopolitics of moral panic: the influence of Argentinian neo-conservatism in the genesis of the discourse of 'gender ideology'." Int Sociol 34(4):402–417.https://doi.org/10.1177/0268580919856488

Ford CJ (2018) Transgender bodies, catholic schools, and a queer natural law theology of exploration. J Moral Theol 7(1):70–98

Garbagnoli S (2016) Against the heresy of immanence: Vatican's 'gender' as a new rhetorical device against the denaturalization of the sexual order. Religion Gender 6(2):187–204. https://doi.org/10.18352/rg.10156

Giddens A (1991) The consequences of modernity. Polity Press, Cambridge, UK

Giddens A (1992) The transformation of intimacy: sexuality, love, and eroticism in modern societies. Polity, Cambridge

Goode E, Ben-Yehuda N (1994) Moral panics: the social construction of deviance. Blackwell, Oxford

Graff A (2016) 'Gender ideology': weak concepts, powerful politics. Religion Gender 6(2):268–272. https://doi.org/10.18352/rg.10177

Haag C (2016) Emergence of a new type of family? Parenting intentions of homosexual women and men. Bamberger Beiträge zur Soziologie 16. Bamberg, Germany: University of Bamberg Press

Hall S, Critcher C, Jefferson T, Clarke J, Roberts B (1978) Policing the crisis. Mugging, the State, and Law and Order. London: Macmillan

Kováts E, Põim M (eds) (2015) Gender as symbolic glue: the position and role of conservative and far right parties in the anti-gender mobilization in Europe. Foundation for European progressive studies and Friedrich-Ebert-Stiftung Budapest, Brussels

Kuby G (2015) The global sexual revolution: destruction of freedom in the name of freedom. LifeSite/Angelico Press, Brooklyn, NY

Kuby G (2022) The abandoned generation. St. Augustine's Press, South Bend, IN

Kuhar R (2007) The family secret: parents of homosexual sons and daughters. In: Kuhar R, Takács J (eds), Beyond the pink curtain. Everyday life of LGBT people in Eastern Europe. The Peace Institute, pp 35–48

Long SA (2013) Fundamental errors of the new natural law theory. The national catholic bioethics quarterly (Spring 2013), pp 105–131

Pentin E (2015) Gender ideology's 'completely mad attack' on the family and society." National Catholic Register (10 July 2010). https://www.ncregister.com/news/gender-ideology-s-completely-mad-attack-on-the-family-and-society

Plummer K (1995) Telling sexual stories. Routledge, London

Pope Francis (2016) Post-Synodal Exhortation Amoris Laetitia [The Joy of Love]. Vatican: Dicastero per la Comunicazione—Libreria Editrice Vaticana. https://www.vatican.va/content/francesco/en/apost_exhortations/documents/papa-francesco_esortazione-ap_20160319_amoris-laetitia.html

Sharma R (2013) The family and family structure classification redefined for the current times. J Family Med Primary Care 2(4):306–310

Rohlinger DA (2007) Primary socialization. In: Ritzer G (ed), The blackwell Encyclopedia of sociology, pp 590–591. https://doi.org/10.1002/9781405165518.wbeoss194

Roy-Steier S (2021) Coming up short: the Catholic Church's pastoral response to the transgender crisis in America. Religions 12(337):1–20. https://doi.org/10.3390/rel12050337

Ruether RR (2008) Catholic does not equal the Vatican: a vision for progressive Catholicism. New Press, New York

Santillian D (2011) Cultural relativism. In: Ritzer G, Michael Ryan J (eds), The concise Encyclopedia of sociology, pp 109–110. Malden, MA: Blackwell Publishing Ltd

Sroczynski M (2016) A year of conflict—the 'war on gender ideology' discourse of the polish catholic church, and the liberal Backlash. AG AboutGender: Int J Gender Studies 5(10):75–106

Tveitereid K (2022) Lived theology and theology in the lived. In: Ward P, Tveitereid K (eds), The wiley blackwell companion to theology and qualitative research. Chichester, UK: Wiley, 66–77. https://doi.org/10.1002/9781119756927.ch8

Ungar S (1992) The rise and (Relative) decline of global warming as a social problem. Sociol Quart 33(4):483–501

Ungar S (2003) Moral panic versus the risk society: the implications of the changing sites of social anxiety. Br J Sociol 52(2):271–291. https://doi.org/10.1080/00071310120044980

Waddington PA (1986) Mugging as a moral panic: a question of proportion. Br J Sociol 37(2):245–259. https://doi.org/10.2307/590356

Walby S (2020) Varieties of gender regimes. Soc Polit Int Stud Gend State Soc 27(3):414–431. https://doi.org/10.1093/sp/jxaa018

Wunder DF (2007) Socialization, agents of. In: Ritzer G (ed), The blackwell Encyclopedia of sociology, 59–590. https://doi.org/10.1002/9781405165518.wbeoss194

Chapter 6
"Gender Ideology's" Alleged Threats to Children's Welfare: A Sociological-Synodal Analysis

Abstract This chapter sociologically investigates the Roman Catholic Church's moral panic on the alleged threats of the so-called "gender ideology" to the welfare of children in same-sex families, using Pope Francis's synodal approach and drawing on secondary literature, media reports, and Church documents. It argues that the alleged threats of homosexual couples in same-sex families to the children's welfare are an exaggeration and moral panic in the sociological sense. It contends that negative perception of same-sex parenthood on the children's welfare is largely a structural influence of societal homophobia and social discrimination against same-sex parents under the rigid gender complementary and heterosexual standards of the Catholic Church's moral magisterium, founded on the philosophical approach of natural law theory. It recommends a synodal openness to diverse family structures and definitions of children's welfare and a reappraisal of the empirical foundations of the gender complementarity interpretation of Genesis.

Keywords Synodality · Sociology · Same-sex family · Welfare of children · Synodal church

Introduction

It was Pope Benedict XVI who first raised the alarm over the alleged serious threat of GI to children's welfare in same-sex families, because homosexual parenthood is understood as morally opposing the RCC's moral principle on natural complementary of the sexes. To him, only a biological male and female can receive the sacrament of marriage in the Church and become parents to their biological or adopted children. Benedict upheld the traditional Church teaching on the gender complementary of male and female based on the Bible as inviolable. The essence of human beings as created by God is being male and female: "This duality is an essential aspect of what being human is all about, as ordained by God" (Pope Benedict XVI 2012, para. 6). Thus, only a man and a woman in a sacramental heterosexual marriage can raise a family and provide the best Christian welfare for children.

V. O. Ballano, *Gender Ideology and the Contemporary Catholic Church*,
https://doi.org/10.1007/978-981-97-8124-9_6

The RCC Congregation for Catholic Education's (2019) document entitled "Male and Female He Created Them" (2019) blamed the popularity of "gender" promoted by feminists, sociologists, and LGBTQI leaders, and gender ideology (GI), for the current educational crisis in the field of affectivity and sexuality that was destabilizing the family as a basic institution in society. By cancelling out the differences between men and women, GI was said to threaten the very survival of humanity.

Indeed, one strong objection of the RCC to GI is its opposition to Church doctrine on the immutability and inseparability of sex and gender, and the heterosexual model of the family, and GI's negative effect on children's welfare. As Potter (2012, 556), explains, GI poses "new threats to children's minds and bodies, as well as to their family relationships... [It] substitutes a scientific understanding of the male and female sexes with a person's self-determined sense of 'gender identity'."

In the early 2000s, Pope John Paul II saw gender ideologies as causing misleading concepts about the sexuality, dignity, and mission of the woman. The Pontifical Council for the Family also labeled as "gender" the "feminist ideology" that resulted in the rejection of the gender complementarity between a man and a woman in marriage and "a growing confusion about sexual identity" that "complicates the assumption of roles and the sharing of tasks in the home" (Corredor 2016, 615).

The RCC blames GI for promoting gender diversity that views members of the lesbian, gay, bisexual, transgender, queer, and intersexual (LGBTQI) communities as "normal" persons like heterosexuals with the right to marry and raise children. The RCC's moral magisterium strictly teaches that children should be born and raised by biological and heterosexual parents under the bond of sacramental marriage. It traditionally conceives the family as consisting of a man, his wife, and their children. The father was the provider, and the mother stayed at home to raise coitally conceived children" (Omani-Samani et al. 2007, 127).

The RCC allows only heterosexual families based on the moral principle of the complementarity of the sexes as interpreted from the Scriptures. Thus, same-sex families consisting of lesbian or gay parents are a morally unacceptable environment in which to raise children. Same-sex families are seen as "unnatural" and deviations from the natural law-based moral doctrines of the RCC. Under this model, same-sex parenthood is seen as detrimental to children's welfare.

This ecclesiastical argument coincides with some critics of same-sex parent families who argue that children should be raised by their biological parents for healthy emotional and psychological development. Same-sex families with two fathers or two mothers cannot produce the essential socialization experiences for children (Popenoe 1996; Dobson 2004).

Aims, Major Arguments, and Main Sections

Applying sociological theories on deviance, ethnocentrism, and cultural relativism and Pope Francis's synodal teachings, and drawing on secondary scholarly literature, media reports, and Church documents, this chapter aims to unpack the moral panic of the alleged threats of gender and GI to children's welfare. It demonstrates that the existence of non-heterosexual and same-sex families poses no real threat to the welfare of children. It attempts to sociologically show that same-sex parenting does not greatly differ from that of heterosexual families.

Overall, it argues that the RCC's claim of the dangers of GI to children's welfare are unwarranted, given its philosophical approach to resolving moral issues and the heterosexual definition of the family that views children in same-sex families as deviant and morally unacceptable in the Christian community. Owing to the prevailing societal and institutional homophobia in the RCC, no amount of research can convince conservative moralists who follow the strict Thomistic natural law theory (TNLT) approach that children in same-sex families are safe and undergo similar socialization as those of heterosexual families.

This chapter recommends revisiting and updating the empirical foundation of gender complementarity teaching in Genesis and a synodal dialogue between the Catholic hierarchy and moral theologians, sociologists, and feminists, to achieve an interdisciplinary and scientific approach to gender, family life, and children's welfare in the contemporar world, and to overcome the alleged threat of GI to the family and children's welfare.

This chapter is divided into three major sections. The first explains the synodal and sociological approach to resolving moral issues such as GI and children's welfare in homosexual family structures and relations. It also broadly discusses the sociological understanding of deviance, ethnocentrism, and cultural relativism in dealing with issues of children's welfare. The second section attempts to clarify the exaggeration of GI's alleged dangers to children's welfare, or what sociologists call a moral panic. GI is used by popes and Catholic moralists as a political signifier rather than a scientific concept that correctly captures the nature of gender and sexuality in society. It argues that the RCC's warning of the impact of gender on children's welfare is more of a distortion rather than a true reflection of gender and same-sex family relations in contemporary society. The last section aims to resolve the conceptual conflict between the RCC's traditional philosophical definitions of the family and children's welfare, based on its strict gender complementarity teaching, and those of sociologists and feminists, through synodal dialogue and scientific research.

Theoretical Orientation

Basic Conflict in Approaching Gender

The document entitled "Male and Female He Created Them" (Congregation for Catholic Education 2019) speaks of an anthropological disorientation that characterizes the cultural climate contributing to "the destabilization of the family" in the current age. But this anthropological perspective is different from the scientific study of human anthropology in the social science discipline called social anthropology, which specializes in the study of cultures around the globe. This document speaks of anthropological disorientation from philosophical and theological perspectives. Thus, its concept of human anthropology is different from the social science view on sex, gender, and human culture.

The document is critical of social science theories that oppose the biological complementarity of the sexes. It upholds the RCC's teaching on sex and gender as intrinsically linked and ontologically ordained by God, regardless of social and cultural experiences. Following Pope Francis's *Amoris Laetitia* (2016a), it characterizes "gender" as a type of ideology that supports "a personal identity and emotional intimacy radically separated from the biological difference between male and female." Indeed, gender identities such as those of the LGBTQI group are conceived by sociologists and social scientists as radically distinct from heterosexuals and need to be recognized as such by the Church and society.

The RCC approaches sex and gender conceptually and philosophically through logic and deductive reasoning, without the need for empirical data to support it, while the behavioral sciences view them empirically through scientific research methodology. To Bhattacherjee (2012, 5), scientific methodology is "a standardized set of techniques for building scientific knowledge, such as how to make valid observations, how to interpret results, and how to generalize those results."

Scientific methodology can apply quantitative or qualitative research. Understanding people's sexuality and gender today can be resolved using inductive research. "In inductive research, the goal of a researcher is to infer theoretical concepts and patterns from observed data" (Bhattacherjee 2012, 3). This approach is also suitable for Pope's Francis's paradigm shift in Catholic theology which emphasizes the inductive process, that is, knowing first the concrete experiences of believers before theological reflection (Francis 2023).

The philosophical approach is appropriate when dealing with the dogmatic and metaphysical aspects of faith, but not for resolving contemporary moral issues such as gender and GI, since research data are required before the moral situation can be resolved. Thus, the main obstacle to dialogue is the insistence of the RCC's moral magisterium on applying the philosophical–theological approach to resolve GI issues, including the impact on children's welfare, without regard to the growing complexity of gender in the contemporary world that is largely being studied by gender sociologists and feminists.

The RCC's moral magisterium also assumes, inaccurately, that gender identity is a choice rather than a product of socialization and social learning, as sociologists and feminists have largely claimed, and is thus largely unintentional on the part of actors. To be gay or lesbian is not an inborn condition primarily intended by the person, but socially learned unconsciously through gender socialization. Gender-socialization theory posits that individuals develop schemas about gender from an early age through interaction with socializing agents (e.g., parents, siblings, and peers) and exposure to socializing channels (e.g., schools and media) (Burt and Scott 2002; Katz and Ksansnak 1994). Social learning theories also contend that parents as primary socializing agents are highly influential in their children's early gender socialization (Bussey and Bandura 1999).

Despite strong papal and ecclesiastical declarations against GI and the alleged threats of same-sex families to children's welfare, there is no convincing evidence that gender, as understood by sociologists, feminists, and pro-gender activists as social and cultural experience, can result in the exploitation and social misorientation of children. If this alleged threat of gender to children's welfare is an exaggeration intended to create unjustified fear of and antagonism to social science perspectives, then GI is what sociologists call a moral panic. Its alleged threat to children's welfare needs sociological and synodal analysis.

Understanding Moral Panics and GI

A moral panic is a sociological term that attempts to explain a specific form of overreaction to a perceived social problem. The primary objective of the term is to expose processes involved in creating concern about a social problem that have little empirical support in society (Rohloff and Wright 2010). The concept of moral panics was popularized by the sociologist Stanley Cohen in his book *Folk Devils and Moral Panics*. To Cohen, a moral panic is "a condition, episode, person or group of persons that emerges to become defined as a threat to societal values and interests; its nature is presented in a stylized and stereotypical fashion by the mass media; the moral barricades are manned by editors, bishops, politicians and other right-thinking people" (Cohen 1972, 1).

Crossman (2019: para. 1), defines a moral panic as "a widespread fear, most often an irrational one, that someone or something is a threat to the values, safety, and interests of a community or society at large." Despite the repeated use of the term GI in papal writings, the RCC has not provided it with adequate empirical definition and indicators. What, precisely, is GI? In "Male and Female He Created Them," the Congregation for Catholic Education (2019) differentiated the concept of gender as pursued by social scientists from that of pro-gender advocates. It made a distinction:

> between the ideology of gender on the one hand, and the whole field of research on gender that the human sciences have undertaken, on the other...while the ideologies of gender...seek 'to assert themselves as absolute and unquestionable, even dictating how children should be raised', and thus preclude dialogue.

Despite this broad clarification, the RCC remains unclear what GI really means. It seems to have overlooked the fact that there are a variety of gender theories in the social sciences that may overlap with the gender advocacies of feminists and members of the LGBTQI community. What is clear, however, is that whatever gender theories and advocacies tend to separate sex and gender, metaphysically understood by the Church's magisterium as immutable and inseparable, are labeled, panic-stricken, as GI:

> The problem here does not lie in the distinction between the two terms, which can be interpreted correctly, but in the separation of sex from gender. This separation is at the root of the distinctions proposed between various "sexual orientations" which are no longer

> defined by the sexual difference between male and female, and can then assume other forms, determined solely by the individual, who is seen as radically autonomous. Further, the concept of gender is seen as dependent upon the subjective mindset of each person, who can choose a gender not corresponding to his or her biological sex, and therefore with the way others see that person (transgenderism). (Congregation for Catholic Education 2019, #11)

The insistence of this document that "gender is dependent upon the subjective mindset of each person, who can choose a gender not corresponding to his or her biological sex" seems a great misunderstanding of how social scientists view sex, gender, and transgenderism. Social scientists do not deny that gender and sex are inseparable insofar as they are founded on the same person. However, sex is primarily based on aspects of the person's biological make-up, such as genitalia and chromosomes, but gender, that is, how he or she experiences and expresses masculinity and femininity in society, is socially and culturally learned through the process of gender socialization, which is largely not intentional and purely a matter of personal choice, as the RCC assumes.

Synodality, Sociology, and Children's Welfare

Garbagnoli (2016) contends that the RCC's GI is a misleading construct of a single enemy, since its religious and secular actors and groups are diverse. In a meeting with Polish bishops preceding World Youth Day in July 2016, Pope Francis (2016b) condemned GI – which he called ideological colonization – for miseducating children in schools and threatening their welfare:

> In Europe, America, Latin America, Africa, and in some countries of Asia, there are genuine forms of ideological colonization taking place. And one of these – I will call it clearly by its name – is [the ideology of] gender. Today children – children! – are taught in school that everyone can choose his or her sex. Why are they teaching this?

Some scholars agree that the RCC's description of GI's threats to the family, the Church, and society are exaggerated and are used as a political tool to create a moral panic against a common enemy. GI is the common glue in its war against gender and feminism (Graff 2016; Garbagnoli; 2016; Kováts and Põim 2015). To Anna Odrowąż-Coates (2015, 27), the "anti-gender" debate initiated by the RCC has proclaimed a deepening crisis of family and society as being caused by GI. Popes and bishops blame gender theories and gender theorists for the societal problems of families in contemporary society. This discourse has been elaborated in the media, resulting in animosity and friction between gender scholars and Church representatives.

The way to resolve opposing views on "gender" and the welfare of children in the RCC, and to dissolve the signifier of GI in the Church today, is through Pope Francis's synodality, inductive theology, and the incorporation of sociology and the social sciences in the study of sexuality and gender. When St. Thomas Aquinas incorporated the pagan Aristotelian philosophy into Catholic theology, thus popularizing philosophical theology, the dominant ecclesiastical concern was doctrinal, that is, providing correct and rational justification for the Christian faith to address heresies and erroneous teachings.

But contemporary society is characterized by growing liquidity and the main concern for the RCC is now moral and ethical, that is, how to apply the Church's moral teachings accurately amid the growing evolution of moral situations in globalizing society. This includes massive transformations to family structures and relations as well as their impacts on children's welfare. The Catholic hierarchy of clerics that acts as the RCC's moral teachers and arbiters, however, with their fundamental training still rooted in philosophy and philosophical theology, tend to tend view moral issues theoretically rather than empirically.

The philosophical method, and philosophical–theological approaches, have inherent limitations in terms of perspective and methodology. Philosophers and theologians have no scientific methods of ascertaining whether their theorizing on human behavior and societal issues has empirical support. Thus, resolving moral issues is a largely deductive and theoretical process that does not necessarily inquire into people's social and cultural experiences, such in the case of sexuality and gender.

Can the RCC continue to maintain the philosophical approach when dealing with complex contemporary issues such as gender, sexuality, and family relations? St. Thomas's adoption of Aristotelian philosophy is obviously culture bound and not timeless. When he first attempted to incorporate the philosophy in Catholic theology, not all in the RCC were happy. He encountered opposition to his approach but eventually prevailed on its importance for addressing the signs of the times that required rational justification to the Christian faith to debunk heresies and false teachings.

The contemporary world is very different from St. Thomas's medieval world. Change is now so swift that today's society can be characterized metaphorically as undergoing "liquidity," with people, information, goods, services, or social networks becoming very mobile and in a state of flux owing to the process of globalization (Ritzer 2010). With globalization integrating the economic, political, social, and cultural life of the current age, patterns of human behavior and societal structures are undergoing constant cultural recycling and evolution. Cultures are also changing, challenging medieval and modern social orders that emphasized solidity, stability, and commitment.

While Thomistic philosophical theology is indeed indispensable in defending Church dogmas and doctrines, it has inherent limitations in dealing with contemporary moral issues that need the empirical approaches of sociology and the social sciences. Aspects of Aquinas's philosophical TNLT approach that supported the RCC's rigid view on gender as immutable and ordained by God require some updating in the light of the cultural revolution and the advent of the social sciences as a new way of gaining knowledge.

Pope Francis, being educated in the philosophical and theological Catholic tradition, may not have fully realized the implications of his synodality and synodal theology. However, these approaches encourage Catholic theologians and scholars to first explore people's lived experiences before reflecting theologically, welcoming other branches of knowledge such as sociology and the social sciences to assist theologians with scientific studies on human behavior and moral issues in synodal theologizing. To determine whether GI does indeed threaten children's welfare requires sociological research and synodal inductive theology.

GI and Defining Children's Welfare

The main conflict between the RCC's concept of gender and children's welfare and those of sociologists, feminists, and LGBTQI advocates is the fundamental difference in perspectives. Despite newer developments in the RCC, such as Francis's synodality and inductive theology, which is open to empirical and scientific perspectives, the RCC's moral magisterium still rigidly maintains the philosophical perspective based on TNLT in its approach to gender and sexuality.

Although the document "Male and Female He Created Them" made a distinction "between the ideology of gender on the one hand, and the whole field of research on gender that the human sciences have undertaken, on the other," it did clarify their fundamental difference. While encouraging dialogue to resolve the GI issue, it had already precluded this dialogue by condemning gender as understood in the social sciences.

The document inaccurately noted that "while the ideologies of gender claim to respond ... 'to what are at times understandable aspirations', they also seek 'to assert themselves as absolute and unquestionable, even dictating how children should be raised'" (Congregation of Catholic Education 2019). Research on children's welfare in same-sex families, like any scientific studies, only provides recommendations based on results rather than dictating how children should be raised, as assumed by this declaration.

The RCC's position on gender and children's welfare continues to be based on the philosophical approach, which has inappropriately judged the social science approach as "scientism" – without clearly understanding the scientific method owing to the lack of social science education for the clerics who act as moral guardians in the Church. This bias against the social sciences reflects the prevailing anti-science and anti-positivist attitudes of several Catholic bishops and theologians. As Cross (2019, para. 1) inaccurately argues:

> Many people have difficulty with the Catholic Church's teaching on sex and gender because they fail to recognize its philosophical dimension. As inheritors of twentieth-century positivism, many today assume that the quantitative sciences are the arbiters of truth, and that any other way of knowing, except that privileged and direct access to one's own internal subjectivity, can be no more than private opinion or pseudoscience. This philosophical error silences objection and shuts down dialogue by defining disagreement with itself as hateful and anathematizing.

This quote misunderstands the nature of scientific research and method. It suggests that the social sciences are pseudoscience that is primarily based on the positivist quantitative approach. It fails to understand that a positivist attitude is temporarily assumed by social scientists when doing research to minimize personal biases and subjectivity in scientific judgment. It also ignores the fact that behavioral sciences also employ qualitative approaches to understand people's motives and the meanings of their actions as well as social processes.

Behavioral and social sciences such as sociology only provide descriptive knowledge of the world and behavior and do not pretend to be absolute arbiters of truth. Scientific research is always open to dialogue. That is why research studies are always subjected to peer review and dialogue between researchers and other scholars and experts to enhance scientific knowledge.

Following its logic and deductive reasoning based on TNLT, the RCC defines children's welfare within the context of the traditional view of the family as heterosexual, with only a biological male and female as parents. Because it only recognizes gender complementarity in family relations, it ignores that fact that same-sex parents can also provide the best welfare for their children. That is why the dominance of the "traditional" family has increasingly been challenged as a larger number and proportion of individuals create more fluid and flexible family structures, redefining what it means to be a family (Teachman et al. 2004).

According to the UCLA William Institute's study (2022) "How Many Adults and Youth Identify as Transgender in the United States?" the number of people who identify as transgender has increased through the years. Around 1.3 million adults, or 0.5%, and 300,000 youth aged 13 to 17 (1.4%) were identified by the survey as transgender. With a growing number of transgender individuals, a rise in same-sex families that deviate from the RCC's standard of a heterosexual family with two biological parents can be expected.

"The term family is no longer reserved for households with children and two married biological parents but consists of an assortment of family structures, such as stepparents, single parents, and cohabiting parents" (Potter 2012, 556). Hence the rise of nontraditional families such as same-sex families. As these nontraditional families become more prominent, researchers have attempted to better understand how they affect children's outcomes (Powell, Bolzendahl, Geist, and Steelman, 2010).

Children's Welfare in Same-Sex Families

Some opponents of gay parenthood fear the homosexual orientation of the parents would affect their children's sexual orientation. But this is an unsubstantiated idea. Gay and lesbian parents are no different from heterosexual parents. "There is no actual reliable evidence that gay parents would turn their children's sexuality to homosexual because the environment is different from the others" (Chen 2017, 1). Advocates argue that children's development is unaffected by living with same-sex parents and have cited mounting evidence supporting their claim (Fairtlough 2008; Golombok et al. 2003). In general, "research on same-sex parent families has found little to suggest that children are negatively affected by living in such a family structure, although this conclusion is based on a body of research whose methodological veracity has been challenged" (Potter 2012, 556–557).

In the area of academic performance, critics of same-sex families argue that children in traditional families, understood as households having two married biological parents, tend to perform well in school compared to their peers from nontraditional families (e.g., children living with divorced parents, a single parent, or step-parents) on several indicators of academic achievement (Potter 2012). However, children of same-sex parent families tend to be an exception to this pattern: "Children with lesbian mothers or gay fathers do not exhibit the poorer outcomes typically associated with nontraditional families" (Potter 2012, 556).

There are also research studies supporting GI's moral panic that views the same-sex family as jeopardizing children's welfare. Children of homosexual couples are said to be more likely to be bullied, stigmatized, teased, harassed, and victimized by their peers in schools. They are also perceived to have trouble in social relationships. However, Chen (2018, 4) argues that "most of the cases are due to different reasons. For example, some students are bullied because they wear glasses, are less popular, are over or underweight, are of a different race or religion, are gay or lesbian, or have a disability. Students who are raised by same-sex parents would not be the only reason for facing difficulty in social relationships."

Societal Context, Homophobia, and Children's Welfare

The ultimate reason why being in same-sex families tends to be seen as detrimental to children's welfare is the prevailing societal and institutional homophobia in the RCC that sees homosexuality and same-sex parenthood as deviant and abnormal. "[H]omophobia—in its various (in)visible forms, guises, modes, patterns, and styles—constitutes a dynamic and insidious force driving and (re)shaping people's ideas, beliefs, behaviors, and discourses with respect to their sense of (im)morality, normalcy, acceptance, health, respect, sexuality, and citizenship" (Da Silva Pereira 2023, 17).

Homophobia, a term coined by the psychologist George Weinberg (2000) in the early 1970s, became widely used after the publication of his book *Society and the Healthy Homosexual*. To him, homophobia consists of:

> (a) belief systems which hold that discrimination on the basis of sexual orientation is justifiable; (b) the use of language or slang, e.g., "queer," which is offensive to gay people; and/or (c) any belief system which does not value homosexual lifestyles equally with heterosexual lifestyles. (Weinberg 2000, 46)

Contemporary scholars such as Renzetti and Edleson (2008, 338) understand homophobia as "a range of behaviors, feelings, negative attitudes towards sexual variations and people identified or perceived as LGBTQI." To West et al. (2016), "homophobia" is a shorthand for stigmatizing attitudes and practices towards people who demonstrate sexual diversity. In Christian churches such as the Roman Catholic

Church (RCC), homophobia is still considered a silent "disease" that continues to hound Catholic institutions up to the present times (Congregation for Catholic Education 2005; Cozzens 2000, 2006; Junker 2019; Callaghan 2018; Callaghan and Van Leent 2019).

In a homophobic society, no amount of empirical research can convince people such as anti-gender clerics and critics who see families of lesbians or gay parents as abnormal and different from heterosexual families. As Pennings (2011, 1609) argues, "the discrimination against same-sex families will not be overturned by empirical evidence about the welfare of the children. Children in same-sex families are generally doing well but their situation could be improved if their parents' relationship were to be socially and legally recognized." Homophobes consider that only biological parents in a heterosexual marriage can provide the best welfare for children. Indeed, homophobia is the greater evil. As Omani-Samani et al. (2007) contend, bringing up children in same-sex families in a homophobic society is completely contrary to their welfare.

The fear of homosexuality and homosexuals, which remains dominant in today's world, specifically in Christian churches such as the RCC, despite LGBTQI activism and gender research, is the main reason that same-sex parenthood is alleged to be dangerous to children's welfare and deviant in the eyes of society. To Ventriglio et al. (2021, 1), "Homophobia is still a scourge in the modern era and the fight against this social and cultural phenomenon ought to be an immediate priority."

Despite the advancement of sociological and social science research and literature on gender, sexuality, and the LGBTQI group in today's postmodern age, the fear of homosexuals and homosexuality is still dominant in Catholic theology and official doctrines. The RCC's fear of GI as jeopardizing children's welfare is one of the consequences of institutional homophobia. Gerard Loughlin (2018) argues that the institutional culture of the RCC, which is formed through the teaching of the Church's magisterium, is basically homophobic, especially in its teaching on sex and homosexuality.

The Catechism of the Catholic Church (1993), in defining homosexual attraction as "an exclusive or predominant sexual attraction toward persons of the same sex," (#2357), which is "objectively disordered" (#2358) and a sign of affective immaturity, is promoting the fear of homosexuality of any kind or homophobia in the universal Church. Yolanda Dyer (2006) contends that homophobia in the Church is a product of the hegemony of heteronormativity that sidelines sexual minorities with transgender identity and sexuality. Thus, Catholic homosexuals such as gays and lesbians who intend to marry and raise children are viewed with suspicion in the prevailing institutional homophobia of the Church.

Sociological Approach to Defining Children's Welfare

How to define and understand children's welfare in nontraditional families such as same-sex households depends on what definition one uses to judge moral situations. The RCC needs to recognize that it has no monopoly on the correct normative standard for the general welfare of children in the family, given the normative pluralism in society. Normative pluralism is increasingly pronounced in contemporary society where behavioral justification of people's actions is multiplying (Ballano 2017). Indeed, behavioral standards that guide people's actions in today's world are increasing and competing with Christian moral standards. Despite the RCC's more than 2,000 years of history and Christ's mandate to preach the Good News to all nations, society is always culturally diverse and pluralistic in judging and justifying human behavior and social norms. In their contemporary theory called the Sociology of Worth, French sociologists Boltanski and Thévenot (1991) argued that actors rely on various normative standards to justify their actions to others. People, including Christians, justify their actions to others by drawing on their experience to appeal to principles they hope will command respect. In sociology of deviance, judging human action and social condition as deviant or deviating from a behavioral standard would depend on the definition or normative standard used by the observer (Goode 2003).

The sociologist Eric Goode (2019) identified the normative definition as one of the several definitions of deviance. Under this definition, an act, person, or condition is deviant if it violates a social norm. Thus, evaluating whether children in a same-sex family are in a deviant or normal condition would depend on the moralist's normative definition. If moralists apply the RCC's heterosexual normative definition of a family, then children in a same-sex family are in a deviant and abnormal environment, thus detrimental to their personal growth and welfare. But if they uses a different definition that recognizes transgender individuals and the LGBTQI people as legitimate genders with similar rights to heterosexuals, such as the right to raise a family, then children in same-sex families can be judged as in a normal situation that is not necessarily dangerous to their welfare.

Unfortunately, no amount of convincing through scientific studies that children are safe with same-sex parents can convince people who rigidly use the heteronormative definition of the family with the prevailing societal homophobia (Pennings 2011). That is why LGBTQI groups and gender social movements lobby for the enactment of laws that protect gender equality and diversity and the rights of LGBTQI people to raise a normal family like heterosexuals. Maintaining the traditional heterosexual definition of the family based on gender complementarity that only recognizes a biological male and female couple as legitimate parents to protect children's welfare is ethnocentric.

Ethnocentrism that sees one's own culture as the best culture while others are inferior is contrary to Pope Francis's concepts of inclusivity, synodality and synodal theology, which allow divergent views and consultations with the voiceless as well as prioritizing the accurate understanding of people's lived experience before applying theological reflection and moral judgment. Thus, children's welfare should be judged appropriately using the transgender or homosexual definition of the family, not just the heterosexual standard that is currently maintained by the RCC.

Church authorities and moral theologians need to revisit the empirical foundations of gender complementarity in Genesis, to establish whether the literal interpretation of having male and a female in marital union is what the human authors intend to convey in the Biblical message.[1] This literal traditional gender complementarity interpretation of Genesis is the root cause of why homosexual marriage with the right to raise children, transgender identity, and the LGBTQI group and its non-heterosexual lifestyle and parenting are seen as GI and dangerous to children's welfare and thus cannot be fully accepted in the Christian community, despite Pope Francis's *Fiducia Supplicans* [Supplicating Trust] which allows pastoral blessing of homosexual couples (DDF 2023).

Conclusion

This chapter has unpacked the alleged claim of the RCC's GI that gender threatens children's welfare, especially children in non-heterosexual or same-sex families, using Pope Francis's synodal approach and sociological analysis. It argued that the alleged threats of same-sex couples in a same-sex family to the children's welfare are largely an exaggeration or moral panic based on an ethnocentric definition and normative standard that is biased against same-sex parenting. It contends that negative perceptions of the influence of same-sex parenthood on the children's welfare is largely a structural influence of societal homophobia and social discrimination against same-sex parents under the rigid gender complementary and heterosexual standards of the Catholic Church's moral magisterium, founded on the philosophical approach of TNLT.

This chapter recommends a synodal openness to cultural diversity and diverse family structures and definitions of children's welfare in contemporary society, as well as a sociological re-evaluation of the empirical foundations of gender complementarity as traditionally interpreted in the Book of Genesis.

References

Ballano VO (2017) Law, normative pluralism, and post-disaster recovery: evaluating the post-disaster relocation and housing project of Typhoon Ketsana Victims in the Philippines. Springer, Singapore

Bhattacherjee A (2012) Social science research: principles, methods, and practices. Textbooks Collection. Book 3. http://scholarcommons.usf.edu/oa_textbooks/3

---

[1] See Ballano 2024. "Chapter 4: Reappraising Gender Complementarity and Heterosexual Marriage in the Catholic Church." *LGBTQI Inclusivity, Homosexuality, and Same-Sex Marriage in the Catholic Church.* Singapore: Springer Nature.

Boltanski L, Thévenot L (1991) On justification: economies of worth. Princeton University Press, Trans. Catherine Porter
Burt KB, Scott J (2002) Parent and adolescent gender role attitudes in 1990s Great Britain. Sex Roles 46(7–8):239–245. https://doi.org/10.1023/A:1019919331967
Bussey K, Bandura A (1999) Social cognitive theory of gender development and differentiation. Psychol Rev 106(4):676. https://doi.org/10.1037/0033-295x.106.4.676
Callaghan TD (2018) Homophobia in the Hallways: Heterosexism and transphobia in Canadian catholic schools. University of Toronto Press, Toronto, ON
Callaghan TD, Van Leent L (2019) Homophobia in catholic schools: an exploration of teachers’ rights and experiences in Canada and Australia. J Catholic Educ 22(3):36–57. http://dx.doi.org/https://doi.org/10.15365/joce.2203032019
Catechism of the Catholic Church (1993) Vatican: Libreria Editrice Vaticana. https://www.vatican.va/archive/ENG0015/_INDEX.HTM#fonte.
Chen YJ (2018) Right of adoption for same-sex parents. Lesley University Community of Scholars Day. 11. https://digitalcommons.lesley.edu/community_of_scholars/2018/session_b/11
Cohen S (1972) Folk devils and moral panics. Paladin, Herts
Congregation for Catholic Education (2005) Instruction concerning the criteria for the discernment of vocations with regard to persons with homosexual tendencies in view of their admission to the seminary and to holy orders. Vatican.
Congregation for Catholic Education (2019) Male and female he created them: towards the path to dialogue on the question of gender theory in education. Vatican Press, Vatican
Corredor ES (2016) Unpacking ‘gender ideology’ and the global right’s anti-gender countermovement. Signs J Women Culture Society 44(3):613–638. https://doi.org/10.1086/701171
Cozzens DB (2000) The changing face of the priesthood: a reflection on the priest’s crisis of soul. Liturgical Press, Collegeville, MN
Cross BR (2019) Gender ideology and the catholic church. Life, issues.net. Available at: https://www.lifeissues.net/writers/cro/cro_01genderiddeologyandchurch.html
Da Silva Pereira R (2023) Protect the children, Save the family: ‘Gender Ideology’ in the classroom: a case study of moral panic in Brazil. MA Thesis Submitted to the Faculty of Graduate and Postdoctoral Studies, University of British Columbia, Vancouver
DDF (Dicastery of the Doctrine of the Faith) (2023) Fiducia Supplicans: on the pastoral meaning of blessings. Vatican: The Roman Curia. Available at: https://www.vatican.va/roman_curia/congregations/cfaith/documents/rc_ddf_doc_20231218_fiducia-supplicans_en.html
Dobson J (2004) Marriage under fire: why we must win this battle. Sisters, OR: Multnomah
Fairtlough A (2008) Growing up with a lesbian or gay parent: young people’s perspectives. Health Soc Care Community 16(5):521–528
Garbagnoli S (2016) Against the heresy of immanence: Vatican’s ‘gender’ as a new rhetorical device against the denaturalization of the sexual order. Religion Gender 6(2):187–204. https://doi.org/10.18352/rg.10156
Golombok S, Perry B, Burston A, Murray C, Mooney-Somers J, Stevens M, Golding J (2003) Children with lesbian parents: a community study. Dev Psychol 39(1):20–33. https://doi.org/10.1037/0012-1649.39.1.20. PMID: 12518806
Goode E (2019) Deviant behavior, 12th edn. Routledge, New York
Graff A (2016) ‘Gender Ideology’: weak concepts, powerful politics. Religion Gender 6(2):268–272. https://doi.org/10.18352/rg.10177
Junker M (2019) Ending LGBTQ employment discrimination by catholic institutions. Berkeley J Employment Labor Law 40(2):403–42. https://www.jstor.org/stable/26795249
Katz PA, Ksansnak K (1994) Developmental aspects of gender role flexibility and traditionality in middle childhood and adolescence. Dev Psychol 30(2):272–282. https://doi.org/10.1037/0012-1649.30.2.272
Loughlin G (2018) Catholic homophobia. Theology 121(3):188–196. https://doi.org/10.1177/0040571X17749147

Omani-Samani R, Dizaj AV, Taghi M, Rezania MR, Taha MS, Leila A (2007) Access to fertility treatments for homosexual and unmarried persons, through Iranian law and Islamic perspective. Iranian J Fertility Sterility 1:127–130

Pennings G (2011) Evaluating the welfare of the child in same-sex families. Hum Reprod 26(7):1609–1615

Popenoe D (1996) Life without father: compelling new evidence that fatherhood and marriage are indispensable for the good of children and society. Simon & Schuster, New York

Pope Benedict XVI (2012) Address of his holiness benedict XVI on the occasion of Christmas greetings to the Roman Curia. Vatican: Libreria Editrice Vaticana. https://www.vatican.va/content/benedict-xvi/en/speeches/2012/december/documents/hf_ben-xvi_spe_20121221_auguri-curia.html

Pope Francis (2016a) Post-Synodal exhortation Amoris Laetitia. Vatican: Dicastero per la Comunicazione—Libreria Editrice Vaticana. https://www.vatican.va/content/francesco/en/apost_exhortations/documents/papa-francesco_esortazione-ap_20160319_amoris-laetitia.html

Pope Francis (2016b) Meeting with the polish bishops: address of his holiness pope francis, 27 July 2016. Vatican: Dicastero per la Comunicazione – Libreria Editrice Vaticana https://www.vatican.va/content/francesco/en/speeches/2016/july/documents/papa-francesco_20160727_polonia-vescovi.html. Accessed 30Aoril 2024

Pope Francis (2023) Apostolic letter issued "Motu Proprio" Ad Theologiam Promovendam [To Promote Theology]. Unofficial full English translation available at: https://returntotradition.org/unofficial-full-english-translation-of-francis-revolutionary-motu-proprio-ad-theologiam-promovendam-plus-breaking-news-report-on-text/

Potter D (2012) Same-sex parent families and children's academic achievement. J Marriage Family 74:556–571. https://doi.org/10.1111/j.1741-3737.2012.00966.x

Powell B, Bolzendahl C, Geist C, Steelman LC (2010) Counted out: same-sex relations and Americans' definitions of family. Russell Sage Foundation, New York

Renzetti CM, Edleson JL (2008) Homophobia. In: Renzetti CM, Edleson Jeffrey L (eds) Encyclopedia of interpersonal violence. New York: SAGE Publications

Ritzer G (2010) Globalization: a basic text. Wiley, Hoboken, NJ

Rohloff A, Wright S (2010) Moral panic and social theory: beyond the heuristic. Curr Sociol 58(3):403–419. https://doi.org/10.1177/0011392110364039

Teachman JD, Tedrow LM, Crowder KD (2004) The changing demography of America's families. J Marriage Fam 62(4):1234–1246. https://doi.org/10.1111/j.1741-3737.2000.01234.x

UCLA William Institute (2022) Report: how many adults and youth identify as transgender in the United States? Available at: https://williamsinstitute.law.ucla.edu/publications/trans-adults-united-states/. Accessed 2 April 2024

Ventriglio A, Castaldelli-Maia JM, Torales J, DeBerardis D, Bhugra D (2021) Homophobia and mental health: a scourge of modern era. Epidemiol Psychiatric Sci 30(e52):1–3. https://doi.org/10.1017/S2045796021000391

West G, Van Der Walt C, Kaoma KJ (2016) When faith does violence: reimagining engagement between churches and LGBTI groups on homophobia in Africa. HTS: Theol Studies 72(1, a3511):1–8. https://doi.org/10.4102/hts.v72i1.3511

Wickberg D (2000) Homophobia: on the cultural history of an idea. Critical Inquiry 27(1):42–57. https://www.jstor.org/stable/1344226

Part III
Transgenderism, Human Dignity, and the Inculturation of Gender Diversity

Chapter 7
"Gender Ideology" and the Catholic Morality of Gender-Enhancing Treatment and Sex Change

Abstract This chapter aims to sociologically unpack and clarify the Catholic Church's concept of "gender ideology" and analyze the morality of gender-enhancing treatment and surgical procedures in light of Pope Francis's synodal inductive approach. It argues that the traditional philosophical moral approach grounded in natural law theory is inadequate to morally analyze these contemporary sexual issues. It recommends the sociological approach of inquiring into the motives and not just the meaning of these "unnatural" external acts before passing moral judgment, and applying the principle of double effect to understand the morality of transgenderism, gender-enhancing treatment, and transgender sexuality to resolve the moral panic of "gender ideology" in the Catholic Church.

Keywords Gender ideology · Synodality · Sociology of morality · Transgenderism · Gender dysphoria · Gender-enhancing treatment · Sex change

Introduction

Transgenderism and gender diversity have become a growing moral concern for the Roman Catholic Church (RCC) in the contemporary world where an increasing number of young people have become transgender. "Transgender" describes a person whose gender identity does not match their natal sex or does not align with traditional notions of masculinity or femininity" (Edwards-Leeper and Spack 2012, 321). Transgender people are individuals whose gender identity, that is, the internal knowledge of their gender, whether a man, woman, or other gender, is different from their sex or biological make-up at birth (National Center for Transgender Equality 2023).

Transgender people generally experience social stigma, discrimination, and harassment in society and in their church when they reveal their gender identity as a transgender woman or transgender man. Transgenderism is a growing complex moral and sexual issue that cannot be resolved by mere deductive philosophical reasoning using the traditional Thomistic natural law theory (TNLT) and the RCC's metaphysical view of sex and gender. In sociology and the social sciences, gender is a product

V. O. Ballano, *Gender Ideology and the Contemporary Catholic Church*,
https://doi.org/10.1007/978-981-97-8124-9_7

of social and cultural experience of the person. How a person develops a transgender identity during their formative years requires inductive scientific research.

One of the greatest moral challenges for the RCC in the contemporary world is how to deal with gender diversity and transgenderism. Recent papal declarations have categorized all conceptions of sex and gender that are contrary to the Church's gender complementary teaching as "gender ideology" (GI). GI as a concept originated within Catholicism, and is said to have been coined, circulated, and legitimized by Pope Benedict XVI during his pontificate (Vaggione 2020). The history of the conflict between those who support and those who resist GI is complex. It has revealed "a complicated interchange between the constellation of liberatory movements castigated by the Vatican as 'gender ideology' and the constellation of reactionary movements the Vatican and other religious conservatives developed to counter them" (Case 2019, 659).

One of the major issues raised by those who oppose GI is the alleged complete freedom of people to determine their gender in society beyond God's plan on the immutability and inseparability between sex and gender. Specifically, it condemns gender-enhancing treatment for young boys and girls. The RCC, following a strict philosophical view of morality based on TNLT, views artificial intervention in the person's body as unnatural and therefore immoral.

However, circumstances exist when children and adolescents experienced incongruence between their expressions of gender and their sex assigned at birth. This discrepancy often leads to serious mental anguish and psychological trauma, which is identified by psychologists and psychiatrists as gender dysphoria (GD). According to the American Psychiatric Association (2000, para.1), GD is "psychological distress that results from an incongruence between one's sex assigned at birth and one's gender identity. Though gender dysphoria often begins in childhood, some people may not experience it until after puberty or much later."

GD is rising among young people. Recent studies indicate a rising self-reported transgender identity among children, adolescents, and adults from 0.5 to 1.3%. This increase is much higher than the prevalence rates in clinic-referred samples of adults only, which implies an increasing prevalence of GD among the young (Hayes 2018). To address this increasing psychological problem among transgender children and adolescents, doctors usually prescribe gender-affirming hormones or drugs as the proper treatment after discovery and proper diagnosis to improve the psychological functioning and quality of life for transgender or non-binary individuals.

Access to these gender-affirming hormones is thus crucial to address the mental health and well-being of transgender people (Restar et al. 2022). GD can result in serious psychological consequences and even death or suicide among transgender youth. "Transgender youth have higher rates of anxiety, depression, substance abuse, and suicide than their peers" (SAHM 2013). Research has revealed that delaying gender-affirming treatment (GET), including puberty blockers and subsequent cross-sex hormones, is correlated with increased psychiatric comorbidity among increasingly young transgender individuals (De Vries et al. 2011).

Gender-enhancing hormones are not given indiscriminately to children and adolescents by doctors but only to those who are medically certified with GD. Yet, despite medical and psychological proof showing that gender-enhancing hormones can reduce risks of mental anguish and suicide due to GD, the RCC still views any attempt to change one's God-given gender as immoral and part of the GI discourse promoted by sociologists, feminists, and the LGBTQI group. Thus, one wonders: Is deductive philosophical reasoning to resolve the issue of the use of GET the appropriate approach to address the risk of mental anguish among young people that can result in suicide or serious psychological illness?

GET, sex change, and other medical interventions to alter one's gender are strongly condemned by the RCC as part of GI, a grave sin that violates God's divine teaching on the immutability and inseparability of sex and gender. The RCC's moral teachings subscribe to heteronormativity and cisgender, that is, one's gender should correspond to the sex one is assigned at birth. The recent Vatican declaration issued by the Dicastery for the Doctrine of the Faith (DDF 2024) entitled *Dignitas Infinita* [Infinite Dignity] strongly rejects GET and sex change as violating human dignity.

Aims and Major Arguments

The primary aim of this chapter is to sociologically evaluate the nature of the RCC's concept of GI and the morality of gender-enhancing treatment and sex change procedures to align transgender people's experience of masculinity and femininity in society with their biological sex assigned during birth to address GD and other serious psychological problems in light of Pope Francis's synodal inductive approach. Following a philosophical and metaphysical approach to sex and gender as inseparable and divinely ordained, the RCC assesses and judges sexual morality based on TNLT and deductive moral reasoning without prioritizing people's gender experience in society.

The RCC only recognizes cisgender, that is, a person's gender or expression of masculinity and femininity should align with their assigned sex at birth, applying the traditional interpretation of human creation in Genesis on natural complementary of the sexes. Thus, all human attempts to alter the ontological nature and unity of sex and gender, such as gender-enhancing drugs, puberty blockers, or medical procedures and sex change, are judged as immoral and part of GI promoted by gender sociologists, feminists, and activists to destroy humanity as created by God.

However, the traditional philosophical moral approach grounded in natural law theory is inadequate to morally analyze these contemporary sexual issues. Applying the principles of the sociology of morality and double effect, as well as Pope Francis's inductive synodal theological approach, which prioritizes people's experiences in society as the starting point for theological reflection, this chapter argues that an understanding of the personal struggles, motives, and intentions of adult transgender people and parents of minor transgender individuals availing themselves of GET or undergoing sex change is necessary to morally understand and judge their Catholic morality in today's technological age.

To frame and achieve these arguments, this chapter is divided into three main parts. The first part briefly discusses the basic concept of the emerging sub-discipline called the sociology of morality, the nature of GI, the limitations of the RCC's philosophical approach to sex, gender, and transgenderism, and the application of Pope Francis's synodality and inductive synodal theology for investigating transgenderism in contemporary society. The second part examines the Catholic morality of GET and sex change employing the inductive sociological and synodal approaches that begins with the scientific understanding of human experiences, motives, and moral situations as foundations for moral judgment and social action to resolve transgender moral issues. The final part highlights the importance of modern sociology rather than deductive philosophy for inquiring into the personal moral motives and facts of the case in transgenderism and sex change. It also applies the traditional moral principle of double effect to illustrate that transgenderism or sex change are not naturally disordered.

Theoretical Foundation

Sociology of Morality

The revival of interest in the sociology of morality has returned morality to the center stage of the sociological enterprise. Indeed, sociology was once an integral component in the scientific study of morality in society. However, its explicit focus has waned over the past half-century (Hitlin and Vaisey 2013). It is only in recent years that it has experienced a revival. The emerging field called the sociology of morality has made morality a central concern again in sociology (Abend 2010).

"Traditionally, as seen in the work of Durkheim, Goffman, and Collins, the sociology of morality emphasizes how morality binds people together through a common system of rules and expectations during interactions" (Stets and Carter 2012, 121). To them, morality is inseparable from social life (Hitlin and Vaisey 2013). Social scientists have now started to investigate and recognize the social dimensions of morality in society, but unfortunately, there is little systematic guidance for these scholars (Hitlin and Vaisey 2013, 3).

In the RCC, the anti-positivist and anti-science attitude of the Catholic hierarchy in the nineteenth century prevented a science-engaged theology and sociological morality from flourishing in Catholic research and scholarship. The strong influence of scholastic philosophy and TNLT since the medieval period has stunted the growth of sociological and social science research in the RCC. Seeing homosexuality deductively through philosophical reasoning rather than knowing the real lives of the LGBTQI group through consultation and dialogue, several Catholic bishops remain antipathetic to transgender people in the Church.

Church Teaching and Transgenderism

Although the RCC and Pope Francis have issued several pronouncements about homosexuality, homosexual union, and the LGBTQI group in the Church, no specific ecclesiastical teaching and pronouncements have been released on transgender sexuality of Catholics and people who have undergone sex change to suit their sexual and gender orientation. As Ford Jr. claims:

> At present, there is no official Catholic document that engages transgender persons directly as its principal subject. The result is that a determination about what exactly counts as "official church teaching" on the matter is complex, since any answer will essentially involve a collation of teachings, comments, and resources put out by the magisterium—more or less in passing—while focusing on other matters. (Ford Jr. 2018, 75)

Official Church documents that specifically provide moral guidelines on the ministry and pastoral care of transgender Catholics and members of the LGBTQI community in the RCC are scarce and vague (Ford 2018; Canales 2018; Herriot and Callaghan 2019). Discussions that deal with the morality of transgender sexuality and gender identity in the Church usually occur in passing as part of a larger conversation focused on family life, Catholic youth, and the environment (Roy-Steier 2021).

Pope Francis has issued some statements that relate to transgender sexuality and LGBTQI. But these statements merely reflect the traditional stance of the RCC on sex and gender. In his comments relating to transgender persons in the documents *Laudato Si'* (Pope Francis 2015) and *Amoris Laetitia* (Pope Francis 2016), for instance, Francis reiterated the magisterial teaching on sex and gender as "inseparably linked aspects of a singular reality and human identities as immutable and created by God."

Like his predecessors Pope John Paul II and Pope Benedict XVI, Francis has clearly re-echoed traditional teaching that sees the inseparability of sex and gender, and those who oppose this teaching as people who advocate "gender ideology." As Ford Jr. (2018, 77) contends:

> Francis gathers all opposition to current magisterial teaching with respect to sex and gender and gives it the name of 'ideology.' To do this, he creates a dichotomy between those who believe the truth, which is coextensive with the magisterium's position, and those who do not so believe the truth, who choose instead to give in to 'ideology.'

Medical Intervention in Transgenderism as GI

Instead of seeing the empirical situation and inquiring into the real experiences of children and young people suffering with GD, the RCC immediately dismisses any gender transition process that changes the person's gender assigned at birth as part the GI discourse that one has the absolute freedom to choose whatever gender one wants to be without regard to God's plan.

The misunderstanding of the true nature of gender and gender theory in society espoused by sociologists, feminists, and gender reformers has magnified the RCC's perception of the threats of GI to society's moral order. Without scientifically verifying the intricacies and diversity of gender theories through scientific research, the RCC perceives GI as directly attacking the Church's traditional teachings on gender, gender complementarity, and heterosexual marriage and family life.

In Catholic Poland, for instance, GI has been condemned with empirical support "as responsible for low birth rates, the collapse of traditional family models, the breakdown of marriages, abortion, homosexuality, sexual freedom due to contraception, the early sexualization of children and many other…negative phenomenon that are a threat to family, society and the whole of humanity" (Odrowąż-Coates, 2015, 28). Bracke and Paternotte (2016, 145) claim that:

> [t]he Catholic Church…has a legacy of enabling various kinds of spaces for those whose lives are not easily molded into heteronormative marriage and has eagerly and lavishly entertained homosociability and also homoeroticism. It is, therefore, all but helpful to cast 'gender ideology' as a return to a traditional Catholic regime of sexual difference, yet that is often the claim that those who resist 'gender' seek to make.

Currently, powerful conservative actors and organizations continue to uphold the ideology of the healthy and traditional heterosexual family that opposes transgenderism, gender diversity, and LGBTQI rights. They propagate an anti-gender discourse that promotes the notion that society will disintegrate if human sexuality is not controlled (Baird, 2007). The only acceptable way of preserving society and the "traditional family" as well as ensuring public health and safety under this discourse is promoting traditional sexual practices that maintain the religious concept of a "natural" sexual order (Baird 2007).

From the mid-1990s onwards, the RCC has strengthened its moral guardianship of a strict sexual morality that defends "culture of life" and has started employing GI as a rhetorical device to counter "the denaturalization of the family and the degendering of social relationships" (Corredor 2016: 620). In the early 2000s, Pope John Paul II stated that "misleading concepts concerning sexuality and the dignity and mission of the woman" were driven by specific gender ideologies (Corredor 2016: 615).

The Pontifical Council for the Family further declared that a "feminist ideology … known as 'gender' had produced misunderstandings of the complementary difference between man and woman and "a growing confusion about sexual identity" that "complicates the assumption of roles and the sharing of tasks in the home" (Corredor 2016: 615). Pope John Paul II upheld the traditional Church teaching that saw male and female as naturally complementary in his theology of the body. To John Paul II, "When considered together [as man and woman], they produce a unified reality, forming a whole that neither of them could form alone": "Masculinity and femininity express the twofold aspect of man's somatic constitution… [which] consists in reciprocal enrichment" (Ford Jr. 2018, 81).

The RCC believes in gender equality but relates it to gender complementarity. To the Catholic hierarchy, "transgressing the assigned identities means denial of the 'natural' role, that is, given by God" (Szwed and Zielinska 2017, 121). The RCC further views heterosexuality as natural and closely related to male and female bodies.

Synodality in Analyzing Transgender Realities

If GI is constructed as a moral panic rather than a reflection of people's gender experiences in society, then it runs contrary to Pope Francis's synodality and his paradigm shift in Catholic theology that calls for an inductive synodal theological approach. Synodality implies the adoption of an inductive theological approach that begins with human experience, consulting people from below, especially those on the peripheries of the Church and society. It includes the application of other branches of knowledge to understand the cultural revolution of the current age. In his document *Ad Theologiam Promovendam* [To Promote Theology] (*ATP*), issued after the first roundtable discussions of the Synod on Synodality (SoS) in Rome in October 2023, Pope Francis (2023) wants an inductive theology rather than a deductive one based on abstract concepts of the past. He encourages multi-disciplinary approaches and science-engaged theologies to give an accurate account of human experience before theological reflection. Following Francis's inductive synodal theology to resolve the issue of GI implies first understanding people's experiences of gender in society, reading the descriptive sociological and scientific studies on gender and women's movements against gender inequality, before passing judgments on the perceived threats and evils of GI to the Church and society.

Transgender people are persons "whose gender identity does not match their natal sex or does not align with traditional notions of masculinity or femininity" (Edwards-Leeper and Spack 2012, 321). This situation is largely unintentional and a product of the person's socialization and social learning. The nonconformity of their gender identity to their biological sex causes grave psychological consequences that the RCC and moral theologians should not ignore. "Transgender youth have higher rates of anxiety, depression, substance abuse, and suicide than their peers (SAHM 2013). Delaying gender-affirming treatment, including puberty blockers and subsequent cross-sex hormones, is correlated with further increased psychiatric comorbidity within this population (De Vries et al. 2011). Parents also face psychological traumas on how to deal with their transgender children as Howe (2021, 78) argues:

> Parents, even when they are optimally supportive, may face multiple traumas. In some cases, traumas may include deciding what to name their child and how to dress their child, and, later, whether and when to approve puberty-blocking drugs, gender-enhancing medications, and surgeries that may be irreversible. Their greatest challenge may be, however, to become able to love their child just as the child is.

Indeed, for transgender people and parents of transgender children, it is not easy to decide whether to undergo gender-enhancing treatment or surgical procedures that are irreversible because of the biological consequences of the sex change or GET. The moral dilemma is whether to give priority to an intervention that will help adolescents become who they are, or to withhold an intervention to better protect adolescents from making choices that they may later want to reverse. "The needs of transgender individuals are unique, and the importance of their needs may transcend those of most other patients" (Howe 2021, 284).

Puberty blockers are offered in clinics to help the child avoid puberty and GD. The prescribing of puberty blockers (PBs) for children with GD is highly contentious and has polarized views among both clinicians and bioethicists (Dyer 2020; McGregor, and Phillips 2021). "In the past, PBs were primarily used to treat precocious puberty but more recently they have, increasingly, been given to children presenting with GD" (Latham 2022, 269).

Several research studies have shown positive results in the use of gender-enhancing drugs and PBs by transgender people. These benefits include returning to normal limits in adulthood (Cohen-Kettenis et al. 2011), better results for biological female patients undergoing mastectomy (Khatchadourian et al., 2014), improvement in secondary sexual traits (Schagen et al. 2016), enhancement in psychological and social life (Schneider et al. 2017), progress in general functioning, a decline in depressive symptoms as well as emotional and behavioral problems (De Vries et al. 2011), and most importantly, lower lifetime rates of suicide (Turban et al. 2020).

The benefits of using gender-enhancing drugs and treatment are also accompanied by risks, as some studies reveal. Among children, one negative effect consisted of mood swings and emotional liability (Khatchadourian et al., 2014). Another negative outcome included various bodily changes such as increased fat (Klaver et al. 2018). The higher cost of obtaining these gender medical procedures, especially for those who have no insurance, is also a problem (Nahata et al. 2017). Other risks included slow growth, decline in lean body mass, decreased height velocity (Schagen et al., 2016), and a lowering of bone turnover markers (Vlot et al. 2017).

Of course, the health of the individual is also a paramount consideration in analyzing the morality of GET for overcoming GD, which might lead to serious psychological problems or suicide. Hormonal treatment offers hope and risks, and needs more research to understand the long-term effects. But this does not prevent young transgenders and their parents with good intention to avail of this treatment to address the adverse effects of GD" (Rew et al. 2021, 9). Not all cases involving hormone injections and surgical procedures for transgender people end up in total failure.

As Rew et al. (2021, 4) argue:

> Hormonal treatment, including the use of puberty suppressing drugs, provides a potentially life-saving solution for these patients, yet for this specific population of patients, the long-term consequences of these drugs are relatively unknown…For children and adolescents who experience gender dysphoria (GD), the possibility of receiving this treatment provides hope; however, the lack of longitudinal evidence may lead to barriers in accessing and receiving treatment.

Advances of gender technology in transforming biological sex into the desired gender mean that the mere deductive reasoning and philosophical approach of the traditional TNLT would be inadequate to address these complexities. Clinically, transgender people have unique needs. Selvaggi and Giordano (2014) argue that "trans people are necessarily an 'inherently complex,' separate category of patients because their motivations are different, and the purposes of surgery are different" (Latham 2017, 40).

> Increasingly, early adolescents who are transgender or gender diverse (TGD) are seeking gender affirming healthcare services. Pediatric healthcare providers supported by professional guidelines are treating many of these children with gonadotropin-releasing hormone agonists (GnRHa), which reversibly block pubertal development, giving the child and their family more time in which to explore the possibility of medical transition. (Rew et al. 2021, 3)

A review by Rew et al. (2021) of studies on puberty suppression in young transgender people with gender dysphoria revealed positive results such as decreased suicidality in adulthood, improved affect and psychological functioning, and improved social life:

> Adverse factors associated with use were changes in body composition, slow growth, decreased height velocity, decreased bone turnover, cost of drugs, and lack of insurance coverage. Given the potentially life-saving benefits of these medications for TGD youth, it is critical that rigorous longitudinal and mixed methods research be conducted that includes stakeholders and members of the gender diverse community with representative samples. (Rew et al. 2021, 3)

Sociology of Morality and Inquiry into Motives

Modern sociology, with its emphasis on the understanding of human behavior through scientific methods, has much to offer the RCC and Catholic theology. Sociology can generate reliable and cumulative knowledge of the regular patterns of social phenomena to be used by Catholic moral theologians as the empirical foundation before applying the Church's ethical principles in their theological reflection. The revival of interest in the sociology of morality has returned morality to the center stage of the sociological enterprise. Indeed, sociology was once an integral component of the scientific study of morality in society.

Despite Auguste Comte's intention of establishing sociology as a rational religion in society, sociological enterprise does not intend to disprove the doctrinal and moral claims of the Church and its theologians, but insists on the empirical understanding of human behavior and social issues as the starting point of moral analysis. To Max Weber, one of the main pillars of modern sociology, a moral (value-laden) action is a vital force in society and an empirical analysis of this type of action is a fundamental component of the sociological method (Weber 1978).

In his classic work *The Protestant Ethic and the Spirit of Capitalism*, Weber (2009) emphasized the study of motives in moral actions. In studying moral action as a social action, Weber identified two forms of understanding: the observational understanding that aims to interpret the meaning of the external act; and the interpretive understanding that intends to know the real motive of the act. In his concept of *Verstehen* or interpretive understanding, he emphasized knowing the person's motives beyond understanding the meaning of their external acts or stereotypes. It implies putting oneself into the shoes of the other to understand the true meaning of their external action.

Resolving the moral issue of GET and other cosmetic surgeries transforming gender to address the mental anguish and risk of suicide among transgender youth needs inductive inquiry into human motives. This approach is backed up by the traditional moral approach that requires to know the person's intention before judging whether an action constitutes a grave sin or a venial sin. In evaluating the sources of morality in the RCC, the Catechism of the Catholic Church (1993, #1750) highlights the following components: the object chosen, the end in view or the intention, and the circumstance of the action. Thus, the intention or motive of the actor in an act is crucial to evaluate morality:

> **1752** In contrast to the object, the intention resides in the acting subject. Because it lies at the voluntary source of an action and determines it by its end, intention is an element essential to the moral evaluation of an action. The end is the first goal of the intention and indicates the purpose pursued in the action. The intention is a movement of the will toward the end: it is concerned with the goal of the activity. It aims at the good anticipated from the action undertaken.

Understanding the morality of an action through understanding human intention and not just the external act is in keeping with Max Weber's sociological concept of *Verstehen*. This also requires – as Pope Francis always insists in his synodality – listening to people's concerns before passing theological or moral judgment.

Moral Situations and Motives in GET and Sex Change

In the latest document from the Dicastery of the Doctrine of the Faith (DDF 2024), entitled *Dignitas Infinita* [Infinite Dignity] (*DI*), the RCC reiterated the metaphysical view of human dignity that is tied to its teaching on gender complementarity, which interprets the creation of a man and a woman in Genesis literally, thus retaining the strict heteronormativity that rejects all forms of gender diversity as well as GET and sex change. However, *DI*'s moral teaching on human dignity has to be applied carefully by transgender Catholics (and their parents in the case of minors) in their assessment of the evolving moral situation and purification of motives.

As yet there are no longitudinal studies on GET and sex change to judge conclusively their risks to transgender individuals (Rew et al. 2021). GET and gender surgical procedures carry benefits and risks, and can be irreversible. Sex change can also make people sterile. However, all cases of sex change are different and thus subject to inductive inquiry and Christian discernment. Externally, according to *DI,* these acts appear to be immoral and violative of human dignity. However, for transgender individuals who experience GD and all sorts of social discrimination in society, GET and sex change can be the only way to "redeem" their human dignity. Thus, morally judging these actions requires careful inductive and sociological analysis of the entire meaning of these acts. The morality must be judged based on the transgender individual's intention and those of the parents. Basically, transforming one's assigned biological sex to treat serious psychological disorder such as GD is morally good or at least morally neutral. Internally, transgender people resorting to GET and sex change are aiming to align their gender identity with their biological sex in order to achieve personal wholeness, happiness, and social acceptance. Their primary motive is to cure GD and attain social integration. Overcoming mental anguish and maintaining psychological balance and mental health are primary ethical concerns. By insisting on the ontological approach to transgenderism detached from actual human experience, the RCC unintentionally appears uncaring to the non-binary people and LGBTQI people that Pope Francis aims to welcome as part of his synodal church.

Applying the Principle of Double Effect[1]

The complex moral issue of GET and sex change needs inductive synodal and sociological analysis. The traditional tool for moral analysis in the RCC called the "principle of double effect" (PDE) which first investigates human motives may also be relevant. Under PDE, there are human actions which have two effects – one good and the other bad – that need to be resolved by inquiring into motives. This method is appropriate for analyzing the Catholic morality of GET and sex change. As Dr Carol Bayley (2016, 3) contends on sex change:

> This tool allows us to think through whether a negative outcome is morally permissible when it is foreseen but not intended. The action undertaken must be good or at least neutral; the desired effect must be good; the bad effect must not be the means to the good effect and the action undertaken must be proportionate to the desired good outcome" (Bayley 2016, 3).

Using the moral principle of double effect, Bayley (2016) then morally justifies sex change to suit the person's gender. She explains the unforeseen effect of sterility in sex change for transgender people. But the act of surgery is morally neutral. And the ultimate intention or motive of the intended effect is not evil but good:

> In the case of bottom surgery that will sterilize the person, I believe that we can use the rule of double effect in a similar way. The surgery itself is neutral. The good effect, from the perspective of the person undergoing it, is that his or her body will come to present to the world the person in the gender he or she experiences inside. The relief of suffering this represents is profound. (Bayley 2016, 4)

Sex change not only provides personal satisfaction for transgender individuals but also the legal recognition of changing their gender and name. Like the RCC, most current legal systems only recognize heterosexuality and sex as the basis for gender. "Courts generally will not recognize a transgender person's chosen sex or gender without the undergoing sex change surgery, and preoperative transgender individuals are sometimes precluded from legal name change as well" (Ben-Asher 2006, 55). Transgender people can then enjoy legal status and other societal benefits if their gender is aligned with their sex.

---

[1] This section is largely based on Chap. 8 of the book by the author entitled "LGBTQI Inclusivity, Homosexuality, and Same-Sex Marriage in the Catholic Church: Pope Francis's Synodal Theology, Sociology, and Moral Issues. Singapore: Springer Nature.

The crux of the issue why the RCC still rejects transgender sexuality and identity, as well as sex change, is the traditional belief based on a metaphysical understanding that sex and gender are inseparable and immutable, and that heterosexuality is the only norm for sexual and gender identity. This is contrary to the sociological and inductive approach that first investigates the empirical reality and the real intentions and motives of the person in judging transgender sexuality and identity.

Clearly, sex is biological, but gender is social and experiential, learned by the person through the normal socialization process in society. Gender is not a personal intention, but a social product not primarily planned by the person. Thus, it is not a sign of immaturity on the part of the person, as the traditional moral teaching of the Church still claims, if he or she assumes a transgender sexuality and identity after birth. "Gender" is a social behavior or norm while "sex," based on biology, is permanent, non-negotiable, and objective. While gender is often considered to be something that bodies *do*, sex is often considered what *are*" (Ben-Asher 2006, 52–53).

Synodal-Sociological Approach to GET and Sex Change

The serious psychological consequences of GD are legitimate empirical and moral concerns that cannot be resolved by mere logic and philosophical moral reasoning. It requires discernment, as Pope Francis suggested during his Christmas address to the Roman Curia – that life is bigger than ideas and theories. Thus, applying Francis's inductive synodal theology, facts and motives for transgender people (and their parents) who have opted to undergo GET or sex change to address GD and attain happiness and social well-being should be carefully examined. Obviously, GET and surgical procedures have short-term and long-term good and bad effects, as research studies show, although no longitudinal research has yet been done to measure their long-term effects on the person's health and mental well-being (Rew et al. 2021). Thus, facts are necessary, requiring social science research to guide doctors, parents, and caregivers who are involved in GET and sex change to address GD and the social exclusion related to transgenderism before making moral judgments and decision.

If Church tradition is living, evolving and not static, constantly adapting to societal and cultural changes, then moral teachings should also be updated as the moral situation today has also greatly changed. Transgender sexuality, for instance, is part of the technological advancement of society that nowadays allows people to change their sex However, owing to a lack of dialogue between Catholic theologians and sociologists and anthropologists, the RCC's understanding of gender and transgenderism lacks scientific grounding.

Moral teachings are not like creedal or dogmatic teachings, which do not largely depend on the moral situation to be morally acceptable. The latter are a non-negotiable matter of belief and assent for Catholics. The former are different, their applicability depending on accurate understanding of the social and cultural contexts of the moral situations, which are fast evolving, and the application of Church's moral principles are largely dependent on scientific readings of these contexts.

Sociology of morality applies what Max Weber calls an "interpretive understanding" of moral actions; inquiring into people's motives for their actions to fully understand the meaning of their external acts is in consonance with Francis's inductive theology that sees life and empirical reality as larger than the philosophical and theological ideas of Catholic theologians and top clerics. As Francis claimed during his BBC interview, "If a person is gay and seeks God and has good will, who am I to judge?" (BBC 2013).

Thus, if gay and transgender people, as well as parents of transgender children, sincerely examine the facts about GET and sex change, discerning to sincerely find God's will, and ultimately decide to avail themselves of GET and sex change, who are we to judge their external acts as morally evil? The RCC's difficulty understanding the human experience of transgender people and inquiring into their motives for GET and sex change is the hegemony of the deductive philosophical moral framework of the TNLT – which, as a purely philosophical approach to morality, is insensitive to human experience and gender relations in the contemporary world. It conceives Catholic morality in the metaphysical sense that sees gender as immutable, ahistorical, and divinely ordained. Thus, a shift to a more inductive, sociological, and synodal moral framework in the spirit of the RCC's teaching on inculturation and Francis's inductive theology is necessary if LGBTQI people are finally to be fully welcomed in the RCC.

Conclusion

This chapter has sociologically clarified the Catholic Church's concept of "gender ideology" and analyzed the morality of gender-enhancing treatment and sex change to align transgender people's gender identity with their biological sex to address gender dysphoria and other psychological problems in light of Pope Francis's synodal inductive approach. It contended that the traditional philosophical moral approach grounded in natural law theory is inadequate to morally analyze these contemporary sexual issues. It recommended the sociological approach of inquiring into the motives and not just the meaning of these "unnatural" external acts before passing moral judgment, as well as applying the principle of double effect as appropriate to understand the morality of transgenderism, gender-enhancing treatment, and transgender sexuality, thus dissolving the moral panic of GI in the Catholic Church.

References

Abend G (2010) What's new and what's old about the new sociology of morality, pp 561–86 in Handbook of the sociology of morality, edited by S Hitlin and S Vaisey. New York: Springer

American Psychiatric Association (2000) What is gender dysphoria? Available at: https://www.psychiatry.org/patients-families/gender-dysphoria/what-is-gender-dysphoria
Baird V (2007) The no-nonsense guide to sexual diversity (No-Nonsense Guides). New Internationalist, Oxford, UK
Bayley C (2016) Transgender persons and catholic healthcare. Healthcare Ethics USA 24(1):1–17
BBC (2013) Pope Francis: who am I to judge gay people? BBC News Website. https://www.bbc.com/news/world-europe-23489702
Ben-Asher N (2006) The necessity of sex change: a struggle for intersex and Transsex liberties. 29 Harvard J Law Gender 51, http://digitalcommons.pace.edu/lawfaculty/591/
Bracke S, Paternotte D (2016) Unpacking the sin of gender. Religion Gender 6(2):143–154. https://doi.org/10.18352/rg.10167
Canales AD (2018) Ministry to transgender teenagers (part one): pursuing awareness and understanding about trans youth. J Pastoral Care Counseling 72(3):195–201. https://doi.org/10.1177/1542305018790216
Case MA (2019) Trans Formations in the Vatican's War on 'gender ideology'. Signs J Women Culture Society 44(3):639–664
Catechism of the Catholic Church (1993) Libreria Editrice Vaticana. https://www.vatican.va/archive/ENG0015/_INDEX.HTM#fonte
Cohen-Kettenis PT, Schagen SEE, Steensma TD, DeVries ALC, Delemarre-van de Waal HA (2011) Puberty suppression in a gender-dysphoric adolescent: A 22-year follow-up. Arch Sex Behav 40:843–847
Corredor ES (2016) Unpacking 'gender ideology' and the global right's anti-gender countermovement. Signs J Women Culture Society 44(3):613–638. https://doi.org/10.1086/701171
DDF (Dicastery of the Doctrine of the Faith) (2024) Declaration Dignitas Infinita on human dignity. Vatican: The Roman Curia. https://www.vatican.va/roman_curia/congregations/cfaith/documents/rc_ddf_doc_20240402_dignitas-infinita_en.html
De Vries ALC, Steensma TD, Doreleijers TAH, Cohen-Kettenis PT (2011) Puberty suppression in adolescents with gender identity disorder: a prospective follow-up study. J Sexual Med 8:2276–2283
Dyer C (2020) Children are "highly unlikely" to be able to consent to taking puberty blockers. Rules High Court. British Medical Journal 371:m4699
Edwards-Leeper L, Spack NP (2012) Psychological evaluation and medical treatment of transgender youth in an interdisciplinary "Gender Management Service" (GeMS) in a major pediatric center. J Homosexuality 59:321e36
Ford CJ (2018) Transgender bodies, catholic schools, and a queer natural law theology of exploration. J Moral Theol 7(1):70–98
Hayes K (2018) Ethical implications of treatment for gender dysphoria in youth. J Health Ethics 14(2). https://doi.org/10.18785/ojhe.1402.03
Herriot L, Callaghan TD (2019) Possibilities for trans-affirming policy potential: a case study of a Canadian Catholic school. J Catholicc 22(3):57–83. Education. https://doi.org/10.15365/joce.2203042019
Hitlin S, Vaisey S (2013) The new sociology of morality. Annual Rev Sociol 39(1):51–68
Howe EG (2021) At the bedside: caring for transgender adolescents. J Clin Ethics 32(4):277–286
Khatchadourian K, Amed S, Metzer DL (2014) Clinical management of youth with gender dysphoria in vancouver. J Pediatr 164:906–911
Klaver M, de Mutsert R, Wiepjes CM, Twisk JWR, den Heijer M, Rotteveel J, Klink DT (2018) Early hormonal treatment affects body composition and body shape in young transgender adolescents. J Sexual Med 15:251–260
Latham JR (2017) Making and treating trans problems: the ontological politics of clinical practices. Studies Gender Sexuality 18(1):40–61. https://doi.org/10.1080/15240657.2016.1238682
McGregor D, Phillips C (2021) High court ruling on puberty blockers will worsen trans healthcare. BMJ 372:n219

Nahata L, Quinn GP, Caltabellotta NM, Tishelman AC (2017) Mental health concerns and insurance among transgender adolescents. LGBT Health 4:188–193

National Center for Transgender Equality (2023) Understanding transgender people: the basics. National Center for Transgender Equality Website. https://transequality.org/issues/resources/understanding-transgender-people-the-basics

Odroważ-Coates A (2015) Is gender neutrality a post-human phenomenon? The concept of ‘gender neutral’ in Swedish education. J Gender Power 3(1):113–133

Pope Francis (2015) Laudato si [Praise Be To You]: Encyclical Letter of Pope Francis on the Care on Care of Our Common Home.” Vatican: Dicastero per la Comunicazione—Libreria Editrice Vaticana.https://www.vatican.va/content/francesco/en/encyclicals/documents/papa-francesco_20150524_enciclica-laudato-si.html

Pope Francis (2016) Post-Synodal exhortation Amoris Laetitia. Vatican: Dicastero per la Comunicazione—Libreria Editrice Vaticana. https://www.vatican.va/content/francesco/en/apost_exhortations/documents/papa-francesco_esortazione-ap_20160319_amoris-laetitia.html

Pope Francis (2023) Apostolic Letter Issued “Motu Proprio” Ad Theologiam Promovendam [To Promote Theology]. Unofficial full English translation available at: https://returntotradition.org/unofficial-full-english-translation-of-francis-revolutionary-motu-proprio-ad-theologiam-promovendam-plus-breaking-news-report-on-text/

Restar A, Dusic EJ, Garrison-Desany H et al (2022) Gender affirming hormone therapy dosing behaviors among transgender and Nonbinary adults. Humanities Soc Sci Commun 9(304):1–11. https://doi.org/10.1057/s41599-022-01291-5

Rew L, Young CC, Monge M, Bogucka R (2021) Review: puberty blockers for transgender and gender diverse youth—a critical review of the literature. Child Adolescent Mental Health 26(1):3–14. https://doi.org/10.1111/camh.12437

Romeo M, Cruz M, A new priest for a new society? The masculinity of the Priesthood in Liberal Spain. J Religious History 45(4):540–558. https://doi.org/10.1111/1467-9809.12799

Roy-Steier S (2021) Coming up short: the Catholic Church’s pastoral response to the transgender crisis in America. Religions 12(337):1–20. https://doi.org/10.3390/rel12050337

SAHM (Society for Adolescent Health and Medicine) (2013) Recommendations for promoting the health and well-being of lesbian, gay, bisexual, and transgender adolescents: a position paper of the society for adolescent health and medicine. J Adolescent Health 52:506e10

Schagen SEE, Cohen-Kettenis PT, Delemarre-van de Waal HA, Hannema SE (2016) Efficacy and safety of gonadotropin-releasing hormone agonist treatment to suppress puberty in gender dysphoric adolescents. J Sex Med 13:1125–1132

Schneider MA, Spritzer PM, Soll BMB, Fontanari AMV, Carneiro M, Tovar-Moll F, … Lobato MIR (2017) Brain maturation, cognition, and voice pattern in a gender dysphoria case under pubertal suppression. Frontiers Human Neuroscience 11:528

Selvaggi G, Giordano S (2014) The role of mental health professionals in gender reassignment surgeries: unjust discrimination or responsible care? Aesthetic Plast Surg 38:1177–1183

Stets JE, Carter MJ (2012) A theory of the self for the sociology of morality. Am Sociol Rev 77(1):120–140

Szwed A, Zielińska K (2017) A war on gender? The Roman catholic Church’s discourse on gender in Poland. In: Ramet S, Borowik I (eds), Religion, politics, and values in Poland. Palgrave Studies in Religion, Politics, and Policy. Palgrave Macmillan, New York. https://doi.org/10.1057/978-1-137-43751-8_6

Turban JL, King D, Carswell JM, Keuroghlian AS (2020) Pubertal suppression for transgender youth and risk of suicidal ideation. Pediatrics 145:e20191725

Vaggione JM (2020) The conservative uses of law: the catholic mobilization against gender ideology. Social Compass 67(2):252–266. https://doi.org/10.1177/0037768620907561journals.sagepub.com/home/scp

Vlot MC, Klink D, den Heijer M, Blankenstein MA, Rotteveel J, Heijboer A (2017) Effect of pubertal suppression and cross-sex hormone therapy on bone turnover markers and bone mineral apparent density (BMAD) in transgender adolescents. Bone 95:11–19

Weber M (1978) Economy and society. University of California Press, Berkeley
Weber M (2009) From max weber: essays in sociology, 1st edn. Routledge, London

Chapter 8
Human Dignity and Gender Issues in Contemporary Society: A Synodal-Sociological Exploration

Abstract This chapter sociologically explores how the Catholic Church's teaching on human dignity can be applied in the field of sex and gender in today's contemporary world in accordance with Pope Francis's inductive synodal theology and the Vatican's declaration on human dignity known as *Dignitas Infinita* [Infinite Dignity]. It argues that teaching on human dignity is central to the Christian faith for Catholics and must always be observed in resolving moral issues. However, in the spirit of Francis's inductive theology, the application of this teaching in concrete cases such as the morality of gender-enhancing treatment and sex change requires inductive synodal and sociological assessment to scientifically describe the complex moral situation and motives of actors. The chapter also sociologically re-examines the empirical basis of Genesis on gender complementarity—the root cause of why transgenderism, gender-enhancing treatment, and sex change are generally seen as violative of human dignity.

Keywords Human dignity · Inductive synodal theology · Sociology · Gender · Gender diversity · Transgenderism · LGBTQI

Introduction

Social and Conceptual Background

The fluid modern world continues to manifest complex behavioral patterns and human situations that pose serious moral challenges to the Roman Catholic Church's (RCC) deductive philosophical moral framework based on natural law, especially on the complex issues of sex, gender, and transgenderism. Unlike the previous medieval and modern periods, today's social structure is very fluid, "liquid," and always in a state of flux (Bauman 2000, 2003; Giddens 2002; Ritzer and Dean 2019). The advent of sociology and the social sciences has also challenged scholastic philosophy and philosophical theology in the RCC as the primary conceptual tools to understand human society and behavior.

V. O. Ballano, *Gender Ideology and the Contemporary Catholic Church*,
https://doi.org/10.1007/978-981-97-8124-9_8

The primary challenge of the RCC in today's globalizing and liquid world is not primarily doctrinal but moral, that is, how to apply the Church's various moral teachings in the highly evolving social structure of postmodern society. With the growing complexity of human behavior patterns, specifically on gender identity and diversity, that is facilitated by the swift advancement of biomedicine, biotechnology, and gender-enhancing therapies and sex-change surgical procedures, applying moral principles in concrete human and medical situations such as human dignity may appear very complicated to most clerics and Catholic moral theologians who have been primarily educated in the normative disciplines of philosophy and theology.

Despite the growing integration of all aspects of life because of globalization, which in the current age needs the scientific method to accurately understand behavioral and moral issues, the RCC still sees philosophy as the main conceptual tool to address moral problems and questions about life for clerics and seminarians. Thus, it retains philosophy as the primary preparatory course for theological studies in Catholic seminaries, colleges, and universities. Vatican II's *Optatam, Totius* (Decree on Priestly Training) (1965) still acknowledges the central role of the philosophical disciplines in priestly formation, despite the significant historical, cultural, and social changes of modern times (Ballano 2021).

After centuries of fighting heresies and doctrinal errors using the philosophical approach to provide rational justification for the Christian faith, the RCC has gradually organized and codified its doctrinal and moral teachings. Catholic doctrines on faith and morals that protect Catholic orthodoxy are largely fixed and codified. The philosophical approach of the Thomistic natural law theory (TNLT) became the theological foundation of Catholic morality. The main pastoral challenge for the RCC, however, is how to apply moral doctrines in contemporary moral situations which are always in a constant state of flux, with the advancement of technology and the increasing globalization of society.

The synthesis of the pagan Aristotelian philosophy and Catholic theology as well as the adaptation of the stoic natural law theory by St. Thomas Aquinas during the medieval period have played a crucial role in clarifying and organizing Church moral doctrines. The Second Vatican Council (Vatican II), a universal gathering of all Catholic bishops with the Pope in the early 1960s to update Catholic teachings in society, also played a crucial role in adapting Church teachings in modern and postmodern times.

Despite Vatican II's Church reforms and *aggriornamiento* [renewal] to make the Church mission more relevant and responsive to the needs of the times, the RCC remains cautious and conservative, and continues to embrace philosophy with its deductive reasoning based on TNLT to deal with contemporary social and moral issues. However, the pontificate of Pope Francis has made great strides to supplement philosophical approaches with scientific methods to understand people's lived experiences in society as the starting point of doing theology.

Recently, Francis convened the ecclesiastical reform project, the Synod on Synodality (SoS), to implement Vatican II's reforms for contemporary times. In his document *Ad Theologiam Promovendam* (*ATP*), he called for a paradigm shift in doing theology and stressed the need for understanding the cultural revolution of the times through an inductive, interdisciplinary, and scientific approach to apply Church doctrines in accordance with people's lived experiences in society (Francis 2023).

How the RCC's moral guardians—still largely trained in the prescriptive disciplines of scholastic philosophy and philosophical theology—are to apply Church doctrines within constantly evolving human behavioral patterns and moral cases in the current technological age is a difficult challenge for the contemporary Church. The moral theologians and guardians of the Dicastery of the Doctrine of the Faith (DDF) are still thinking in prescriptive, deductive, or normative terms of philosophy and philosophical theology in resolving moral issues, while the moral situations of these issues that require specialized knowledge of the social sciences and scientific method have greatly evolved.

Evolving moral situations in the contemporary world need the social or behavioral sciences to fully understand facts, cases, and motives, as well as behavioral patterns and their holistic sociological meanings, before applying the RCC's moral principles to resolve them. With their lack of empirical methods, philosophy and philosophical theology as normative and prescriptive disciplines primarily apply deductive reasoning to assess moral issues in society—failing to use immersion and inductive research to completely know the human experience of people from below before passing moral judgment.

Human Dignity and Gender Complementarity

Recently, the RCC's Dicastery for the Doctrine of the Faith (DDF) published a declaration entitled *Dignitas Infinita* [Infinite Dignity] (*DI*), a 20-page document, which is said to have been five years in the making and was approved by Pope Francis on March 25, 2024. It was aimed as an ethical guide for Catholics to expound the Church's moral doctrine on human dignity and to analyze a range of contemporary moral issues such as gender, gender ideology, and gender-enhancing treatment and sex change (DDF 2024). Using a deductive philosophical–theological approach, it highlights the ontological nature of human dignity that is intrinsically connected to the gender complementary of the sexes.

DI particularly stated that each person has human dignity because they are willed, created, and loved by God. It teaches that ontological dignity is infinite and indelible. It is valid beyond any circumstances in which the person may find themselves: "This dignity of every human being can be understood as "infinite" (dignitas infinita) … as Pope St. John Paul II affirmed…[that] human dignity transcends all outward appearances and specific aspects of people's lives" (DDF 2024, 2). According to *DI*, the metaphysical nature of human dignity is linked with the gender complementary teaching of Genesis, thus excluding any form of gender diversity and suggesting that gender alteration is violative of this dignity:

> Biblical Revelation teaches that all human beings possess inherent dignity because they are created in the image and likeness of God: "God said, 'Let us make man in our image, after our likeness' [...] So God created man in his own image, in the image of God he created him; male and female he created them" (Gen. 1:26-27). With this, humanity has a specific quality that means it is not reducible to purely material elements. Moreover, the "image" does not define the soul or its intellectual abilities but the dignity of man and woman. Because of this, to be created in the image of God means to possess a sacred value that transcends every distinction of a sexual, social, political, cultural, and religious nature. Our dignity is bestowed upon us by God; it is neither claimed nor deserved. Every human being is loved and willed by God and, thus, has an inviolable dignity.

By teaching that human dignity is rooted in the gender complementarity teaching of the Scriptures and divinely ordained, *DI* maintains the strict heteronormativity that only allows heterosexuality and cisgender, that is, the correspondence of one's biological sex and gender, as the only way of upholding human dignity in gender issues. It re-emphasized the RCC's traditional teaching on the biological complementary of the sexes, reaffirming the literal interpretation that God created man and woman as biologically different but ontologically inseparable gendered beings.

Thus, any human attempt to tinker with the divine plan on the immutability of sex and gender is trying to "make oneself God." With this stance, it is logically understandable that the RCC and *DI* would condemn gender-affirming treatment and sex-change operations as interfering with God's plan and thus grave violations of human dignity, on a par with abortion and euthanasia (DDF 2024). However, *DI* has not given clear empirical justification for this stance. In paragraph 10, *DI* acknowledges that it only provides philosophical points for reflections to address these complex moral issues: "This Declaration does not set out to exhaust such a rich and crucial subject. Instead, its aim is to offer some points for reflection that can help us maintain an awareness of human dignity amid the complex historical moment in which we are living" (DDF 2024, 2).

Thus, *DI* only offers philosophical reflections or conceptualization and has no empirical evidence or illustration to back up its moral judgments on the complex gender issues it has investigated—a clear disciplinal limitation of philosophy and theology as normative disciplines that do not offer scientific evidence to back up their theoretical claims. *DI* also reiterated previous papal condemnations of so-called "gender theory" or "gender ideology" (henceforth called GI) without clear conceptualization and behavioral indicators of this concept for clarity and pastoral guidance for Catholics.

DI also does not provide clear conceptual and empirical explanations as to why sex change and other gender-enhancing treatment (GET) are specifically violative of human dignity, given their complex nature, except for a general assessment that they contravene gender complementarity. Thus, it disregards the complexity of the moral situations and motives of adult transgender people as well as parents of young transgender people for opting to avail themselves of gender-enhancement drugs or undergoing medical sex-change procedures. Doctors and psychologists only recommend GET or sex change to transgender individuals to address gender dysphoria (GD) and other serious psychological traumas that could ultimately lead to suicide if not addressed in time.

Objectives, Main Sections, and Arguments

The primary objective of this chapter is to sociologically assess *DI*'s concept of human dignity, taking account of Pope Francis's synodality and inductive synodal theology. Specifically, it explores the strengths and weaknesses of its philosophical treatment of human dignity in relation to contemporary moral issues of gender, transgenderism, GET, and sex change. It also attempts to re-examine the empirical basis of the RCC's teaching of human dignity as founded on gender complementarity—the root cause of why homosexuality as well as all forms of transgenderism such as gender-enhancing medical procedures and sex change are violative of human dignity and thus morally unacceptable to the Church's moral magisterium.

To achieve this end, this chapter is structured into three main sections. The first section briefly expounds Pope Francis's synodality and inductive synodal theology and their affinity with the inductive sociological approach to human behavior and moral actions. The second section critically examines the conceptual and methodological limitations of *DI*'s concept of human dignity in relation to the moral issues of transgenderism, GET, and sex change. It particularly evaluates the limitations of the four types of human dignity and explains why *DI*'s philosophical approach, founded on the TNLT, undermines Pope Francis's inductive synodal theology in *ATP*. The third section attempts to revisit and reappraise the empirical basis of the Biblical foundation of human dignity which is founded on the literal interpretation of gender complementarity as found in Genesis, which accepts heterosexuality as the only divinely ordained gender, rejecting all forms of gender diversity and transgenderism as moral transgressions.

Pope Francis may not be fully aware of the sociological consequences of his synodal approach and inductive synodal theology in his *ATP*, but this document mandates a paradigm shift towards inductive and interdisciplinary approaches that can incorporate social science methods and perspectives to fully understand people's lived experiences before applying theological reflection.

This theological shift of direction, which prioritizes empirical reality before theologizing, implies careful and scientific analysis of the complex issues of transgenderism, GET, and sex change, informed by the latest scientific research, as well as inquiring into the motives of transgender people and the parents of transgender minors for deciding to undergo medical and psychological interventions for sex change. While the ontological concept of human dignity is the overall doctrinal and conceptual guide to resolving moral issues, it is the individual who will actualize the concept through discerning how it can be applied in complex moral situations.

Owing to the logic that human dignity is intrinsically connected with the literal Biblical interpretation of gender complementarity from Genesis that "God created them male and female," it is not difficult to see why the RCC generally judges all forms of gender-enhancing drugs and sex-change procedures as immoral and violative of human dignity, despite genuine and good intentions of people, the application of Christian discernment, and analysis of the benefits and risks of these biotechnological interventions.

Thus, the fundamental conflict over why gender diversity and all types of gender are violations of human dignity, according to *DI*, is its strict logic which intrinsically links dignity with the biological complementary of the sexes, which is non-negotiable despite honest and good motives. Although Francis approved *DI*'s content, this chapter argues that his declaration could have gone in a more inductive scientific direction if the authors and drafters had specifically incorporated sociological and social science research and perspectives in their approach to the complex moral issues of gender, gender-enhancing medical treatment, and sex change.

This chapter contends that the RCC needs to sociologically re-examine the empirical foundation of the Scriptures, specifically the teaching of Genesis on gender complementarity, the root cause of why transgenderism, sex change, and other related issues such as homosexual marriage and LGBTQI inclusivity in the Church cannot be fully achieved despite Francis's synodality and call for inductive synodal theology.

Overall Theoretical Framework

Pope Francis's Synodal Inductive Approach

Through his writings and media interviews, Pope Francis has been known to welcome the LGBTQI group in his concept of a synodal church, a church that embraces marginalized groups such as the gay community. In *Fiducia Supplicans* [Supplicating Trust] (*FS*) (DDF 2023), he approves the pastoral blessing of homosexual couples by priests, as well as gays acting as godparents in baptism.

Despite his strong support for LGBTQI inclusivity in the RCC, Francis remains steadfast in his stand against so-called gender ideology (GI), which ironically includes advocacy for LGBTQI inclusivity. GI as a broad political signifier that opposes gender theories has not been clearly defined and operationalized in the RCC and yet is being used as a political tool to oppose feminism and gender diversity in contemporary society. *DI*'s latest declaration on human dignity has reflected Francis's opposition to GI as a new colonization and a serious threat to humanity for cancelling the biological distinction between male and female as taught in the Scriptures.

Although he strongly condemns GI and gender diversity, Francis's holistic and inductive outlook in his concept of synodality and inductive synodal theology tends to go beyond the traditional philosophical perspectives and deductive approach of *DI* to address the cultural transformation of the current age. His inductive synodal theology in *ATP* encourages an interdisciplinary approach that allows other branches of knowledge to assist Catholic theologians to deal with the intricate theological and moral issues of today.

Francis's synodality also implies listening to and understanding the lived experiences of Catholics and those who are voiceless at the peripheries of the Church, such as the LGBTQI group. To him, listening to and learning from people's experiences in current society necessitates an accurate understanding of the empirical reality inductively to discern God's will among people. In the same Christmas address to the members of the RCC's Roman Curia, he emphasized that discernment is important as part of the spiritual life that strip clerics of:

> the illusion of omniscience, from the danger of thinking that it is enough simply to apply rules, from the temptation to carry on, even in the life of the Curia, by simply repeating what we have always done. And in this way failing to realize that the Mystery of God is always beyond us and that the lives of people and the world around us are, and will always remain, superior to ideas and theories. Life is always superior to ideas. (Francis 2023, para. 9)

In this address, Francis clearly underscores the need for the entire Church to discern and go beyond rules and dogmas to understand God's mystery, highlighting that the lives of people and actual human experience in the world are beyond preconceived theological and philosophical theories and ideas. This inductive approach reflects his synodal theology in the document *ATP* in which he recommends Catholic theologians to commence their theologizing with accurate knowledge of people's lived experience in the contemporary world before theological reflection and moral judgment (Francis 2023).

To Francis, "Good theologians, like good pastors, also smell of the people and the street and, by their reflection, pour oil and wine on the wounds of men." Openness to the world, to man in the concreteness of his existential situation, with its problems, wounds, challenges, and potential, cannot, however, be reduced to a "tactical" attitude, extrinsically adapting now crystallized content to new situations, but must urge theology to an epistemological and methodological rethinking" (Pope Francis 2023, para. 3). This implies a shifting of focus and method in theological reflection, one that begins with human experience and empirical reality before the application of Biblical or Church teachings.

The *ATP* encourages Catholic theologians to use the scientific methods of other branches of knowledge such as sociology and social sciences to comprehend the cultural revolution of the current age to inductively and empirically ground theologizing. For Pope Francis, the new mission of Catholic theology is "promoting engagement and dialogue in every sphere of knowledge, in order to reach and involve the whole People of God in theological research, so that the life of the people may become theological life" (Campisi 2023 para. 16).

Francis further encourages them to engage in synodal listening and empathizing with homosexuals and the LGBTQI who have long been ostracized silently in the Church because of homophobia. This listening and openness to the concerns of the gay community "resonated with the spirit of the ongoing synodal process, which asks the Church to listen, discern, and walk together with the faithful so that everyone can participate in the dynamism of missionary communion" (Bordoni 2023, para. 1).

The Sociological Approach

Resolving the current moral issues of homosexuality, same-sex marriage, and LGBTQI inclusivity in the RCC through synodality needs the traditional "see, judge, and act" methodology to be applied, which starts with the empirical knowledge of the moral situation before applying the Church moral principles and undertaking social action to resolve them. Pope John XXIII described these steps as follows:

> First, one reviews the concrete situation; secondly, one forms a judgment on it in the light of these same principles; thirdly, one decides what the circumstances can and should be done to implement these principles (*Mater et Magistra* [Mother and Teacher] 1961, para. 235).

Understanding the moral situation, or "to see," requires sociology and the social sciences to aid Catholic philosophers and moral theologians to understand transgenderism, GET, and sex change. The first step of understanding accurately the moral situation is crucial, because moral judgment and social action to resolve the moral issue depend on it. An erroneous or unscientific evaluation of the concrete situation can result in moral misjudgment, incorrect implementation of moral principles, and an inappropriate plan of action to address it.

Scientific and sociological research methods are highly important tools for the SoS's participants to attain certainty in all three stages of the see-judge-act methodology to resolve moral issues, especially in the first stage, which requires objectivity and a scientific account of the empirical situation so as not to err in the next two stages. Sociology's positivism has some limitations in understanding the empirical world. It can, however, serve as a potent tool to check against the subjectivism and inaccuracies of common-sense judgment of moral situations.

In *DI,* philosophy and reasoning play a dominant role in resolving moral issues, despite their complexity in the postmodern world. Despite the advent and popularity of the social sciences in the current age, philosophy is predominantly seen by the hierarchy as playing a significant role in resolving moral issues. Catholic theology has always relied on human reasoning and philosophy to justify the Catholic belief (O' Mahony 1967). However, it is generally understood by social scientists that it is not really the task of philosophers to provide empirical evidence to prove their theoretical positions, which is the province of science. Sociology as a social science that specializes in the scientific study of social behavior and contemporary society and culture, specifically in the study of gender relations, is thus the most appropriate discipline to aid the RCC's moral theology in providing an account for sex and resolving moral issues about gender and transgenderism.

Analyzing DI's Human Dignity and Gender Issues

Gender Diversity and DI's Human Dignity

The growing liquidity of globalizing contemporary society has unintentionally resulted in gender diversity and fluidity (Bauman 2000; Giddens 2002). With the advent of sophisticated medical technology for gender-enhancing treatment and sex change, a product of human ingenuity, nonbinary people and members of the LGBTQI community can now align their biological sex with their gender. Transgender individuals or people whose gender does not correspond with their biological sex have existed since time immemorial but remain unrecognized and discriminated against owing to societal homophobia which accepts heterosexuality as the only true gender in society.

Unlike the RCC's metaphysical approach to sex and gender as immutable, inseparable, and divinely ordained, sociology and the social sciences as empirical and scientific disciplines distinguish sex from gender. For sociologists, sex is biological, and gender is social and cultural, although both are connected in one person. Gender is determined by human experience through the process termed by sociologists gender socialization.

This basic perspective of sociology that sees gender as socially and culturally conditioned conflicts with the current philosophical view of the RCC, which sees gender as immutable and metaphysical, denying the experiential aspect of gender. Sociologists and social scientists, using a naturalistic and empirical approach, view gender as human experience. Sex is biological and assigned at birth while gender, that is, a person's expression of femininity and masculinity, is socially learned through human interaction in society. The Church's moral magisterium and Catholic moral theologians who subscribe to the philosophical–theological view that follows logic and deductive reasoning view gender as ontologically linked to biological sex which is ordained by God.

This conceptual conflict in looking at gender, instead of being resolved through Pope Francis's inductive synodal theology, which encourages an interdisciplinary and scientific approach to theologizing, has exacerbated the divide created by DDF's *DI*. *DI* reiterated the ontological view of human dignity and retains its view on gender as immutable, ahistorical, and divinely ordained. It also subscribes to the exaggeration, or what sociologists call "moral panic," of GI as the greatest threat, extremely dangerous to humanity, that "intends to deny the greatest possible difference that exists between living beings: sexual difference."

DI upholds gender complementarity and rejects any form of gender diversity and transgenderism, despite a portion of the document defending the human dignity of gay and transgender people, affirming that "every person, regardless of sexual orientation, ought to be respected in his or her dignity and treated with consideration, while 'every sign of unjust discrimination' is to be carefully avoided, particularly any form of aggression and violence."

Although *DI* talks about defending the human dignity of the LGBTQI group, it also condemns transgenderism, specifically gender-enhancing medical care and sex change, basing this condemnation on the traditional and philosophical argument that they tinker with the divine plan on the immutability of gender and contravene the ontological view of human dignity that is based on the literal interpretation of Genesis that God "created them as male and female." As Amy Welborn (2024, paras. 19–20) contends:

> The new Vatican document, *Dignitas Infinita*, fails terribly by offering transgender and nonbinary people not infinite, but limited human dignity. While it lays out a wonderful rationale for why each human being, regardless of condition in life, must be respected, honored, and loved, it does not apply this principle to gender-diverse people…The document's attempt to uphold and defend human dignity is weakened by its stunning lack of awareness of the actual lives of transgender and nonbinary people.

DI has broadly explained the ontological, moral, social, and existential meaning of human dignity, but its treatment remains largely in the conceptual realm. It still applies philosophy and reasoning to deal with human dignity, but it does not provide behavioral indicators of how this dignity can be realized in the various complex gender issues of GET and sex change. A philosophical approach has limitations regarding the empirical. As Sandu (2020, 47) argues, "Philosophy, as we have become accustomed to it, at least since modernity, is less interested in concrete, particular situations, while privileging a universalized understanding of the investigated situation and detaching itself from a particular context."

Gender Complementarity and Human Dignity

Traditionally, human dignity in the RCC is based on the Biblical teaching of Genesis that God created man in his own image and likeness, and is always correlated with gender complementarity. However, it is noticeable that in recent years, since Pope John Paul's theology of the body which emphasized gender complementarity, human dignity has been often linked to the biological complementarity of male and female. In *DI*, human dignity is attached to gender complementarity by reiterating that Biblical passage in Genesis that God created man as male and female:

> [A]ll human beings possess inherent dignity because they are created in the image and likeness of God: "God said, 'Let us make man in our image, after our likeness' … So God created man in his own image, in the image of God he created him; male and female he created them" (Gen. 1:26-27). With this, humanity has a specific quality that means it is not reducible to purely material elements. Moreover, the "image" does not define the soul or its intellectual abilities but the dignity of man and woman. (DDF 2024, para. 11)

The inseparability of sex and gender based on natural law is emphasized in Catholic sexual teaching: "Masculinity and femininity express the twofold aspect of man's somatic constitution…This meaning, one can say, consists in reciprocal enrichment. Refracting this theological perspective into the natural law tradition, this gender essentialism paired with gender complementarity is understood to be a natural complementarity between the genders" (Ford 2018, 81).

Pope John Paul II's Letter to Families entitled *Gratissimam Sane* [For His Own Sake] (1994, #6), also declares, "Man is created 'from the very beginning' as male and female: the light of all humanity… is marked by this primordial duality. From it there derive the 'masculinity' and the 'femininity' of individuals, just as from it every community draws its own unique richness in the mutual fulfillment of persons… Hence one can discover, at the very origins of human society, the qualities of communion and of complementarity."

The result of this influential theology, espoused by Pope John Paul II and reaffirmed by Pope Benedict XVI and Pope Francis, is that the RCC has inappropriately and indiscriminately categorized all views and explanations that oppose this theology and official sexual teachings of the Magisterium, including the inductive scientific approaches of the social sciences, as "gender ideology" (Ford Jr. 2018). This labeling does acknowledge, however, the basic difference in perspective and method between traditional Catholic morality and the social sciences.

The current Catholic moral theology sees the ontological unity between sex and gender, while sociology and the social sciences view sex as biological and gender as social and cultural. As Davis and Evans (2019, 273) aptly argue:

> When a baby is born doctors immediately categorize the infant as either male or female based on the appearance of the baby's external genitalia. This genital categorization is the child's sex, which is often viewed as synonymous with gender given those with penises are typically raised as boys, and those with vaginas are typically raised as girls. However, sex and gender are not synonymous with one another, nor is each a simple two-category phenomenon.

Dr Carol Bayley (2016, 1) comments:

> People tend to say "gender" when they are actually referring to sex, there is a difference. Both terms can refer to the male/female division of the human species, but "sex" refers to the reproductive aspects of that difference, while "gender" refers especially to the social or behavioral aspects of it. Learning how to express masculinity and femininity is socially learned by the person in society and this does not necessarily reflect his or her sex or biological make-up.

To some authors, the emphasis on gender complementarity is a recent invention of the RCC as an ideology to combat GI, gender diversity, and feminism. In her article, "The Role of the Popes in the Invention of Complementarity and the Vatican's Anathematization of Gender," Mary Anne Case (2016) contends that sexual complementarity is a twentieth-century theological innovation. Adherents of the papal teaching on the theology of the body popularized it in the RCC as the appropriate response to the sexual crises of late modernity. Gender complementarity has become a doctrinal tool of the RCC to resist feminism, women's reproductive rights, and gay rights, as well as to defend the masculinity of Catholic priesthood (Beattie 2016).

As Joan Scott (2007, 71) also contends, "the male/female opposition" serves to "vindicate political power" by making references to gendered, hierarchical relationships "seem sure and fixed, outside human construction, part of the natural or divine order." In this sense, the RCC has turned the gender complementarity issue into a "Catholic ideology" to resist feminism and other gender and reproductive rights issues. It upholds the heteronormativity that marginalizes LGBTQI people in the Church. The traditional "Christian interpretations of Genesis continue to lend divine legitimation to a heterosexual social order predicated upon male authority and female subordination" (Beattie 2016).

> The Vatican first to embrace sexual complementarity as the foundation of its theological anthropology and then to mobilize that anthropology in an attempt to influence secular law in settings as diverse as the United Nations' 1995 Beijing Conference on Women and *La manif pour tous*, the protest movement that brought thousands of French citizens out to demonstrate against the inclusion of same-sex couples in a law extending 'mariage pour tous' (Marriage for Everyone) in the spring of 2013. (Case 2016, 156)

It is therefore unsurprising that the RCC's latest declaration in *DI* intrinsically connects human dignity to gender complementarity to resist GI, gender diversity, transgenderism, and medical procedures for gender enhancement and sex change. *DI* condemns all forms of changing the person's divinely ordained immutable sex and gender as violative of human dignity. Using a deductive and philosophical approach, *DI* becomes blind to transgender people's intense psychological trauma and the risk of suicide among children and young people due to GD, contrary to *ATP*'s approach of first understanding the lived experiences of people before theological reflection or moral judgment (Francis 2023).

DI's Four-Fold Distinction of Human Dignity

DI recommends human dignity a general ethical framework to morally analyze gender and transgender issues such as sex change and GET using philosophical and theological reasoning. However, it underscores the primacy of reasoning in recognizing this dignity:

> (Dignitas infinita) Every human person possesses an infinite dignity, inalienably grounded in his or her very being, which prevails in and beyond every circumstance, state, or situation the person may ever encounter. This principle, which is fully recognizable even by reason alone, underlies the primacy of the human person and the protection of human rights…. (DDF 2024, para. 1)

To accommodate social and existential contingencies and avoid misinterpretations, *DI* breaks down the concept of human dignity into four types. Despite this four-fold distinction to accommodate contingencies, *DI* has not provided sufficient behavioral indicators and guidelines on how to discern whether complex and evolving moral situations affirm or reject human dignity:

> [T]he phrase "the dignity of the human person" risks lending itself to a variety of interpretations that can yield potential ambiguities [15] and "contradictions that lead us to wonder whether the equal dignity of all human beings … is truly recognized, respected, protected and promoted in every situation."[16] This brings us to recognize the possibility of a fourfold distinction of the concept of dignity: ontological dignity, moral dignity, social dignity, and

> existential dignity. The most important among these is the ontological dignity that belongs to the person as such simply because he or she exists and is willed, created, and loved by God. (DDF 2024, para. 7)

Human dignity as perceived by *DI* is a non-negotiable religious belief or doctrine for Catholics. In Catholic orthodoxy, all persons are indeed thought to be created by God and redeemed by Christ and thus possess this indelible metaphysical dignity, which must be always respected. In its concept of moral dignity, *DI* attempts to relate this ontological dignity to the actual exercise of people's freedom. Moral dignity is described at some length as referring to:

> How people exercise their freedom. While people are endowed with conscience, they can always act against it. However, were they to do so, they would behave in a way that is "not dignified" with respect to their nature as creatures who are loved by God and called to love others. Yet, this possibility always exists for human freedom, and history illustrates how individuals—when exercising their freedom against the law of love revealed by the Gospel—can commit inestimably profound acts of evil against others. Those who act this way seem to have lost any trace of humanity and dignity. This is where the present distinction can help us discern between the moral dignity that de facto can be "lost" and the ontological dignity that can never be annulled. And it is precisely because of this latter point that we must work with all our might so that all those who have done evil may repent and convert.

Again, *DI* speaks of moral dignity in abstract and theological terms that still lack empirical guidance on how to exercise human freedom to uphold ontological dignity in moral situations that are developing as a result of biotechnological advancement and gender diversity. It states that moral human dignity can be lost by committing sin against the law of God, but clearer behavioral guidance is needed for ordinary Catholics amid the growing plurality of normative standards in secular society.

Aside from moral dignity, *DI* also identifies social dignity as intrinsically linked to ontological dignity, defining it broadly as:

> the quality of a person's living conditions. For example, in cases of extreme poverty, where individuals do not even have what is minimally necessary to live according to their ontological dignity, it is said that those poor people are living in an "undignified" manner. This expression does not imply a judgment on those individuals but highlights how the situation in which they are forced to live contradicts their inalienable dignity. (DDF 2024, para. 8)

This claim merely supplements the philosophical argument that human dignity cannot be lost even amid undignified situations, but it does not clarify how to apply social dignity in complicated social and moral situations such as transgenderism, gender diversity, GD, GET, and sex change.

The last type of human dignity that *DI* identifies is existential dignity. This is:

> the type of dignity implied in the ever-increasing discussion about a "dignified" life and one that is "not dignified." For instance, while some people may appear to lack nothing essential for life, for various reasons, they may still struggle to live with peace, joy, and hope. In other situations, the presence of serious illnesses, violent family environments, pathological addictions, and other hardships may drive people to experience their life conditions as "undignified" vis-à-vis their perception of that ontological dignity that can never be obscured. These distinctions remind us of the inalienable value of the ontological dignity that is rooted in the very being of the human person in all circumstances. (DDF 2024, para. 8)

DI here attempts to relate human dignity to people's lived experiences, albeit giving only a very limited example. It only refers to certain types of people who, despite material deprivation, serious illnesses, violence, and other "undignified situations," still find peace, joy, and hope, and retain their sense of ontological dignity. This existential description of human dignity still follows the philosophical logic that human dignity is indelible regardless of human and social conditions.

Based as it is on philosophical deductive reasoning, *DI* fails to appreciate inductively the intricacy and complexity of today's evolving moral issues. Scientific research is, rather, the basis for discernment and moral judgment as to whether pursuing transgenderism or sex change affirms or violates human dignity.

Pope Francis's synodality and inductive synodal theology implies learning people's experiences before resolving theological or moral issues rather than relying on ideas, concepts, and abstract formulas from the past (Pope Francis 2023). Given the complex and evolving moral issues behind gender diversity, transgenderism, GET, and other gender-transforming medical procedures, *DI* should have withheld its moral condemnations, instead comprehensively reviewing the complicated medical, psychological, sociological, and bioethical contingencies concerned in continuous synodal dialogue between philosophers, ethicists, and theologians of the DDF and sociologists, social scientists, doctors, and feminists specializing in gender, GET, and sex change. The sociologist-priest Andrew Greely once lamented that when the RCC aims to resolve issues, it brings in its own experts who usually advise what bishops want to hear rather than the dissenting views of scholars, experts or social scientists which can nevertheless be helpful for the resolution of the issues.

Pope Francis's synodality encourages listening and dialogue with people with divergent views, the voiceless, and those on the peripheries of the Church. Now is the time for theologians, philosophers, and authorities in the DDF to start listening to the divergent views of gender sociologists, social scientists, feminists, and the LGBTQI community, and learning from their scientific, inductive, and experiential approaches to gender and gender diversity in the contemporary world. Basically, this is what Francis wants in his *ATP*—an interdisciplinary approach to theological issues amid the cultural revolution of the current age.

DI's Philosophical Approach and Pope Francis's Synodality

The philosophical approach to human dignity, according to the TNLT tradition, is clarified in paragraph 9 of *DI*:

> Finally, it is worth mentioning that the classical definition of a person as an "individual substance of a rational nature" [17] clarifies the foundation of human dignity. As an "individual substance," the person possesses ontological dignity (that is, at the metaphysical level of being itself). Having received existence from God, humans are subjects who "subsist" – that is, they exercise their existence autonomously. The term "rational" encompasses all the capacities of the human person, including the capacities of knowing and understanding,

as well as those of wanting, loving, choosing, and desiring; it also includes all corporeal functions closely related to these abilities.

But how this dignity is expressed in empirical reality needs to be defined operationally. GET and sex change are complex medical and behavioral issues that cannot be resolved by mere application of the ontological and theological exposition of human dignity. *DI* deductively judges all gender theories and ideologies that cancel humanity, as well as gender transition procedures, as violations of human dignity, without a careful and scientific investigation of the moral situations.

Understanding human dignity at the conceptual level presents no problem for Catholics, for whom it is a matter of faith that people are created in the image and likeness of God and redeemed by Christ, thus possessing an ontological worth that cannot be changed by human and societal contingencies. The problem lies in its application in the human and cultural realm, dealing with concrete situations related to gender issues.

Overall, *DI* seems a setback to what Pope Francis started in *ATP*, which encouraged interdisciplinary and scientific approaches to understanding people's lived experiences before theological reflection and moral judgment on urgent contemporary moral issues. Sociologists, social scientists, medical and gender specialists did not take part in the formulation and drafting of *DI* in the DFF, so it cannot be expected to have advanced Francis's inductive and synodal approach, which stresses consultation and knowing empirical situations, despite his approval of this document.

In *ATP*, Francis proposes a paradigm change in Catholic theologizing to stress the limitations of the deductive philosophical approach based on abstract formulas of the past. With the growing complexity of contemporary moral situations and bioethical questions, scholars are beginning to question the appropriateness of this approach for resolving current moral issues. Philosophy is useful for establishing ethical principles, developing analytical frameworks, and mapping out concepts, but now that these theoretical foundations have been established, clinicians, ethics consultants, policy makers, and scholars need only to be trained in how to apply these foundations to cases" (Blumenthal-Barby et al. 2022, 1). "Biotechnology and the life sciences have astonished the world in recent years, but they have also disoriented people by raising a whole new set of ethical issues" (Lanigan 2009, x).

Thus, a paradigm shift and an interdisciplinary approach that involves sociology and the social sciences as suggested by Pope Francis in his inductive synodal theology is urgently needed to fully understand urgent contemporary issues of gender, transgenderism, gender diversity, and gender-enhancing technologies. It requires a sociological ethics that can investigate the empirical and scientific foundations of these intricate moral situations, and people's motives, before applying moral principles and making judgments as to whether pursuing gender-enhancing technologies promotes or undermines human dignity.

Resolving the Empirical Basis of Gender Complementarity[1]

No amount of empirical and scientific research on sex, gender, and gender diversity can alter the RCC's basic philosophical stance on gender complementarity. The root cause why members of the LGBTQI community cannot be fully accepted in the RCC as "normal" and "moral" persons is the literal interpretation of the Genesis story that God created a man and a woman in His own image and likeness. Only a humanity inhabited by heterosexuals as ordained by God is recognized, and only a man and a woman can be sacramentally married in the Church. Homosexuality and transgenderism remain abominable and violative of human dignity, originally designed by God as founded on heterosexuality.

Francis has reached out to the LGBTQI community to show his synodal concern to people with diverse genders with his approval of the declaration *FS* that allowed pastoral blessings to homosexual couples by priests. Following substantial revision, the 20-page *DI*, five years in the making, was recently approved by Pope Francis and issued by the Vatican's DDF. However, the traditional and philosophical approach to sex, gender, and gender complementarity contained in *DI* is seen by transgender people as a setback. Leaders of LGBTQI Catholics immediately criticized *DI* as outdated, harmful, and even contrary to the stated goal of recognizing the "infinite dignity" of all God's children.

Francis DeBernardo of New Ways Ministry, which advocates for LGBTQI Catholics, criticized DI, saying: "While it lays out a wonderful rationale for why each human being, regardless of condition in life, must be respected, honored, and loved, it does not apply this principle to gender-diverse people" (The Associated Press 2024, para. 7).

Sex and Gender Complementarity in Genesis

In its most eagerly anticipated section, the DI continues to reject GI and the idea that one's biological sex can change. Those who attempt to tinker with the divinely ordained design that sees a man and a woman as biologically different and separate beings are said to be making themselves God. However, sociologists and feminists, and LGBTQI leaders, disagree with the RCC's view on the immutability and inseparability of sex and gender. Sociology and the social sciences always believe that sex is biological, whereas gender is a social and cultural experience and not a fixed and immutable reality, contrary to the RCC's philosophical and theological interpretation, which applies the Thomistic natural law theory and the literal interpretation of Biblical gender complementarity. For sociologists, gender is a socio-cultural

[1] This section is largely based on "Chapter 4: Reappraising Gender Complementarity and Heterosexual Marriage in the Catholic Church" of the 2024 book by the author entitled *LGBTQI Inclusivity, Homosexuality, and Same-Sex Marriage in the Catholic Church: Pope Francis's Synodal theology, Sociology, and Moral Issues*. Singapore: Springer Nature.

reality that is historical, as culture and society advance in complexity and development. Thus, evolving sexuality and gender identity have resulted in LGBTQI categorizations of people.

There are various ways of expressing one's gender in terms of femininity and masculinity, depending on one's social and cultural norms. Winkler (2021) argues that to be a "male" man implies following certain societal rules. There are various cultural expressions of masculinities, not only the one commonly interpreted by Catholic theologians to defend heterosexuality as the only way to be human.

> To be regarded as a 'male' man, one has to act and perform according to specific ideas, norms, expectations and standards within a specific culture at a specific time. Masculinity – that is what we call this set of ideas, norms and so forth – is part of a culture and its agents who want to perform successfully within a specific social sector and role. It differs, develops and is performed in various ways by 'masculine' agents, so we might better speak of masculinities (plural!). It is a pluralistic and variable set of notions, norms, standards, and cultural practices. (Winkler 2021, 269–270)

In the traditional interpretation of gender complementarity, only a biological male and female can enter a moral marriage. One may recall in particular the slogan of those opposing marriage equality in the years before it was instituted in the US: "It's Adam and Eve, not Adam and Steve," is a particularly revealing example of embedded prescriptivist assumptions about the creation narrative. This interpretation is, however, debatable, since Genesis cannot be interpreted literally. The names Adam and Eve are symbolic names representing humanity as created by God rather than a reference to historical heterosexual couples.

The common interpretation of Genesis's gender complementarity that recognizes only heterosexuality and cisgender, that is, the gender identity of the person should correspond to their sex as male or female, is thus a social construction by theologians and Biblical scholars of what the human authors of Genesis meant. Gender as a social experience was not within the cultural awareness and intention of the authors, who used biological make-up as the basis for the divine message that God created the whole of humanity as male and female, without specifying the cultural and social meaning of what it meant to live as male and female in society.

The traditional Catholic moral teaching that sex and gender are one inseparable reality, that one's sex determines one gender and sexuality in society, can have a rival empirical interpretation when applying Weber's "interpretive understanding" of the authors' real motives in Genesis. To James Brownson (2013), "God created males and females after God's image (Gen 1:27), which is intended to convey the value, dominion, and relationality shared by both men and women, but not the idea that the gender complementarity is somehow necessary to fully express or embody the divine image" (Sim 2023, 8).

Gender as biological sex rather than a social experience and relationality was what the authors of Genesis most probably had in mind in their gender complementarity message. Stiebert and Walsh (2001, 121) explain, "It is important to note that the idea of sexuality necessarily entails an idea of relationality. A person may be gendered (i.e., male or female) without necessary reference to another, but a person is sexual only in relation to another person." Thus, while a person's sex is biologically assigned at birth, how they actualize their gender to express their masculinity and femininity in society is highly influenced by their relationality and socialization in society.

James Brownson (2013) made four important claims to debunk the literal interpretation of gender complementarity in Genesis:

> 1. That the original Adam was not an undifferentiated being that was divided into male and female; 2. Similarity as opposed to complementarity; 3. Both male and female are created in the divine image (and that complementarity is not necessary to fully express the divine image); 4. That "one-flesh" connotes a kinship bond, as opposed to physical complementarity. (Henegar 2011, 5)

Other scholars also doubt whether the interpretation of the biological and procreative complementarity of Genesis 2, which is the popular basis for rejecting homosexuality and homosexual marriage, is tenable (Sim 2023). To Caleb Day (2016), interpreting gender complementarity in these ancient texts without regard to their cultural context of patriarchy is anachronistic.

Re-examining the Empirical Foundation of Gender Complementarity

The traditional interpretation of gender complementarity in Genesis is cisgender, that is, the person's sex or genitalia, determines their gender as a heterosexual. Transgenderism, where one's gender as a social experience differs from the assigned sex at birth, is seen as abominable and deviant. In short, the traditional interpretation of gender complementarity only accepts heteronormativity as the only way to become a "normal human being" and that only a biological male and female can enter a moral marriage. Transgenders or people whose gender identity is different from their gender they were thought to be when they were born" (National Center for Transgender Equality 2023, para. 2), contradicting their sex, are "immature" and "unnatural" in the eyes of traditional Catholic moralists and thus ineligible for Christian marriage.

The problem is that "to the traditionalist/behavioralist, the question of same sex relationships appears decisively closed. This is because neither male-male nor female-female relationships can fully embody the complementarity nature of humanity intended by God in creation" (Henegar 2011, 4). However, this traditional view that rejects same-sex marriage has been challenged more and more by contemporary social science scholars specializing on gender and sexuality. "What was previously relegated to the silence of 'the closet' and to euphemistic speech is now being discussed more directly and openly. And with this greater directness and openness of speech comes the need to face questions that the church has not faced so directly and explicitly before" (Henegar 2021).

Biblical Gender Complementarity as Prototypical

Since the early Church, Christian communities have generally been against people with same-sex orientation. Consequently, "their treatment of [transgenders] as created in God's image, have been harsh and rejecting. The psychological damage that has been inflected as a result has been devastating" (Russell 2011, 2). Archaeologist and Hebrew Bible scholar Carol Meyers (1988) cautions scholars that there can be two approaches to understanding gender complementarity in the Bible. It can either be prototypical, explaining how things came to be, or archetypal, revealing some timeless essential truths about human nature. For Meyers, these two approaches can have serious implications for the construction of ideals well beyond the period of the story.

A closer inductive sociological analysis of the creation of humans in Genesis 2 as "male and female" would most likely reveal the prototypical approach rather than the archetypal. The story only explains how things came to be: that humanity, both male and female, was created by God. But it does not teach that heterosexuals are the only ideal human beings who are allowed by God to enter marriage beyond the period of the story. Thus, it is not a timeless message. What is timeless is that God created humanity. But an archetypal interpretation of the Biblical gender complementarity in Genesis to the effect that only male and female are the true genders is debatable and subject to scientific reappraisal.

Judging whether God, through the human authors of Genesis, really intends to convey gender complementarity as heterosexual union in Genesis 2 is an empirical question rather than a philosophical and theological one. It requires a scientific reappraisal of the social and cultural contexts of Genesis as well as an interpretive understanding of the motives and intentions of the human authors.

Therefore, a comprehensive understanding of whether gender complementarity as expressed in Genesis only refers to biological sex and heterosexuality, thus condemning same-sex union, requires us to conduct a scientific investigation into "the ancient Eastern and Graeco-Roman context of the Bible, study the perspective of same-sex relations in Judaism and early Christianity, and consult recent works in psychology, sociology, and biology" (Sprinkle 2016, 9).

Conclusion

This chapter has examined the RCC's teaching on human dignity as explained by the DDF's latest declaration, *DI,* through a sociological lens and Pope Francis's inductive synodal theology. It reviewed the limitations of the philosophical–theological approach of *DI,* which basically views human dignity in the conceptual and metaphysical realm despite briefly explaining its four-fold dimension. Owing to its strictly philosophical approach, *DI* did not provide empirical indicators and guidelines as to how ontological dignity can be applied in complex evolving moral situations to resolve contemporary gender issues such as transgenderism, GET, GD, and sex change.

The chapter also argued that the fundamental reason why homosexuality, homosexual marriage, and transgenderism cannot be morally accepted and the LGBTQI community cannot be fully incorporated in the RCC is the traditional and literal interpretation of gender complementarity in Genesis that strictly upholds heteronormativity and its philosophical understanding based on natural law theory that sex and gender are metaphysically immutable, inseparable, and ordained by God.

This chapter recommends a re-evaluation of the empirical basis of Genesis regarding gender complementarity and the incorporation of modern sociology and the social sciences in understanding sex and gender as well as transgenderism, GET, and sex change to achieve a deductive and inductive view of human dignity in the spirit of Pope Francis's inductive synodal theology.

References

Ballano VO (2021) Inculturation, philosophy, and the social sciences as the emerging handmaid of theology: time to update catholic clerical education? Int J Religion Spirituality Society 11(2):1–13. https://doi.org/10.18848/2154-8633/CGP/v11i02/1-13

Bauman Z (2000) Liquid modernity. Polity Press, Cambridge

Bauman Z (2003) Liquid love: on the frailty of human bonds. Polity Press, Cambridge

Bayley C (2016) Transgender persons and catholic healthcare. Healthcare Ethics USA 24(1):1–17

Beattie T (2016) Gendering genesis, engendering difference. a catholic theological quest. Svensk Teologisk Kvartalskrift 92(3–4):102–117

Blumenthal-Barby J, Aas S, Brudney D, Flanigan J, Liao SM, London A, Sumner W, Savulescu J (2022) The place of philosophy in bioethics today. Am J Bioeth 22(12):10–21. https://doi.org/10.1080/15265161.2021.1940355

Brownson JV (2013) Bible, gender, sexuality: reframing the church's debate on same-sex relationships. Grand Rapids, MI: Eerdmans

Campisi T (2023) Pope: theology must interpret the gospel for today's world. Vatican News. https://www.vaticannews.va/en/pope/news/2023-11/pope-francis-motu-proprio-pontifical-theology-academy.html

Case MA (2016) The role of the popes in the invention of complementarity and the Vatican's anathematization of gender. Religion Gender 6(2):155–172

Davis G, Evans MJ (2019) Surgically shaping sex: a gender structure analysis of the violation of intersex people's human rights. In: Risman BJ, Froyum CM, Scarborough WJ (eds) Handbook of the sociology of gender second Edition. Cham: Springer Nature

Day C (2016) 'A time to throw away'? Rethinking the Gender requirement for leg2timate Christian sex. M.T.S. Colloquium presentation, University of Notre Dame, Notre Dame, IN, USA

DDF (Dicastery of the Doctrine of the Faith) (2023) Fiducia Supplicans: on the pastoral meaning of blessings. Vatican: The Roman Curia. Available at: https://www.vatican.va/roman_curia/congregations/cfaith/documents/rc_ddf_doc_20231218_fiducia-supplicans_en.html

DDF (Dicastery of the Doctrine of the Faith) (2024) Declaration Dignitas Infinita on human dignity. Vatican: The Roman Curia. https://www.vatican.va/roman_curia/congregations/cfaith/documents/rc_ddf_doc_20240402_dignitas-infinita_en.html

Edwards A (2017) Beyond a cisgender genesis: reading the creation narratives through a transgender feminist lens.

Ford CJ (2018) Transgender bodies, catholic schools, and a queer natural law theology of exploration. J Moral Theol 7(1):70–98
Gaudium et Spes [Hope and Joy]. Pastoral Constitution on the Church in the Modern World." Vatican: Vatican Archives. http://www.vatican.va/archive/hist_councils/ii_vatican_council/documents/vat-ii_const_19651207_gaudium-et-spes_en.html
Giddens A (2002) Runaway world: how globalization is reshaping our lives. Profile Books, London
Henegar M (2011) Mid-day discussion guide for bible, gender, sexuality: reframing church's debate on same-sex relationships by James V Brownson. https://www.efaidnbmnnnibpcajpcglclefindmkaj/http://podcast.manhattanchurch.org/docs/coffee-stretch/Bible-Gender-Sexuality-Notes.pdf
Lanigan BT (2009) Human dignity and bioethics. Nova Science Publishers, New York
Mater et Magistra [Mother and Teacher] (1961) Social encyclical of pope John XXIII on christianity and social progress. Vatican: Libreria Editrice Vaticana, Available online: http://w2.vatican.va/content/john-xxiii/en/encyclicals/documents/hf_j-xxiii_enc_15051961_mater.html
Meyers C (1988) Discovering eve: ancient israelite women in context. Oxford University Press, New York
National Center for Transgender Equality (2023) Understanding transgender people: the basics. National Center for transgender equality website (January 27, 2023). https://transequality.org/issues/resources/understanding-transgender-people-the-basics
O'Mahony B, Cap OFM (1967) The role of philosophy in the formation of priests. Ir Theol Q 34(4):281–300. https://doi.org/10.1177/002114006703400401
Optatam Totius [Decree on Priestly Training] (1965) Decree on priestly training proclaimed by his holiness Pope Paul VI. http://www.vatican.va/archive/hist_councils/ii_vatican_council/documents/vatii_ decree_19651028_optatam-totius_en.html
Pope John Paul II (1994) Letter to the Families, Gratissimam Sane [For His Own Sake]. Vatican: Libreria Editrice Vaticana. https://www.vatican.va/content/john-paul-ii/en/letters/1994/documents/hf_jp-ii_let_02021994_families.html
Pope Francis (2023) Apostolic letter issued "Motu Proprio" Ad Theologiam Promovendam [To Promote Theology]. Unofficial full English translation available at: https://returntotradition.org/unofficial-full-english-translation-of-francis-revolutionary-motu-proprio-ad-theologiam-promovendam-plus-breaking-news-report-on-text/
Ritzer G, Dean P (2019) Globalization: a basic text, 3rd edn. Wiley-Blackwell, Hoboken, NJ
Russell GM (2011) Motives of heterosexual allies in collective action for equality. J Soc Issues 67(2):376–393. https://doi.org/10.1111/j.1540-4560.2011.01703.x
Sandu A (2020) Bioethics—philosophy or science? Logos Universality mentality education novelty: philosophy & humanistic sciences 8(1):44–60. https://doi.org/10.18662/lumenphs/8.1/35
Sim J (2023) What does the creation story tell about homosexuality? TheoRhēma 18(1):5–30
Sprinkle PN (2016) Introduction. In: Sprinkle P (ed) Two views on homosexuality, the bible, and the church, 9–16. Grand Rapids, MI: Zondervan.
Stiebert J, Walsh JT (2001) Does the hebrew bible have anything to say about homosexuality? Old Testament Essays 14(2001):119–152
The Associated Press (2024) Vatican blasts gender-affirming surgery, surrogacy and gender theory as violations of human dignity. NBC News Website. https://www.nbcnews.com/news/world/vatican-blasts-gender-affirming-surgery-surrogacy-gender-theory-rcna146824
Winkler M (2021) The Ancestors' Masculinities in Genesis. J Study Old Testament 46(2):269–88

Chapter 9
Inculturating Gender Diversity and LGBTQI Inclusivity: A Synodal Call for the Catholic Church

Abstract This chapter sociologically argues that the Catholic Church needs to inculturate or adapt sociological concepts of gender diversity and LGBTQI inclusivity in its moral teachings as a synodal response to the call of postmodern times. It specifically contends that gender diversity has existed in human culture since ancient times but is only today in the public eye due to the growing pro-gender and LGBTQI social movements of the current age. Now is the time for the Catholic Church to update its philosophical natural law moral framework on sex and gender and adopt sociological and social science gender research and perspectives to fully welcome the LGBTQI community into the Church.

Keywords Inculturation · Synodality · Sociology · Gender · Gender diversity · LGBTQI inclusivity

Introduction

Since its inception, responding to "the call of the times" to make its teachings relevant to the ever-evolving culture of society has always been an important pastoral challenge for the Roman Catholic Church (RCC). The theological concept of *Ecclesia Semper Reformada* [The Church is Always in Need of Reform] also acknowledges that the Church is an imperfect institution in its pursuit of Christ's mandate. The Second Vatican Council (Vatican II) also called for continuous ecclesiastical renewal in society with the concept of *aggriornamento* [renewal].

In recent years, the RCC has been heavily involved in debates on gender issues such as gender diversity (GD) and lesbian, gay, bisexual, transgender, queer, and intersex (LGBTQI)[1] inclusivity in the Church. Recent papal pronouncements by Pope Benedict XVI and Pope Francis have attacked gender and gender diversity, that is, the existence of other forms of gender aside from heterosexuality as espoused

---

[1] This chapter consistently uses the acronym "LGBTQI" for simplicity and consistency despite its historical evolution.

V. O. Ballano, *Gender Ideology and the Contemporary Catholic Church*,
https://doi.org/10.1007/978-981-97-8124-9_9

by feminists, sociologists, and LGBTQI leaders, and have inaccurately termed them "gender ideology" (GI).

Pope Benedict XVI invented, circulated, and popularized the concept of GI within Catholicism (Vaggione 2020) to counter the influence of feminist, gay rights, and LGBTQI movements which were popular in the United States, Europe, and Latin America. To Benedict XVI, gender is the greatest sin against humanity. He popularized GI as "a concept—a signifier for what conservative Catholics construe as the evils of liberalism in the realm of human sexuality." The new term of GI is thought to have replaced Pope John Paul II's concept of "culture of death" and "bad feminism" (Graff 2016).

Pope Francis, who succeeded Benedict XVI, continues to popularize GI in his media declarations and writings, providing it with new "tactics and strategies for this war, with his rhetoric of anticolonialism and his combination of warm receptivity to individuals with continuing opposition to their rights" (Case 2019, 659). Francis's latest attacks against GI occurred during his address to the participants of a Vatican conference on gender entitled "Man-Woman Image of God: For an Anthropology of Vocations" on March 1, 2024. At this conference, he warned Catholics against GI and its intention to destroy the gender complementarity of humanity by cancelling out all differences between a man and a woman, this time calling it the "ugliest danger" of our time (Zengarini 2024).

The RCC's two main objections to GI are the idea that gender can change in society and that the LGBTQI group constitutes a separate set of genders different from heterosexuality. To the RCC's moral magisterium, biological sex and gender are metaphysically and intrinsically inseparable: God created male and female as the only "normal and moral human beings" who are created in His own image and likeness (*Dignitas Infinita* [Infinite Dignity] 2024). For the RCC, homosexuality and other gender identities are intrinsically disordered under law and are a "sign of immaturity" needing pastoral care to realign the individuals concerned to heterosexuality as the only gender standard in the Church and society.

The nonbinary gender orientation and minority status in society of homosexuals and transgender people has caused them to be generally persecuted and judged as deviant individuals throughout human history. They are still regarded by some as mentally ill despite the depathologization of homosexuality as a form of psychiatric illness in 1973 by the American Psychiatric Association (APA). Nonbinary people with diverse gender identities have remained ostracized in society and Christian churches. As Sheldon et al. (2007, 4) observe, "The link between homosexuality and stigma seems quite resistant to attempts at normalizing gay and lesbian identity."

In the RCC, homosexuality and gender diversity have remained an anathema, a "natural" disorder, and a sign of psychological immaturity. With the prevailing institutional homophobia or dread of homosexuals and homosexuality, nonbinary Catholics and members of the LGBTQI face major obstacles "coming out" and freely revealing their true gender identity in the Christian community without suffering discrimination and rejection by their bishops and fellow Catholics. Pope Francis, however, seeking to counteract the institutional homophobia in the RCC, has shown great sympathy to homosexuals and members of the LGBTQI group. As a pastoral gesture to welcome marginalized LGBTQI Catholics into the Christian community despite their unique gender identity, he also approved the declaration *Fiducia Supplicans* [Supplicating Trust] (*FS*), which allowed same-sex couples to receive pastoral blessings from priests and to become godparents in baptism. In Francis's vision of an inclusive synodal church based on his latest ecclesiastical reform project, the Synod on Synodality (SoS), the marginalized and the voiceless such as homosexuals and the LGBTQI members would feel at home in the RCC.

In October 2021, Pope Francis convened the SoS to further implement the reforms of the Second Vatican Council (Vatican II) and adapt the Church's mission in the contemporary world. It is in the synodal spirit that Francis embraces the LGBTQI community in the RCC, regardless of their gender orientation. To protect their legal rights, he declared that homosexual couples should seek civil union. In his letter known as *Ad Theologiam Promovendam* [To Promote Theology] (ATP), Francis (2023) also stressed the need for an inductive interdisciplinary synodal theology that commences with accurate understanding of people's lived experience.

Despite these ecclesiastical and theological reforms focusing on human experience, the RCC remains committed to the deductive philosophical approach to morality based on natural law that opposes gender diversity and transgenderism as naturally disordered, contravening the immutability and inseparability of sex and gender. Heterosexuality and cisgender, that is, that the person's gender identity and expression should match their biological sex assigned at birth, remain the standard gender norms in the Church. To fully understand gender diversity and LGBTQI activism and movements, which the RCC regards as part of GI, requires sociological and synodal inductive investigations and new ways of inculturating the RCC's moral teachings in contemporary society, as well as a paradigm shift from a philosophical to sociological view of sex and gender as a synodal response to the call of the times.

Aims, Main Sections, and Arguments

This chapter attempts to sociologically illustrate that the growing activism and gender movements for gender diversity and LGBTQI inclusivity, far from being the greatest evils for humanity, are today's "signs of the times," calling for an urgent pastoral response from the RCC that takes account of Pope Francis's concepts of synodality, synodal theology, and synodal church, and requiring an inculturation of sociological and social science research and perspectives on sexuality, gender, gender diversity and inclusivity.

The chapter has three main sections. The first provides a conceptual framework to guide the main argument. The second broadly discusses the major historical and sociological contingencies that have led to the rise of feminism, gender diversity, and LGBTQI groups. It argues that the expanding advocacy and social movement for the recognition of gender diversity and LGBTQI as separate genders in the Church and society have undergone a long history of social, political, and cultural struggle for social and legal acceptance. The last part explores how the RCC can respond to the challenges posed by feminists and LGBTQI leaders, and can apply the inculturation process and synodal approach.

Conceptual Framework

Call for Inculturation and Inductive Synodal Theology

Western philosophy may have been an appropriate conceptual tool during medieval times when the RCC needed to inculturate Church doctrines to provide Christians with adequate rational justification of their faith against heresies and doctrinal challenges. Thus, St. Thomas Aquinas had rightly incorporated the pagan Aristotelian philosophy into Catholic theology, which became popularly known as philosophical theology, adapting the Christian faith to address the "signs of the times" during the intellectual climate of the medieval period.

Modern sociology and the social sciences had been providing an account of the massive changes and complexity of behavioral and social issues that have occurred since the nineteenth century following the three great revolutions – the Industrial, French, and American revolutions. The primary method of acquiring knowing had also evolved from philosophy to modern sciences. Instead of relying on reason or a priori knowledge to understand behavior and the social order, modern sociology and the social sciences utilize the naturalistic and scientific method to understand the world of nature and people. This involves gathering qualitative and quantitative data to support sociological theories that describe and explain social reality, in contrast to the philosophical approach, which does not require empirical data, remains at the conceptual level, and does not scientifically scrutinize social and cultural experiences.

Pope Francis has been introducing welcome reforms to the RCC that prioritize human experience, as well as an inductive approach as the starting point to resolve moral issues such as transgender sexuality and LGBTQI inclusion in the RCC. In light of his latest pronouncements in FS and *Ad Theologiam Promovendam* [To Promote Theology] (*ATP*), and his synodal approach, which encourages an inductive and consultative method of resolving ethical issues. More reforms to Catholic moral theology can be expected from Francis.

As Ford (2018) contends, "Because Catholic tradition holds that both faith and reason come from God and work together to reveal truth, empirical evidence and theoretical knowledge can be used to help inform morality and guide pastoral practice." "The Magisterium has not shied away from utilizing sociological research and scientific data to inform its positions, teachings, and responses to various social, political, cultural, and religious issues" (Roy-Steier 2021, 1).

The paradigm shift in Catholic theology implied by *ATP* suggests a new inculturation process in dealing with empirical reality and the lived experiences of believers. Francis states:

> [W]ithout opposing theory and practice, theological reflection is urged to develop with an inductive method, which starts from the different contexts and concrete situations in which peoples are inserted, allowing itself to be seriously challenged by reality, in order to become discernment of the "signs of the times" in the proclamation of the salvific event of the God-agape, communicated in Jesus Christ. (Francis 2023, para.8)

. This inductive and interdisciplinary approach to understanding the complex empirical world and inculturating the Christian message in society has important implications for current issues such as gender diversity and LGBTQI inclusivity.

Recognizing the Call of the Times and Sociology

Today's LGBTQI campaign for gender diversity and inclusiveness is not accidental. It has a long history. Creating public awareness of the need to change the strict heteronormativity that excludes nonbinary and gay people in society is "the result of long-term and increasingly visible and vibrant activist engagement, drawing on strategies such as media coverage, peer interventions, ally-building and institutional training" (Browne 2019, 3). And the emergence of gender theories has helped to clarify that sex is biological while gender is social and cultural. Gender theories challenge the popular and hegemonic gender complementarity and heteronormativity that discriminate against homosexuals and members of the LGBTQI community in both the Church and society.

The RCC has strongly resisted sociological, feminist, and scientific approaches to sex and gender, upholding instead the tradition of seeing sex and gender as metaphysically inseparable and designed by God. "Natural law tradition continued to be preserved and developed by Roman Catholic moral theologians, with the results that it came to be associated with Catholic thought—an association that persists to this day" (Porter 2005, 32–33).

To address the need to scientifically study the massive changes of the nineteenth century, Auguste Comte conceived of a new science of society which he called sociology. His student Emile Durkheim continued his work and became the founder of modern sociology as an established academic discipline. The birth of sociology and other social sciences that imitated the scientific methods of the natural sciences in their study of human behavior and society has generally shifted the processes of gaining knowledge from the deductive philosophical approach to the inductive naturalist method which blends theory and data to understand people's behavior and society.

Gender Diversity and Fluidity

Gender diversity and nonbinary people who express their masculinity and femininity beyond heterosexuality have existed in the world since ancient times, albeit largely excluded from and unrecognized in society. "Fluid and nonbinary gender identities and presentations can be found across all recorded history" (Feinberg, 1996), but only in the past decade has the notion of gender fluidity achieved widespread familiarity. Psychological research has long presumed rigid categorical notions of gender, but these presumptions have been challenged increasingly by researchers in neuroscience, behavioral endocrinology, genetics, and epigenetics" (Diamond 2020, 2). O' Keefe et al. (2018, 14) observe, "Throughout recorded history, homosexuals have comprised a small but significant cohort of society. Evidence of same sex behavior dates back to the oldest written texts, first noted in Egypt in 4,400 years ago, and subsequently found in ancient Greece, Rome, and China...In Western society today, the prevalence of male homosexuality is between two and eight percent."

Nonbinary people continue to exist today even outside Western society. Some countries recognize gender diversity in their own cultures. In India, the Hijas group, for instance, has been considered the most typical third gender in Hindu culture for more than 2,000 years. People of nonbinary gender expression have been an important part of Hindu society since olden times. They are even mentioned in holy texts such as *Ramayana* and the *Mahabharata*, with the hero Arjuna as the third gender to show their cultural significance. The Bugis tribe in South Sulawesi, Indonesia, recognizes three gender categories beyond the binary: the Calalai, individuals who have female sexual characteristics but express themselves publicly in traditional masculine ways; the Calabai, which includes individuals with male sexual characteristics and traditionally feminine expression; and the Bissu, a meta-gender group which manifest both masculine and feminine ways without identifying any of these traits.

Thus, gender diversity that recognizes nonbinary people has been culturally established in various parts of the world. It is not something that started with feminism and LGBTQI activism in the Western world. To date no specific gene has been found to be associated with homosexuality. Nor have researchers identified credible links to any genetic region in lesbians (Veniegas and Conley 2000). Findings from genetic studies of homosexuality in humans have been confusing –contradictory at worst and tantalizing at best – with no clear, strong, compelling evidence for a distinctly genetic basis for homosexuality.

Sex, Gender, and the Rise of the LBTQI Movement

Historically, the distinction between sex and gender was proposed by gender studies in the 1970s. Since then, the term "gender" has referred not primarily to biological sex as male or female but to social and cultural constructions of masculinities and femininities. Recent gender studies suggest that gender identity is changing and can be performed or experienced in various ways. As Fontanella, Maretti, and Sarra (2014, 2553) contend:

> Gender identity relies on a person's sense of self as male or female or feeling between sexes. The concept of gender identity can be better understood keeping distinguished the notions of "sex", "sexuality" and "gender". Even if gender seems to flow naturally from biological sex,

> gender and sex are not interchangeable terms. While sex principally refers to the biological aspects of male or female, being related to their physical anatomy (sex chromosomes, gonads, sex hormones, internal reproductive structures and external genitalia), gender includes, in addition to the biological elements, the behavioral, psychological and social characteristics of men and women.

Gender identity is the person's intrinsic self-identification of personal femaleness and maleness. In the social sciences, naturalist and empirical explanations understand gender as a social and cultural construction in society (Scott 1999). According to Deutsch (2007), gender is an ongoing emergent aspect of social interaction. It is not something that we are, but something that we do (West and Zimmerman 1987).

Thus, contrary to the RCC's conception of gender as immutable, ahistorical, and divinely ordained, social scientists following methodological naturalism, that is, suspending personal biases such as religious belief in God as the creator in order to achieve a scientific understanding of empirical reality, view gender as continuously changing and socially constructed by people across "time, cultures, contexts, ethnic groups and social situations" (Fontanella, Maretti, and Sarra 2014, 2553). Its evolution depends on both sociological and historical contingencies.

Heterosexuality remains the hegemonic gender norm in most societies, sidelining and discriminating against homosexuals and individuals with diverse genders such as the LGBTQI. "All gender-diverse children, adolescents, and adults face challenges related to social and familial acceptance, and these challenges can lead to lasting mental health concerns" (Diamond 2020, 2). Stigmatization, victimization, and bullying are still the common experience of nonbinary and gender-diverse individuals, especially among young people (James et al. 2016).

Social Discrimination and LGBTQI Protest

Social discrimination, victimization, and denial of the rights of nonbinary and gender-diverse people have historically led to collective action and social movements. The RCC needs to understand empirically that the rise of the LGBTQI movement is the result of a long struggle by gender-diverse individuals around the world against social discrimination and harassment in society, which is also part of the mission of the Church under the ecclesiastical social doctrines of social justice, and the preferential option for the poor and the marginalized in society. Gays and nonbinary people also have human dignity and rights that should respected by heterosexuals.

The LGBTQI movement is a complicated and dynamic set of movements and actors representing the culmination of a long collective struggle against social discrimination and nonrecognition of rights. It is said to have started in the United States with the so-called Stonewall Riots. In the summer of 1969 in Greenwich Village, New York City, a riot broke out between the patrons of the Stonewall Inn and the police. Ordinances in New York during this time prohibited dancing with a same-sex partner. The Stonewall Inn was one of the social clubs or LGBTQ[I] bars where same-sex people felt a sense of kinship and camaraderie. "What followed at the Stonewall Inn would start the evolution of the LGBTQ[I] movement" (Beck 2019, 36–37). It was the first overt collective social resistance by nonbinary people against social and legal discrimination, although the homophile movement of the 1950s and 1960s had already laid down the critical groundwork for the gay liberation movement of the 1970s (Gutterman 2010).

The LGBTQI movement gained political centrality in the late 1980s in the US, greatly altering American perceptions of nonbinary and gender-diverse sexualities and identities. As Marche (2019, 13) aptly observes:

> For more than 40 years, the social movement that is now known as the lesbian, gay, bisexual, transgender, and queer (LGBTQ[I]) movement has been challenging American society's views on LGBTQ[I] mobilizations are among the greatest social transformations that Western societies experienced in the twentieth century. Emerging in the wake of the various protest movements that appeared following the postwar economic boom, these movements have deeply changed the experience of homosexuality, reduced its stigmatization, reinforced its acceptance, and even helped to redefine heterosexuality, conjugality, the family, and the expression of desire.

Like any other social movement, the LGBTQI movement is also characterized by both diversity and inevitable conflict (Ghaziani 2008). Despite these differences, the mainstream LGBTQ movement remains identifiable, although the term LGBTQ has itself undergone an evolution. In the1950s and 1960s, the term "gay" was used to refer to both gay men and lesbians (Stulberg 2018). In the 1990s, the term "transgender" was included in LGBT following claims of sexism in the movement from lesbian feminists, and LGBT became the label that activists used to define their work and their communities. In the past few years, the "Q" for "queer" was further added, though not universally recognized, and the social movement used LGBTQ as a broad and inclusive term for gender and sexual minorities (Stulberg 2018). Eventually, an "I" was added to include the "intersexual."

The LGBTQI movement generally resists heteronormativity and gender complementarity, and advocates gender fluidity and diversity. With great progress in biotechnology and cosmetic surgery, these goals are more achievable if societal homophobia is overcome by legislation. In recent years, the movement has vigorously campaigned for legal rights. National and international fora have also included LGBTQI rights to nondiscrimination, freedom of expression and freedom from violence (Browne 2019). The United Nations, through its UN Human Rights Council report (2017), specifically enjoined nations to create counter measures to resist local and global policies that discriminate against the gay community based on their sexual orientation and unique gender identity (Namaste 2000).

The RCC's Response to the LGBTQ Movement and the Religious Right

The RCC, which philosophically understands sex and gender as immutable, inseparable, and divinely ordained based on Biblical teaching on gender complementarity and the TNLT tradition, has always viewed gender diversity and the LGBTQI movement with suspicion and as part of GI. Pope Benedict XVI warned the Catholic faithful about the dangers of gender questioning the traditional Christian notion of the family as derived from biological sex (Butler 2019). To his successor Pope Francis (2015), social movements that oppose gender complementarity are a form of neo-colonization, in which Western values are being imposed by developed nations on developing countries.

Owing to the dominance of Pope John Paul II's theology of the body in the RCC, Pope Benedict XVI and Pope Francis categorized all views and explanations that oppose this theology as well as the official Church teachings on gender as GI (Ford 2018). Thus, by viewing the advocacy of the gay community for the public recognition of gender diversity and the LGBTQI group as distinct genders as GI, the RCC aligns itself with the anti-gay political coalition known as the religious right (RR).

Instead of empirically examining and recognizing these new challenges posed by the sociologists, feminists, and LGBTQI leaders as "signs of the times" that need inculturation in light of Pope Francis's synodality and inductive synodal theology, the RCC has intensified the social alienation and victimization of nonbinary people in the Church and society. The Religious Right (RR) is a "broad coalition of pro-family organizations and individuals who have come together to struggle for a conservative Christian vision in the political realm" (Herman 1997, 9). The anti-gay RR particularly developed within the New Right from the rising involvement of evangelical Christians in politics in the 1970s. As Stone (2016, 2) observes:

> Since the 1970s, the Religious Right has grown into a highly organized social movement that addresses issues like LGBTQ[I] rights, abortion, pornography, and public education. Scholars are in agreement that over time the Religious Right has escalated, become more organized, and engaged in more proactive rather than reactive opposition to the LGBTQ[I] movement...Initial Religious Right mobilization responded to the progress of the lesbian and gay movement, but in the 1990s the Religious Right began to be more proactive in its opposition to LGBTQ[I] rights, producing anti-gay laws. This escalation impacted the LGBTQ[I] movement by blocking movement advancements, altering the movement agenda, altering framing of movement issues, stifling queer activism, and increasing movement mobilization.

The RR presents a "culture wars" ideology about American society and opposes pro-gay cultural visibility, such as television shows, "out" celebrities, and a pro-gay school curriculum (Bull and Gallagher 1996). It also blocks pro-LGBTQI legislation by raising awareness and increasing campaigns against it. Despite this escalation of the RR campaign against the LGBTQI movement, the gay campaign for social recognition and legal rights continues to flourish. The RR's proactive and repressive actions against the LGBTQI movement have, unintentionally, even helped the latter to grow in recent years.

Although the RCC has aligned with the RR in its campaign against GI, gender diversity, and gay rights, Pope Francis has shown openness and a welcoming attitude towards the LGBTQI community. Despite his strong opposition to GI, Francis allowed the blessing of homosexual couples by Catholic priests as well as making them godparents in baptism (DDF 2023). He also favors civil same-sex marriage to protect the rights of gay couples. In his synodality and synodal church, Francis has urged Catholics to understand and welcome the marginalized and discriminated LGBTQI group in the Christian community. Despite these efforts, the RCC's moral magisterium still cannot fully accept the LGBTQI group into the Church. The group's gender diversity campaign contradicts traditional ecclesiastical teaching that allows only heterosexual as the standard gender in society, complementarity of sexes, and heterosexual marriage.

Unless the Church's moral magisterium re-examines its traditional philosophical stance on sex, gender, and gender complementarity, as well as incorporating sociological and feminist views on gender as social and cultural experiences rather than as simply divinely ordained, the RCC cannot fully comprehend and empathize with the human experiences of members of the LGBTQI community and welcome them into the Church as true Christians with ecclesiastical rights to sacramental union and family life.

Call to Inculturation Concerning Sex and Gender

Gender diversity can only be fully understood by the RCC through immersion in the actual lives and struggles of nonbinary individuals and members of the LGBTQI community. No amount of philosophizing can make Catholic bishops and moral theologians sympathetic to the personal plight and struggle of LGBTQI people and implement Pope Francis's synodal exhortation to love the marginalized, the voiceless, and those on the periphery of the Church and society. Unless the Church's moral magisterium shifts its approach to sex and gender from philosophical to sociological and scientific, without abandoning the fundamental divine teaching that God created persons in his own image and likeness, inculturation will be a formidable task. The philosophical approach to moral issues using the TNLT is not a "dogma" that is not subject to change, but merely a cultural and conceptual tool to apply the RCC's moral principles in society when appropriate. This deductive philosophical approach cannot cover all the social and moral contingencies of gender and gender diversity in the contemporary world.

To what extent will the RCC be able to compromise on its basic philosophical approach, embracing the scientific and inductive approach to sex and gender set out by sociologist, feminists, and LGBTQI activists to achieve inculturation and ultimately Pope Francis's synodal church, one that welcomes the marginalized and people with divergent views?

The Crux of the Matter

The use of philosophy rather than sociology and the social sciences to understand the relationship between sex and gender is ultimately why gender diversity and LGBTQI gender identities remain morally unacceptable for the RCC's moral magisterium despite Francis's *FS,* which blesses homosexual couples. There is a basic conceptual conflict between, on one side, the Catholic hierarchy and moral theologians who still subscribe to the philosophical approach to gender based on the TNLT tradition, and on the other, sociologists, feminists, and LGBTQI leaders who generally view gender as a social and cultural construct which can thus be fluid and diverse. The latter views sex as biological while gender is social and cultural, contrary to the RCC's philosophical view that sees them as ahistorical, immutable, and inseparable. Using the scientific method rather than philosophical reasoning, the social sciences view biological sex as assigned at birth as distinct from gender, which is seen as social and cultural and thus subject to historical change. As Bauman (2000, 2003) argues, gender is fluid, unstable, and sensitive to historical and ideological influences that can result in a plurality of identities.

The queer theory also sees "gender and sexuality as flexible, ever-shifting, and not linearly related to biology" (Browne 2019, 3). Queer scholars argue that "gender is fluid, flexible and subject to change—not rooted in an essential male or female (binary) gender identity" (Browne 2019, 3). To them, the current binary gender system of society prioritizes masculinity and heterosexuality, discriminating against femininity and queerness (Schilt and Westbrook, 2009). Thus, they explore new ways of viewing gender beyond heterosexuality as the global standard for sexuality (Browne 2019).

According to TNLT and recent papal teaching on gender complementarity by Pope John Paul II's theology of the body, only heteronormativity is morally acceptable. Gender fluidity and diversity is a creation and social construction of GI. But the evaluation and application of the Church's moral principles are dependent on accurate reading of the moral and empirical situation. Thus, they require sociological and social science scientific research for a thorough empirical evaluation to achieve correct moral judgment and action. The RCC's teaching on sex and gender cannot remain deductive and metaphysical without investigating human experience, especially that of the gay community. The evolving moral situations of gender and sexuality in contemporary society are characterized by "liquidity" (Bauman 2000), which needs scientific assessment.

The major moral issues on gender diversity and LGBTQI inclusivity are new "calls of the times" that need a paradigm synodal shift from philosophical to sociological and scientific approach to understand sex and gender in the contemporary world in order to fully accept diverse gender identities and LGBTQI inclusivity in the RCC. The blessing of homosexual couples in FS may be a major step towards this direction. But the papal gesture is still inadequate. Complete LGBTQI inclusivity in the Christian community needs recognition of their distinct genders as well as legal and moral rights to marriage and family life.

History shows that the RCC always adapts its teaching to the prevailing culture to preach the Christian faith in society. This process is theologically called inculturation. As the New Testament shows, the early Christian church inculturated the faith during the Apostolic era. Inculturation, which is said to be as old as the Church itself, has been described as merely "a new term for an old issue in Christianity concerning the translation and realization of Christian meanings and practices in different cultural contexts" (Orta 2016: 1). "Paul's interpretation of the Christian faith in a Gentile cultural context whereby he propagated the gospel of noncircumcision for Gentile Christians... is an example of inculturation theology in early Christianity" (Ukpong 1999, 100). Thus, inculturation can be understood as "a new vision of an old problem in the Church or a new approach to a solution of an old problem" (Anthony 2012, 237).

Bosch (1991, 454) broadly defined inculturation as "a process whereby cultural values can be transformed through their exposure to the Christian message and the insertion of Christianity into indigenous cultures." To him, inculturation is a double movement of adaptation of Christianity to culture and the Christianization of culture. But this can only occur if there is already an understanding of the local culture "as it relates to world views, ways of thinking, group solidarity, understanding of history and of modernity and its impact" (Duncan 2014, 2).

Inculturation is adapting the Good News to the thought patterns of the hearers in order that it can be easily and properly understood. It implies adopting the best human means to preach the Christian faith in society. Shorter (1999, 12) argues that "the Christian Faith cannot exist except in a cultural form. When we speak of Christian faith or Christian life, we are necessarily speaking of a cultural phenomenon. It is a distinctive way of life that can only operate culturally."

When St. Thomas Aquinas adopted and synthesized Aristotelian philosophy with Catholic theology, he was obviously inculturating the religious faith in an age that sought for a rational justification of the Christian faith. His natural law theory (TNLT), which become a cornerstone of Catholic moral theology, is an adaptation of the pagan Stoic philosophy to express the Christian message that God is the center of the universe, whose divine law is enshrined in human nature and reasoning.

Inculturating Sociology in the RCC's Teaching

The emergence of modern sciences in the sixteenth and seventeenth centuries shifted the primary mode of gaining knowledge from an a priori philosophical approach to an empirical scientific method, with reasoning prioritized over philosophical scholastic approaches to understanding phenomena in the world (Zakai 2007). Scientific approaches with their empirical and naturalistic methods of understanding the world and human behavior became popular in centers of learning in Europe that challenged theology as the queen of sciences and philosophy as its handmaid (Zakai 2007; Ballano 2021). Science is based on facts and accurate descriptions of social phenomena (Lindberg 2007). As a science, sociology follows the same general principles as apply to all branches of scientific knowledge, despite the peculiarities of social phenomena compared with natural phenomena (Bauman 2014). The study of gender was one of the most significant trends in 20th-century sociology and continues to the present day (Lindsey 2021). No other academic discipline gives more attention to gender issues than sociology.

The way that a person expresses their femininity and masculinity or sexual orientation, which is now in the realm of gender, may not necessarily be in accordance with their biological anatomy (Blank 2012). Gender is socially and cultural conditioned. "Human beings make other human beings into specific male and female genders, and the family remains the main modeling for male heterosexuality" (Hopkins 2008, 576). To shape the individual's gender according to society's expectations, gender socialization is normally introduced in the family and continued as the person becomes more exposed to others in society. Being gay or lesbian is not intentional on the part of the person but is acquired through the process of socialization and largely influenced by social interaction. Thus, the RCC's condemnation of homosexuality is tantamount to "blaming the victim."

Members of the LGBTQI community may be ostracized as deviant for having a nonbinary sexuality and gender identity, and are usually victims of harassment and discrimination in society. They are further victimized by their own churches treating them as psychologically immature, and are denied the basic rights to marriage and family life enjoyed by heterosexual Christians, as well as social acceptance. In the RCC, they are forced to accept pastoral care to "make" them heterosexual. This pattern of social discrimination, victimization, and violence against gay and nonbinary people has been going on since ancient times.

It is only in recent memory – starting with the Stonewall Riot – that these people have found the collective support to resist discrimination. And yet the RCC has regarded the LGBTQ movement as part of those groups advocating GI without first seeking to understand their innermost concerns and struggles against social discrimination and injustice in the Church and society through synodal, inductive, and scientific investigation. Strong institutional homophobia continues to prevent gender diversity and LGBTQI inclusivity flourishing in the RCC.

In recent years, theologians have started to utilize science to ground their empirical understanding of the world before theological reflection. Some have availed themselves of the scientific method of sociology and the social sciences, engaging in inductive theology that begins with people's lived experience – hence the birth of science-engaged theology, lived theology, critical theology, empirical theology, and other forms of contemporary theology that use scientific and sociological methods in addition to traditional theological tools. This is precisely the type of Catholic theology Pope Francis is contemplating in his *ATP*.

Conclusion

This chapter has sociologically argued that, in light of Pope Francis's synodality and inductive synodal theology, the RCC needs to inculturate or adapt gender diversity and the inclusion of the lesbian, gay, bisexual, transgender, queer, and intersex (LGBTQI) community in the Catholic Church as a new "sign of the times." It has contended that while gender diversity has existed throughout history, it has become publicly emphasized in the present age thanks to both biotechnological advancement and the growing gender and LGBTQI social movements and advocacies requiring ecclesiastical recognition and inculturation.

This chapter recommends that the RCC should update its philosophical stance on sex and gender and that the appropriate synodal response to the sign of the times is to inculturate sociological and social science gender research and perspectives for the full recognition of gender diversity and LGBTQI inclusion in the Church and society.

References

Anthony KI (2012) Inculturation and the Christian faith in Africa. Int J Humanit Soc Sci 2(17):236–244

Ballano VO (2021) Inculturation, philosophy, and the social sciences as the emerging handmaid of theology: time to update catholic clerical education? Int J Religion Spirituality Society 11(2):1–13. https://doi.org/10.18848/2154-8633/CGP/v11i02/1-13

Bauman Z (2014) Para que serve a Sociologia? (What is Sociology?). Editora Zahar, Rio de Janeiro

Bauman Z (2000) Liquid modernity. Polity Press, Cambridge.

Bauman Z (2003) Liquid love: on the frailty of human bonds. Polity Press, Cambridge

Beck L (2019) The stonewall riots: then and 50 years later. In: Legacy (National Association for Interpretation), Vol 30, No 1, 2019, 36

Blank H (2012) Straight: the surprisingly short history of heterosexuality. Beacon Press, Boston

Bosch DJ (1991) Transforming mission: Paradigm shifts in theology of mission. (American Society of Missiology Series). Maryknoll, New York: Orbis Books

Browne E (2019) Gender norms, LGBTQI issues and development: a topic guide (Version 1). University of Sussex. https://hdl.handle.net/10779/uos.23466224.v1

Bull C, Gallagher J (1996) The religious right, the gay movement, and the politics of the 1990s. Crown, New York

Butler J (2019) What threat? The campaign against 'gender ideology.' Glocalism J Culture Politics Innov 3:1–12. https://doi.org/10.12893/gjcpi.2019.3.1

Deutsch FM (2007) Undoing gender. Gender Sociology 21(1):106–127

Diamond LM (2020) Gender fluidity and nonbinary gender identities among children and adolescents. Child development perspectives, 1–6: https://doi.org/10.1111/cdep.12366

Duncan GA (2014) Inculturation: adaptation, innovation and reflexivity: an African Christian perspective. HTS Teologiese Studies 70(1):1–11. https://doi.org/10.4102/hts.v70i1.2669

Fontanella L, Maretti M, Sarra A (2014) Gender fluidity across the world: a multilevel item response theory approach. Qual Quant 48:2553–2568. https://doi.org/10.1007/s11135-013-9907-4

Ford CJ (2018) Transgender bodies, catholic schools, and a queer natural law theology of exploration. J Moral Theol 7(1):70–98

Ghaziani A (2008) The dividends of dissent: how conflict and culture work in lesbian and gay marches on Washington. University of Chicago Press, Chicago
Gutterman LJ (2010) OutHistory.org: an Experiment in LGBTQ community history-making. Public Hist 32(4):96–109
Herman D (1997) The antigay agenda: orthodox vision and the Christian right. Chicago University Press, Chicago, IL
Hopkins DN (2008) Toward a positive black male heterosexuality. Angl Theol Rev 90(3):575–581
James SE, Herman JL, Rankin S, Keisling M, Mottet L, Anafi M (2016) The report of the 2015 U.S. transgender survey. Washington, DC. Retrieved from https://www.transequality.org/sites/default/files/docs/USTS-Full-Report-FINAL.PDF
Lindberg DC (2007) The beginnings of western science: the European scientific tradition in the philosophical, religious, and institutional context, 600 B.C. to A.D.1450. Chicago, IL: University of Chicago Press
Lindsey LL (2021) Gender: sociological perspectives, 7th edn. Routledge, New York
Marche G (2019) Sexuality, subjectivity, and LGBTQ Militancy in the United States. Amsterdam University Press, Amsterdam
Namaste V (2000) Invisible lives: the erasure of transsexual and transgendered people. University of Chicago Press, Chicago, IL
Orta A (2016) Inculturation. In: Gooren H (ed) Encyclopedia of Latin American Religions. Springer International Publishing, Cham, pp 1–6
Pope Francis (2023) Apostolic Letter Issued "Motu Proprio" Ad Theologiam Promovendam [To Promote Theology]. Unofficial full English translation available at: https://returntotradition.org/unofficial-full-english-translation-of-francis-revolutionary-motu-proprio-ad-theologiam-promovendam-plus-breaking-news-report-on-text/
Schilt K, Westbrook L (2009) Doing gender, doing heteronormativity. Gend Soc 23(4):440–464. https://doi.org/10.1177/0891243209340034
Scott JW (1999) Gender and the politics of history. Columbia University Press, New York
Sheldon JP, Pfeffer CA, Jayaratne TE, Feldbaum M, Petty EM (2007) Beliefs about the etiology of homosexuality and about the ramifications of discovering its possible genetic origin. J Homosexuality 52(3–4):111–150. https://doi.org/10.1300/J082v52n03_06. PMID: 17594974; PMCID: PMC4545255
Shorter A (1999) Toward a theology of Inculturation. Wipf & Stock Publishers, Eugene, OR
Stone AL (2016) The impact of anti-gay politics on the LGBTQ movement. Sociol Compass 10(6):459–467. https://doi.org/10.1111/soc4.12373
Stulberg L (2018) LGBTQ movements. Polity, Cambridge
United Nations Human Rights Council (2017) Report of the independent expert on protection against a violence and discrimination. Sexual Orientation and Gender Identity. http://www.ohchr.org/EN/Issues/SexualOrientationGender/Pages/Index.aspx
Vaggione JM (2020) The conservative uses of law: the catholic mobilization against gender ideology. Soc Compass 67(2):252–266. https://doi.org/10.1177/0037768620907561journals.sagepub.com/home/scp
Veniegas RC, Conley TD (2000) Biological research on women's sexual orientations: evaluating the scientific evidence. J Soc Issues 56:267–282
Welborn A (2024) Dignitas Infinita and gender ideology. The Catholic World Report (13 April 2024). https://archive.is/vlLmp#selection-909.0-911.20
West C, Zimmerman DH (1987) Doing gender. Gender Sociology 1(2):125–151
Zakai A (2007) The rise of modern science and the decline of theology as the 'queen of sciences' in the early modern era. Reformation Renaissance Rev 9(2):125–152, https://doi.org/10.1558/rrr.v9i2.125

Printed in the USA
CPSIA information can be obtained
at www.ICGtesting.com
CBHW050007251124
17936CB00003B/154

9 789819 781232